Environmentally Devastated Neighborhoods

Environmentally Devastated Neighborhoods

Perceptions, Policies, and Realities

Michael R. Greenberg
and Dona Schneider

HT
156
.G74
1996
West

Rutgers University Press
New Brunswick, New Jersey

Library of Congress Cataloging-in-Publication Data

Greenberg, Michael R.
 Environmentally devastated neighborhoods : perceptions, policies,
and realities / Michael R. Greenberg and Dona Schneider.
   p. cm.
 Includes bibliographical references and index.
 ISBN 0-8135-2279-X
 1. Inner cities. 2. Urban poor—Attitudes. 3. Quality of life—
Public opinion. 4. Urban policy. I. Schneider, Dona, 1946–
II. Title.
 HT156.G74 1996
 333.77—dc20   95-26203
                                                                        CIP

British Cataloging-in-Publication information available

Manufactured in the United States of America

Contents

Illustrations

Tables

Preface

This book is about neighborhoods that can cause nightmares. Most of it is concerned with how residents of neighborhoods with severe crime, physical blight, and pollution rate the quality of those neighborhoods. Local health and planning officials corroborate residents' collective perceptions, which leads us to confront a sobering and uncomfortable issue in the politically conservative climate of the 1990s: how to achieve better environments for those living in appalling environmental conditions.

The immediate stimulus for this book was service by one of us, Michael Greenberg, on a National Research Council committee that examined how federal and state agencies set priorities for cleaning up hazardous-waste sites (Committee on Remedial Action Priorities 1994). Witnesses representing the U.S. Environmental Protection Agency (EPA) and the Departments of Defense (DOD) and Energy (DOE) provided workbooks and accounts of how contaminant emissions into the air, ground, soil, and water are converted into public health and environmental risks. Yet we were astonished to learn that little, sometimes nothing, was done about the social and economic implications of hazardous-waste remediation, such as abandoned industrial properties and reduced property values. One interchange with a government official stands out. When asked about a specific project that doubtless would impact the community, the official responded that people in that area "didn't care," and in the case they really did, consultation would occur later. The blunt brush-off of social and economic impacts was frightening.

Our academic reflex was to challenge the assertion by measuring the problems people living in neighborhoods with hazardous-waste sites really cared about. As the initial survey design was piloted and tested in neighborhoods adjacent to hazardous-waste sites, the study evolved from a hypothesis-testing exercise in areas with a single problem, a hazardous-waste site, to one in which we surveyed neighborhoods with multiple environmental hazards.

During this research, we became convinced that disregarding

social and economic impacts and expecting groups interested in housing and transportation to march in the natural science environmental-risk parade while refusing to step forward to march in theirs' is a serious political mistake. The EPA's Science Advisory Board's recommendation that "EPA should work to ensure that environmental considerations are integrated, where appropriate, into the policy deliberations of [other] agencies" (Science Advisory Board 1990:8) is only half of the message that needs to be heard. The other half is that every environmental organization, private and public, should look for opportunities to integrate social and economic considerations into their environmental programs. Without outreach toward other interests, opportunities are missed to tie together air, land, water, and toxins programs with efforts to rehabilitate housing and abandoned factories and to reduce crime, auto accidents, and various other dangerous activities that occur in neighborhoods. Indeed, ignoring other programs inexorably leads to interagency competition for limited resources instead of cooperation.

Narrowly conceived environmental-risk programs may enjoy broad public support and allow scientists, regulators, and some interest groups to continue to do what they know how to do. But narrowly focused programs are not going to remediate the multiple kinds of devastation found in some U.S. neighborhoods. A conversation with a male aged seventy-five-plus living about two hundred feet from a hazardous-waste site in central New Jersey illustrates the failings of creating narrow environmental-risk programs. When asked about the abandoned pesticide facility down the street, this senior citizen replied: "Why would anyone spend all that money down there [to clean up the waste site] and do nothing to fix my sidewalk and the wrecked playground across the street?" He then pointed to a diesel locomotive about two hundred feet away, emitting a loud whining sound that made it difficult to communicate, and later he talked about blight and a growing fear of crime. It is not possible to come away from such conversations without feeling that the present definition of environmental risk misses the point for these multiple-hazard neighborhoods. People standing outside their homes do not understand why environmental risk excludes most of what really distresses them in their environment. Their concept of "environment" is everything outside their dwelling unit, not just pollution, housing, or crime. When you try to explain our laws, agencies, ideologies, and professional identifications to them, when you try to explain that the site down the street is on the Superfund list because it might increase their risk of cancer by one in a million or one in ten million, they look at you as an idiot, not as co-director of the New Jersey Graduate Program in Public Health.

This book was deliberately written to prick the skin of well-intentioned elected and agency officials, environmentalists, housing experts, criminologists, business leaders, academics, and other Americans who collectively have the power to change the inflexible way we often go about our business of improving the quality of life in stressed neighborhoods. Several of our colleagues have told us that through examples and the literature review, whether intentional or not, the book conveys the message that we believe the concerns about hazardous-waste sites and pollution in general are exaggerated, whereas crime, blight, and other problems are understated. In other words, as one colleague put it: "You are picking on EPA."

It was not our intent to criticize the EPA or any single agency or group. What we have tried to convey is that the United States needs to seriously think about how it defines environment, environmental remediation, environmental protection, and the implicit or explicit moral imperatives involved in those decisions. Before deciding, before planning, and especially before spending, we must ask experts to measure risk as objectively and accurately as they can and to calculate the costs of remediating and protecting the public interest. But as smart as an expert sitting in Washington, D.C., a state capital, or a university office might be about air pollution models and epidemiological studies of air pollution, the American system does not encourage or even allow that expert to be equally smart or focused about the partly collapsed building, drug sales, and a myriad of other land-use, blight, and behavioral problems in a multiple-hazard neighborhood. We must also turn to qualified local experts, like health officers and city planners, because in our experience they are the only experts with enough background to understand the science and enough breadth to understand the neighborhood gestalt. Most important, we need to listen to the people who live in these neighborhoods.

Multiple-hazard neighborhoods are a different species of place. Using scientific principles that work fine in places that have a single hazard, appealing to irrelevant economic and political ideologies, and fighting over who has the authority to improve which parts of these neighborhoods is not going to work. We need deliberate and systematic research, thinking, and consultation about these devastated neighborhoods. And we must consider the ethical implications of continuing to make multiple-hazard neighborhoods such a low priority.

Acknowledgments

Much of the fieldwork reported in this book was done with Rutgers' undergraduate and graduate students, and with students from the Liberty Science Program for outstanding New Jersey high school science students. We thank Jennifer Angner, Nicholas Blake, Daiwoo Choi, Karl Hartkopf, Maegan Mathieu, Jonathan Santos, Bimala Vemulapalli, and Sandra Wong. Jennifer Martell and Jim Parry, in particular, made multiple trips and helped supervise the gathering and entering of data.

Several of the chapters, especially chapter 9, are better than they would have been thanks to comments at speaking engagements at the University of South Maine, Rutgers University, and the New Jersey Department of Environmental Protection, and conversations with staff and members of the New Jersey Congressional Delegation and State Assembly.

Parts of chapters 4 and 6 were published in the *Geographical Review, Environmental Health Perspectives,* and the *Environmentalist.* We thank the editors, reviewers, and readers whose comments on those papers encouraged us to pursue the work.

We would also like to thank our colleagues for their many helpful comments on initial versions of this book: Susan Cutter, University of South Carolina; Bernard Goldstein, University of Medicine and Dentistry of New Jersey, Robert Wood Johnson Medical School; Arthur Kuflik, University of Vermont; Mark Lapping, University of South Maine; G. William Page, Florida Atlantic University; Frank Popper, Rutgers University; Charles Powers, Resources for Responsible Management; Peter Sandman, Rutgers University; William Solecki, Florida State University; Daniel Wartenberg, University of Medicine and Dentistry of New Jersey, Robert Wood Johnson Medical School; and Julian Wolpert, Princeton University. The errors, of course, are ours.

Our greatest debt is to the almost fifteen hundred residents of these beleaguered places who told us what they thought about their neighborhoods. We dedicate this book to them.

Environmentally Devastated Neighborhoods

Choosing a Perspective

The mind is its own place and in it self
Can make a Heav'n of Hell, a Hell of Heav'n.
—*John Milton,* Paradise Lost

All of the almost fifteen hundred respondents to our field surveys live within one-half mile of a garbage dump, hazardous-waste site, incinerator, international airport, petroleum refinery and tank farm, superhighway, or other potentially distressing land use. Many live next to crumbling buildings and littered lots, where they contend with roaming arsonists, thieves, murderers, dogs, and rats. Some residents of cities live near all of these physical and biophysical hazards.

In the midst of a period when the majority of Americans do not want to live within ten to fifty miles of these kinds of dangerous land uses and activities (Lindell and Earle 1983; U.S. Council on Environmental Quality 1980), it is remarkable how little we know about the environmental-risk images of those who do and how little we take their perspective into account in policy development. An attempt is made in this book to extend our understanding of environmental risk by studying the perspectives of those who live in neighborhoods that most of use would label environmentally devastated. Two questions framed the research: (1) How do people who live in the immediate vicinity of potentially hazardous land uses and activities rate their neighborhoods? (2) What factors most influence neighborhood ratings, especially the rating of a neighborhood as poor?

We undertook the study without illusions about building a general theory, a perfect data set, or a unassailable foundation for changing policy. Our approach disclaims an attempt to construct a definitive environmental-risk perception theory applicable to all people who live in environmentally devastated neighborhoods. Confronted by the variety of cultures, ages, educational experiences, and other backgrounds of the residents of these neighborhoods, we assumed that a search for a general theory would be fruitless. Yet we did have expectations about the answers to the two research questions, which are presented at the end of the chapter. We also expected some of the answers to surprise outsiders like ourselves, environmental-risk professionals, and most of the readers of this book.

We had no illusions about acquiring a critique-proof database. Disproportionately, we expected that many potential respondents could not or would not complete a long set of Likert-scaled questions or draw mental maps (see chapters 2 and 8). Disproportionately, we were sampling in neighborhoods where a completely random sample was unobtainable, either over the phone or through field surveys. For example, many people in our study areas have a fence as an initial barrier, a No Trespassing sign as a second, a barking dog as a third, and an alarm as a fourth obstacle. A stray dog in Camden, New Jersey, in fact, responded to our presence in its neighborhood by biting one of us, leading to six sets of shots for rabies. A few residents called their local police department, post office, or city manager to complain about our presence. We also assumed that some residents' perceptions would not be grounded in the realities of what is found the streets. Accordingly, we asked local health officials and city planners to give us their priorities for upgrading neighborhood quality as a way of checking the concerns of our neighborhood respondents.

Also, we did not expect our study to persuade those in power to radically change the way they do the business of environmental risk in multiple-hazard neighborhoods. Through efforts to work with a U.S. Senate committee, a New Jersey Assembly committee, and two federal agencies, we have learned that changing government environmental-risk policy faces stiff opposition from political and professional interests. Our policy suggestions are not radical. Indeed, several of the more radical ones are briefly discussed but dismissed as unattainable in the political climate of the 1990s.

Illusions aside, our major goal is to make a contribution to the field of environmental risk by demonstrating that it is feasible to measure the impact of a broad set of environmental risks, amenities, and personal characteristics on neighborhood quality in highly stressed environments. The reader should come away from this book with a sensitivity to the complex relationships between neighborhood quality and physical and behavioral stresses, amenities, residents' perceptions of previous neighborhoods, and residents' personal characteristics. The reader should gain insights into how residents of environmentally stressed neighborhoods create images of their neighborhoods that are different from those of us who live in more protected environments. Finally, the moral implications of seriously neglecting multiple-hazard neighborhoods leads us to argue for a policy for poor quality, multiple-hazard neighborhoods that we hope will be seriously considered by those with political power. The reader should gain an understanding of not only the science but also the ethical foundations of this proposal.

The Scientific Foundation

An "environmental hazard" is anything outside the individual that can cause adverse health effects or damage the environment. In other words, hazards are threats to people and what they value. Risks are estimates of the likelihood of the occurrence of what is threatened (Cutter 1993; Kates and Kasperson 1983; Whyte and Burton 1980).

Environmental hazards, the focus of this book, are everywhere— near and far. A smoker can be burned or asphyxiated while sleeping in his bed and a bather killed by falling in a bathtub. An astronaut can be killed in outer space, and a diver can die in the depths of the ocean. We are concerned with hazards that are located outside and in the immediate vicinity of the home.

Amenities are good schools, museums, shops, places of worship, friends, relatives, and other characteristics that support local residents and entice outsiders to visit a neighborhood. Inexpensive housing and access to work are other potentially important attractions. Human factors include age, gender, length of residence in the neighborhood, and other personal characteristics that will be described later in the chapter.

The literature about neighborhoods; technological, natural, and behavioral hazards; amenities; and the human factors that transform perceptions is massive. Our review is pointed at neighborhood quality, is necessarily selective, and focuses on the creation of images that influence public perceptions.

Choosing the Neighborhood for Defining Environmental Hazards and Amenities

The neighborhood is the spatial unit that engenders the greatest satisfaction and dissatisfaction with place (Campbell, Converse, and Rodgers 1976; Rapoport 1977). It is these feelings about neighborhoods and what causes them that we wanted to measure, specifically in places with multiple environmental hazards. The census tract or small municipality was our working neighborhood unit rather than special areas such as metropolitan statistical areas or health districts, or political units such as the city or county. Except in tiny municipalities, these areas are too large. Most people do not know the boundaries of health, education, and other special districts. Nor, with the possible exceptions of the local traffic helicopter pilot, a few government officials, and "cosmopolitans" who claim the entire city as their domain (Michelson 1970; Webber 1963), are we likely to learn much about devastated neighborhoods by asking people to relate to characteristics of a unit as large as a city, county, or metropolis.

No consensus exists about the definition of a neighborhood (Clay and Hollister 1983). Neighborhoods typically have been defined with population and housing characteristics derived from survey and census block and tract data (Murdie 1969; Shevky and Bell 1972). We eliminated some standard choices that did not fit our needs. One was census blocks. In urban areas, census blocks are small, compact pieces of land formed by the intersection of physical features and streets. In rural and suburban areas, census blocks may be irregular and large (U.S. Bureau of the Census 1983). The census block corresponds closely to Lee's (1968, 1976) "social acquaintance neighborhood," where everyone knows everyone else, although they may not have anything to do with one another. In areas of interest to us, the social acquaintance neighborhood was too small to capture the effect of physical and behavioral characteristics on neighborhood quality because physical structures and behaviors that most directly impact property values and social activities may not be located on the block.

Census tracts are relatively small subdivisions of counties that are defined by local and national census committees. Tracts usually have twenty-five hundred to eight thousand residents and a homogeneous population and housing characteristics (U.S. Bureau of the Census 1983). The census tract/small town is a good approximation of a neighborhood of similar people living in similar houses, which Lee (1968) calls the "homogeneous neighborhood." But population and housing homogeneity were also too restricted for our purposes because they ignore factories, other nonresidential structures, and behaviors that play a key role in defining neighborhood quality in the collective mind of its residents.

We are most interested in understanding neighborhood activity patterns and associated land uses—that is, what Saarinen (1976) calls the "functional environment" and Lee (1968) the "unit neighborhood." For instance, the young family's neighborhood is likely to be defined by shopping, recreating, attending school and religious services, visiting doctors and friends, and avoiding distressing spaces such as a corner where drug sales occur or the area near a factory emitting noises and odors.

With respect to policy, Clay and Hollister (1983) defined functional neighborhoods for production, consumption, socialization, administration, and political activity. One or two census tracts or a small municipality are the closest approximation of a reasonable planning unit for a neighborhood quality function. These are units where development, infrastructure, schools, recreation, disease and injury prevention, fire fighting, and hazard control can be most effectively integrated into the localized daily routines of individuals.

Chapter 2 details how we began with the census tract or small municipality and adjusted it to the location of environmental hazards using approximately one-half mile as the research area. We have a concern about a spatial framing problem resulting from using the term *neighborhood*. The word contains *neighbor*. It is possible that people do not include federal and state highways, airports, oil refineries, and other prominent nonresidential land uses in their neighborhood. We needed to use the word neighborhood to be consistent with federal databases that use it, and we allowed self-definition of neighborhood to be consistent with the federal data. To deal with the limitations of the word neighborhood and respondent definition of neighborhood, we visited every neighborhood and mapped the land uses so that we could determine instances in which

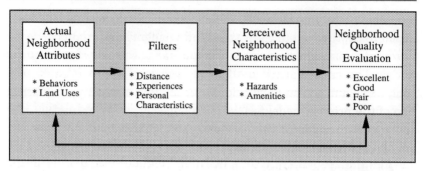

Figure 1.1. Process Model of Neighborhood Characteristics and Perception of Neighborhood Quality

respondents did not recognize the existence of facilities or activities that were present. Two such instances are described in chapters 4 and 7.

Insider and Outsider Perspectives on Neighborhood Quality

Borrowing from the work of Lee (1968), Moore and Golledge (1976), Rapoport (1977), Saarinen (1976), and others, figure 1.1 is a simple process model of how we think people rate their neighborhood quality. The actual neighborhood contains physical attributes such as factories and grocery stores, and behavioral attributes such as barking dogs and baseball games. The actual risks and benefits associated with physical and behavioral attributes are filtered by images and values strongly influenced by age, economic status, ethnicity/race, education, mass media exposure, and experiences with other neighborhoods. Filtering leads to transformation of actual neighborhood characteristics into perceived hazards and amenities.

Perceived characteristics are the database of neighborhood quality ratings—whether people classify their neighborhood as excellent, good, fair, or poor. Perception, in the sense used in this book, is the actual receipt of stimuli from the environment by hearing, sight, smell, taste, and touch. Some of the environmental hazards studied in this book are so powerful that they activate the less well known tactile senses of cold, warmth, pain, pressure, balance, and movement (kinesthetic sense) (see Gold 1980). Perceptions of residents living in neighborhoods with environmental hazards are converted by conscious and unconscious filters into recalled images, which we hoped to capture in our assessment of neighborhood quality.

We use a place with an operating nuclear power station—one type of environmental hazard not included in the case studies in this book—and our personal experiences to initially illustrate the operation of the process model for "insiders" and "outsiders." Insiders live and travel throughout the neighborhood; outsiders do not. Outsiders travel through the neighborhood, may periodically stop in it, but have a limited experience with the neighborhood.

First, we summarize the general public's perception of living near nuclear generating stations—that is, the outsider viewpoint. The U.S. Council on Environmental Quality (1980) commissioned a study of public willingness to live near so-called locally unwanted land uses, or LULUs. Seventy-five percent of respondents did not want to live within ten miles of a nuclear power plant, and half did not to live within fifty miles of one. These results were confirmed by others (Lindell and Earle 1983; Slovic et al. 1991).

Now we turn to insiders perceptions, the population of primary interest to us. In 1984, one of the authors (Greenberg) undertook field survey research for the U.S. Nuclear Regulatory Commission (NRC). He made an informal visit to a small town hosting a nuclear power generating station to talk unofficially with residents. The nuclear power station is located in a suburban town about thirty-five miles from a city. One of the first discussions was with an Asian American male approximately thirty-five years old. This self-described businessman had recently relocated in the neighborhood. He considered the nuclear station, located about two miles from his house, a windfall because it paid such a large proportion of the municipal taxes. His property taxes were low, the school had excellent teachers, and this father of two emphasized that his children already were getting free violin lessons at the school. When asked about the generating station, he remarked that he trusted the utility and government to protect him more than our government could protect him from being "nuked" by the Russians.

The second insider, a Caucasian woman approximately seventy years old, lived about four miles from the nuclear power station. Observed raking leaves in front of her home, she had decided to move. Her multistory house, she said, was too large for her to maintain. When asked about the nuclear power station, she said some people were concerned, but that she felt that "they [the utility] was doing the best they could" and, anyway, the electricity had to be produced somewhere.

We did not expect these two informal conversations to represent the views of township residents. Yet a year later we found that these insider views were not unusual. In 1985, we (Greenberg et al. 1986) examined population change in municipalities hosting all forty-nine operating nuclear generating stations in the United States. Excluding one of the forty-nine municipalities because of census boundary changes, the total population of the forty-eight host communities grew from 335,000 to 450,000 between 1970 and 1980, the decade when nearly all of these plants became operational. The 35 percent increase was more than three times the national growth rate and exceeded that experienced by 87 percent of more than three thousand county government units in the United States. Notably, 76 percent of the host communities experienced greater population growth during that decade than their surrounding (ten-mile radius) regions, compared with only 56 percent during the previous decade.

Because it was their policy to locate facilities in areas at least twenty to thirty miles from population centers, the NRC was distressed by the findings (Greenberg et al. 1986). At their behest, we surveyed the municipal planners of all the host and adjacent townships to try to understand why people were moving into municipalities with a nuclear hazard that supposedly frightens people. This survey was conducted after the Three Mile Island nuclear facility accident (March 28, 1979), when we would have expected great concern on the part of residents and planners about living near a nuclear power reactor.

A response rate of 92 percent was obtained for that survey (191 of 204). The planners said that the greater growth in the host communities was triggered by the tax payments made by the utilities to the local governments and to a much lesser extent the in-migration of people who worked at the nuclear station. Host municipal revenues typically doubled and school district revenues increased by 40 percent. Furthermore, the nuclear power station was not an important factor constraining new developments. Property values appreciated more in the host communities than in adjacent towns.

Financial benefits were not the only explanation for the growth of many of these places. Insiders saw, felt, heard, smelled, and responded to the entire place they lived in, not just the part that outsiders, such as the authors, focused on. Returning to the small town with the generating station, at a local roadside fruit stand, the owner drove home Michael Greenberg's narrow outsider's perspective on this place when he suggested that Greenberg stop "gawking at the station" and go visit the nearby river if he "really wanted to see what this place is like."

Greenberg did. More than a decade later, he can still recall the contrasting images of the generating station area and the nearby river area. The river area was quiet, not noisy like the nuclear power station. Sounds at the river were made by winds, birds, and running water, not turbines, machinery, and trucks. Smells were of flowers and water, not machine oil. Everything at the river could be touched, unlike the inside of the generating station, where Greenberg stared but was reluctant to touch. The view at the river was horizontal, not vertical as it was at the plant site. The topography was primarily natural, not artificial. Objects at the river were light greens, yellow, and blues, not dark as they were at the generating station. Finally, Greenberg's impressions were effected by movement. To get to the river, he had to take a ride along some winding roads and then had to walk down an embankment. He was moving slowly, as was the river. In contrast, his first and continuing impression of the generating station was from the inside of a car driving along a major road with several dips and climbs at fifty-five-plus miles per hour. Overall, Greenberg's outsider perception of this small town was totally different after he visited the river. The vast majority of outsiders will never see the river area and will only see the cooling towers, plume, and reactor building from their cars. Because they will not, outsiders' ratings of this small, neighborhood-sized town will never be like those of most of the residents.

There are many examples in the literature that demonstrate differences in outsider and insider perceptions of places. We have selected five that illustrate the kinds of areas included in this study.

In *Hard Times,* Charles Dickens created a fictitious place called Coketown to express his feelings about the rapid urbanization and industrialization of Victorian England:

> Seen from a distance in such weather (sunny), Coketown lay
> shrouded in a haze of its own, which appeared impervious to the

> sun's rays. You only knew the town was there, because you knew
> there could have been no such sulky blotch . . . without a town.
> The whole town seemed to be frying in oil. There was a stifling
> smell of hot oil everywhere. (1960:145, 147)

Real Coketowns exist all over the world, but not all of them are seen
through Dickens-colored lenses. Dickens's perceptions were filtered
by his feelings that urbanization and industrialization were out of
control and destroying his image of a good environment. Others see
their own, personal Coketowns differently.

For example, the area between northern New Jersey and Staten
Island, New York, that contains the eastern parts of Elizabeth, Newark, and Linden, New Jersey, is a late-twentieth-century Coketown.
It contains or contained breweries, chemical plants, hazardous-waste
sites, landfills, metal-fabricating facilities, petroleum refineries and
tank farms, slaughterhouses, sewerage plants, utility lines and
power plants, and numerous other physical characteristics of
Coketown. The case study of eastern Elizabeth (chapter 5) and one
of the hazardous-waste sites (chapter 6) are located in these municipalities.

Calvin Stillman—the insider—formerly a Rutgers University professor, argued that there are politically dominant viewpoints but no
such thing as a definition of natural beauty for all people. Stillman's
example was this Coketown area of northeastern New Jersey: "I enjoy the landscape of the New Jersey Turnpike north of the Raritan
River. These industrial landscapes belong there, and I'm glad to see
them, sweaty, rusty, smoking, and dirty as they are" (Stillman
1975:25). Stillman was responding to his decades of experiences in
the area, as well as his feeling that the state was taking steps to
control pollution in this New Jersey Coketown.

Another example is Spofford, a youth detention center in the Bronx
(New York). It is not considered a good place for a youthful offender
to be sent. Torres (1989:27) described it as the "boot camp for Riker's
Island, the city's graduate school for criminals," a place that family
court judges—the outsiders—use as a threat to scare youngsters out
of criminal behavior. Former heavyweight boxing champion Mike
Tyson—the insider—was raised in the Brownsville section of Brooklyn. Tyson described his Brownsville neighborhood as "awful living
conditions, poverty, and peer pressure." Trained as a pickpocket,
Tyson was arrested and sent to Spofford. Tyson was "not at all afraid

of it"—his new neighborhood. The former boxing champion described this supposedly fear-inspiring place as a "country club. My friends were there, and I was like a regular. The staff would see me and they were just so nice. They would go to the store outside and buy me stuff in the night . . . bring it to my room" (Torres 1989:31).

Not all environmentally degraded areas are in urbanized and industrialized areas. Chapter 6 presents some that are located in rural and suburban places. Grady Clay (1976) described the Copper Basin, a thirty-five-thousand-acre area located close to the border of Georgia and North Carolina and the rural settlement of Ducktown, Tennessee. From the Civil War to the 1920s, the natural forests were cut to fuel local copper smelting. Later, the area was effected by copper sulfide fumes emanating from the open-air roasting of copper ore. In the early twentieth century, high stacks spread the contaminants. Little remediation was done, even during the 1960s and 1970s. Virtually all the vegetation was destroyed.

Clay picked up twenty-six tourist maps and brochures at a roadside stand in Tennessee. None identified the Copper Basin. Whereas insiders pretty much ignored the area, tourists had strong reactions, including the following colorful descriptions: "A hellhole, a blister, something out of Dante's Inferno, the ugliest place in the South, a moonscape, a red-desert, post holocaust-wasteland, a fascinating wasteland, a ravaged wonder, the largest man-made desert in the United States" (Clay 1976:108).

Outsiders often rate places by looking at the environment through very narrow perspectives. In 1986, Bill Kent, an insider, described "12 great towns that you can still afford" in *New Jersey Monthly*. His descriptions of these twelve places included "relaxing atmosphere, only minutes from New York," "sleepy streets and large white houses," "rural delights with urban advantages," "riverfront homes," "Victorian houses still line the street," and "a homey environment close to the beach." Kent's clear message was that these dozen towns offered high-quality environments. Though not a resident of these towns, the reporter was an insider who had visited and studied New Jersey municipalities with the goal of finding high-quality environments within the state.

Jay Gould was the outsider. In the same year as the publication of Kent's article, using "two environmental measures of exposure to toxic waste as a measure of an area's 'quality of life,'" Gould (1986:8) classified all zip code areas in the United States according to the number of inactive hazardous-waste sites and estimates of the volume of toxic waste generated per capita. We examined Gould's data for the twelve towns in Kent's article. One of the twelve had to be eliminated because it did not have its own zip code. The remaining towns had twenty-nine inactive hazardous-waste sites and averaged 60 percent more toxic waste per capita than the United States as a whole. Through lenses colored with the fear of toxic waste, the towns identified by Kent could not be considered desirable neighborhoods, much less among the most desirable in New Jersey.

Had the *New Jersey Monthly* reporter lied to magazine readers— that is, hidden important information about health and safety from potential buyers? Or does Gould's book represent too narrow a view of what constitutes neighborhood quality? In 1980 the median prices of houses sold in these eleven towns was 22 percent higher than houses sold in New Jersey as a whole and 13 percent higher than houses sold in the United States as a whole. In 1985, the differences were 23 and 37 percent, and in 1988 they were 26 and 99 percent, respectively (Sternlieb and Hughes 1990). In other words, the presence of toxic waste did not seem to hinder the appreciation of house values in these municipalities. Perhaps those that purchased the houses were unaware of the toxic materials. More likely, Gould, the outsider, ignored the information that insiders use when they rate places.

Hull is a British city of more than 200,000 on the North Sea. Burgess (1974) asked 180 inhabitants and 180 outsiders to describe the City of Hull by choosing from a list of forty-eight adjectives. More than two-thirds of the outsiders picked, in order, the following: docks, working-class city, ships, fishing, heavy industry, and slums. Insiders picked good shopping, working-class city, docks, large council estates, friendly people, and trees and parks. In short, outsiders picked Hull's stressful physical and behavioral characteristics; insiders picked shopping, friendly people, and green areas as well as the more obvious negative stressors.

In conclusion, outsiders are drawn to the most prominent characteristics they observe or learn about from secondary sources. If these are negative characteristics, such as an incinerator, landfill, or drug problem, then the neighborhood rating will be negative. Insiders have a much broader experience base. For instance, the street corner that seems harmless to the outsider may be avoided by the insider who recalls the frightening image of a drug-related shooting. On the other hand, the insider may become inured to real dangers because, in their experience, a potentially dangerous facility has never had an accident, a family member or trusted friend works at the plant, or the plant's management has sponsored local activities.

This book focuses on the resident insider perspective. Yet the expert perspective is important. The experts we consulted for the studies described in this book are not officials sitting in state capitals, in Washington, D.C., or in universities. Our experts are local health officers and planning officials. We regard them as insider-outsiders. Nearly all of these officials have advanced degrees and many years of experience in the study areas. They are in the best position to reflect on resident perceptions of the most serious environmental hazards in their neighborhoods.

Classifying Environmental Hazards and Neighborhood Quality

Before presenting the environmental hazards classification we used in this research, we note other classifications of hazards (see Cutter 1993 and Zeigler, Johnson, and Brunn 1983 for summaries). Starr (1969) classified technological risks into voluntary and involuntary categories. Rating hazards according to their probability of occurrence and consequence is another popular approach. More complex typologies have been created, such as Hohenemser, Kates, and Slovic's (1983) seven-group multiple-criteria classification. Another interesting classification was Whyte and Burton's (1980) grouping of hazards by causes, such as economic development, natural resources, new products, and public health. The last comes the closest to our needs, but none fit what we required for this neighborhood-scale research.

Avalanches, blizzards, droughts, earthquakes, hailstorms, heat waves, landslides, lightning, tornadoes, volcanic eruptions, and other geophysical natural hazards were deliberately omitted from our empirical research for two reasons. With the exception of flooding, the national database we used in chapter 3 does not provide natural-hazards data related to neighborhood quality. This void made it impossible to compare the results of the field surveys with a large national database. Furthermore, we had an extremely difficult time finding neighborhoods in the Northeast United States (where our field research was done) that were seriously jeopardized by physical, behavioral, and natural hazards. Some existed, but the physical and behavioral hazards associated with these places were not as obvious as they were in the places we chose.

We divided hazards that should affect insiders' neighborhood quality ratings into four types based on hazard type and scale: (1) massive technology sites and their progeny, (2) local activity spaces, (3) blight, and (4) crime and other behavioral hazards. Before describing each in detail, we explain the rationale for the classification. The four groups are our attempt to organize potential hazards in ways that would contrast outsiders' and insiders' perceptions. For example, large physical hazards such as incinerators are the most frightening identifiable neighborhood hazards to the outsider. But they may be a source of employment and tax revenues to insiders, and insiders may not have experienced an accident or noticed any other problem at the site.

Crime, a biophysical hazard, is unlikely to be noticed by the passing outsider, but is likely to be a major concern to the insider. Burned-out buildings are visible to the outsider, but more subtle forms of blight, such as broken street lights, which are unlikely to be noticed by outsiders, will be noticed by some insiders and linked to an increased chance of mugging. The local bar, restaurant, or nightclub is likely to be perceived as an attraction by the outsider and by many neighborhood residents. But the resident who lives fifty feet away may view the facility as a source of rowdy drunken people.

The literature about these hazards is so large that it would not be feasible to attempt a comprehensive review. Instead we focus on the popular images of these four sets of hazards.

Massive Technology Sites and Their Progeny. Hazardous-waste sites, incinerators, factories, landfills, petrochemical complexes, superhighways, utility towers, and other land uses are massive physical landscape features. These "massive technology sites" attract the outsider gazing through the window of an airplane, automobile, bus, or train. They sometimes produce horrendous odors, noises, and other effluvia. In addition, decades of criticizing corporate industrial giants and their waste-management progeny, and highly controversial sitting disputes (exemplified by NIMBY—the Not in My Back Yard syndrome) have made these massive technology sites the most politically visible features on the environmentally devastated landscape.

During the last two decades, academic scientists, environmental groups, fiction writers, government officials, journalists, and movie and song writers have turned these massive features into caricatures of the physical and social evils brought about by American industrialization. The following examples convey some of the flavor of these caricatures.

Gas tanks, mines, railroads, sewerage and water treatment plants, pipelines, and towers holding electrical transmission lines have been in and out of the news. For instance, the explosion of a liquified natural gas (LNG) facility in Mexico City on November 19, 1984, killed 452 people and injured more than 4,000 (Meislin 1984). Mass media coverage was extensive. This explosion all but stopped efforts to locate LNG facilities in the United States. LNG has not been much in the U.S. news during the last decade, nor in many environmental-risk books. On the other hand, transmission-line corridors and the electromagnetic fields they create have become a major story (Marks 1994). The 1994 explosion of a line carrying natural gas in Edison, New Jersey, about two miles from our offices was a reminder of another potential technological hazard and the news media's great interest in technological hazards.

Massive technology sites can be important perceptual stimuli. We focus here on highways, airports, manufacturing facilities, and hazardous-waste sites because they have attracted uninterrupted attention for a decade or more.

Highways are associated with dirt, dust, dividing neighborhoods, and, especially, the din of noise (Appleyard and Lintell 1972). Kunstler (1993) singled out the automobile industry and highways as the "Evil Empire" for contributing to a *Geography of Nowhere.* Describing the impact of new roads on British neighborhoods, Colin Ward (1989:24) noted: "In retrospect, we would cynically conclude that the more fortunate cities had an engineer who was lazy, close to retirement, or addicted to golf." In other words, fewer roads maintain neighborhood integrity.

Highway traffic is by far the most frequent source of noise complaints. Indoor sound levels no higher than 45 decibels (Db) and outside ones of 55 Db or less are needed for normal activities. Appreciable levels of annoyance and sleep and speech interference occur at 60 Db; physiological stress and hearing damage occur at 90 Db; and startle occurs at 110 Db. At levels of 60 to 70 Db, widespread community complaints and periodic lawsuits are expected. Vigorous political and legal appeals are observed as the noise level increases to about 80 Db (Greenberg 1979).

Airports are associated with traffic jams, airplane crashes, and extraordinarily high levels of noise. When present, low-flying aircraft are an even more distressing source of noise than motor vehicles on highways. Jets, especially jumbo jets that cannot rise quickly, create an extremely high decibel level and a whining sound upon takeoff (Greenberg 1979; Kryter 1970; U.S. Environmental Protection Agency 1974). Unlike a highway where the noise is relatively continuous and can often be masked by sound barriers and air conditioning, airport noise is discontinuous and is virtually impossible to mask. In addition to task interference and the uncontrollable physiological changes observed in people living near highways, those residing near airports suffer from feelings of helplessness and lack of control (Glass and Singer 1978).

During the 1970s, environmental organizations fought against massive technology sites and the people who built them. For example, Environmental Action, Inc. is a political lobbying group located in Washington, D.C. The cover of a 1976 issue of *Environmental Action* showed a picture of the massive U.S. Steel Corporation Clairton works located fifteen miles from Pittsburgh, Pennsylvania. The facility was described as a "pyrolitic monster dominat[ing] the landscape" that contributed to lung cancer, emphysema, landscape destruction, pneumoconiosis, and silicosis (Maize 1976).

Environmental organizations are not the only source of the ugly industrial site image. For instance, the U.S. Environmental Protection Agency (EPA) produced *Fish Kills Caused by Pollution in 1973,* a brief report with a very suggestive front cover: a dead fish in red with a white eye on a black front cover. Even though the authors of the report noted that the rapid increase in fish killed by factories and other fixed facilities could be explained by increased public awareness of pollution, the cover set a negative tone. When this report was shown to a class of our undergraduate students at Rutgers University and discussed a week later, virtually every student remembered the picture of the dead red fish with a white eye and the fact that factory and power plant pollution caused most of the kills. They did not recall the caveats about the data.

Talented writers with a moral cause have left an indelible image of ugly massive technology sites. Commoner's *Closing Circle* (1971), Fallows's *Water Lords* (1971), Meek and Straayer's *Politics of Neglect: The Environmental Crisis* (1971), Zwick's *Water Waste-Land* (1971), and, more recently, Weir's *Bhopal Syndrome* (1987) and Goldman's *Truth About Where You Live: An Atlas for Action on Toxins and Mortality* (1991) conveyed a powerful verbal message about the evils of industrial pollution from massive technology sites.

Although industry has spent billions of dollars to control their emissions, reaffirmations of evil massive technology sites have continued unabated in the 1990s. For example, two new publications arrived as this chapter was being drafted. In *Toxic Circles: The Environmental Hazards from the Workplace into the Community,* Sheehan and Weeden (1993:inside flap) conclude that everybody needs to worry about "the toxic circles of industrial hazards [that] spread in successive waves outward: from the workplace to the home, to the neighborhood, and to the community."

In "A Town Called Morrisonville," Bowermaster (1993) used pictures and carefully crafted and located language to severely criticize Dow Chemical's Plaquemine facility in Louisiana. The subtitle of the article was "In Louisiana's 'Cancer Alley,' Dow Chemical and the other companies are buying out neighboring communities." The first line of the text is "A cemetery sits just behind the Nazarene Baptist." This signal language is keyed to pictures of abandoned houses, and forlorn-looking residents standing with the chemical plant in the background.

Science fiction writers have also contributed to the evil massive technology site image. For example, *The Last Gasp* (Hoyle 1990), *Stark* (Elton 1989), and *Telos* (Versluis 1987) describe the death of Earth by a green bomb that destroyed all the vegetation, a virulent form of dioxin that happens to be contagious, and automobiles described by Hoyle (1990:70) as "movable instruments of death, like Nazi gas ovens on wheels." The only consistent message in these three books is that Earth's destruction was caused by bad-guy billionaires operating from fortresslike technology sites. In short, even in the futures they constructed, these science fiction writers grasped tightly onto the perception that massive technology sites are evil.

Hazardous-waste sites became the major targets of the media during the 1980s. Photo essayists created durable and detailed images of industrial waste disposal, sometimes referred to as "flashbulb memories" because of their ability to arouse emotions (Winograd and Neisser 1992). For instance, Goin's (1991) photos of *Nuclear Landscapes* convey the results of decades of disposing radioactive waste in the American West, and the Smiths' (1975) photos of Minamata cast spellbinding and grotesque pictures of the victims of mercury disposal in Japan. Kaufman and Herz (1984) produced the "first Super-Hero from New Jersey," described as "98 pounds of solid nerd until he became the Toxic Avenger."

Children have also been targeted to receive evil images. For example, Hawkes's (1991) and Hare's (1991) children's books feature page after page of pictures of wastes, dead and deformed people, dead fish and animals. Hawkes's *Toxic Waste and Recycling* shows a world map of the geography of cancer on the same page as a discussion of the "hard facts" of toxic waste. The message conveyed both visually and verbally is that toxic waste is directly associated with the geography of cancer: "The World Health Organization estimates that 60–70 percent of all cancers are environmental in origin. So pollution and toxic waste may already be causing far more deaths than we yet realise" (Hawkes 1991:30).

Finally, Brown's award-winning *Laying Waste: The Poisoning of America by Toxic Chemicals* (1981); Epstein, Brown, and Pope's *Hazardous Waste in America* (1982); and Piller's *The Fail-Safe Society: Community Defiance and the End of American Technological Optimism* (1991) all focus outstanding writing skills and moral outrage on toxic waste disposal. Brown and Mikkelsen's (1990) provocative *No Safe Place* is particularly effective at creating emotion because it draws together industry, hazardous waste, cancer clusters, and lawsuits into a spellbinding story of how economic power takes precedence over environmental interests. A reader of this book would have a difficult time not experiencing the depicted powerlessness and rage felt by the residents of the environmentally devastated Woburn, Massachusetts, neighborhood.

A particularly good example of how government, environmental organizations, academia, and the mass media interact to create and enhance evil massive technology site images is the case of Love Canal in New York. Landy, Roberts, and Thomas (1990) argue that the provocative photographic images and verbal labels "ticking time bomb" and "public health emergency" were first applied to Love Canal by government officials in order to obtain federal and state funds, to justify legal actions against dumpers, and to block opposition to rapid action.

The mass media did not create the emotionally laden phrases, the mistrust, or the scientific uncertainty that led to public responses to Love Canal, but they enhanced them. They took advantage of a summer lull in news and government pronouncements to make Love Canal into a major story. Landy (1986:60) contended that "the . . . sensational language, coupled with the excellent photo opportunities . . . aroused the news media from its late summer torpor. Love Canal became the national news story for days on end." It was featured on the "MacNeil-Lehrer Report," "Sixty Minutes," "Good Morning America," and the "Phil Donahue" show.

Journalists are trained to report human interest. An event that is proximate, important to the audience, unusual, controversial, and, in the case of television, visual, is a potentially a good story that can be made into a great one (Sandman et al. 1987). Hazardous-waste sites have all of these elements. The image of the ticking bomb, good guys (neighborhood residents) and bad ones (chemical companies reluctant to admit guilt), and the evacuation of pregnant women and entire neighborhoods are just a few of the human elements of good story. As some of the most gruesome-looking waste sites happen to be located proximate to major media centers like New York, Washington, D.C., and Los Angeles (Greenberg et al. 1989), good stories were easy to reach and the mass media took advantage of them.

The EPA and elected officials contributed to these negative images by proclaiming unequivocally that hazardous waste was the most important health threat for the 1980s (Stafford 1981). For television, the number one source of news for Americans and that which Adams (1992) sees emerging as its own "gathering place," Love Canal and other hazardous-waste sites provided striking pictures of leaking drums, discolored lawns and basements, and frightened and angry people.

During the period 1978–87, ABC, CBS, and NBC's nightly network flagship news ran ninety-nine Love Canal stories that took 191.2 minutes of news time (Greenberg and Wartenberg 1990). This was more time than the three networks' most expensive news shows

devoted to all the influenza epidemics, Legionnaire's disease out-
breaks, AIDS reports in New York City, San Francisco, and other
locations, and teenage suicides.

The mass media worked to convert a good story into a outstanding one with language, headlines, and photos (Greenberg et al. 1989;
Prato 1991; Sandman et al. 1987; Singer and Endreny 1993). For
example, a 1980 *Time* (September 22, 1980) magazine cover story
was called "The Poisoning of America." The cover showed a man in
a pool. The parts of his face and body submerged in water had dis-
solved to leave only a skeleton.

Kasperson et al. (1988) argue that transfer of hazard risk information to the public has created a feedback loop that has pressured
government officials and industry into programs that are far beyond
what is needed. In other words, the actual risks associated with a
particular hazard are amplified, whereas others are attenuated.

Hazardous waste is clearly a candidate for one hazard that has
been amplified. Both the EPA and American industry have suggested
that priorities ought to be reordered (Foster, Bernstein, and Huber
1993; Grayson and Shepard 1972; U.S. Environmental Protection
Agency 1987; Whelan 1993). We focus here on the cancer and hazardous-waste concern because the dread attached to cancers has his-
torically dominated the concerns of agencies and the public. The
EPA's Cancer Risk Work Group, consisting of twenty-five senior managers and technical staff, analyzed thirty-one environmental problem areas under the agency's jurisdiction. Inactive hazardous-waste
sites were ranked eighth, active hazardous-waste sites thirteenth,
releases from storage tanks nineteenth, direct point discharges to
surface water, indirect point source discharges to surface water, and
accidental releases of toxins and oils spills ranked twenty-third to
twenty-sixth. Worker exposure to chemicals and indoor radon were
ranked tied for first, pesticide residues on food ranked third, and
indoor air pollutants (other than radon) and consumer exposure to
chemicals were tied for fourth. The reality of the EPA's suggested
reordering would be to shift priorities from technology sites to homes
and farms.

Neither the EPA's nor industry's goals are likely to be accepted
by a public that is outraged over industries, generating stations, towers and lines, hazardous-waste sites, and other massive technology
sites. For instance, Edelstein (1988) and Peck (1989) studied the

written record and interviewed residents of neighborhoods with hazardous-waste sites. They reported depressed and pessimistic people who felt betrayed. Odors and sounds from sites were a constant reminder of their helplessness. Many victims moved and many others wished they could. Property values typically drop at least 5 to 10 percent within one-half mile of waste sites, sometimes more (Greenberg and Hughes 1993; McClelland, Shulze, and Hurd 1990).

Public opinion polls confirm these case studies. In 1978, when the United States was first learning about hazardous-waste sites, out of a list of thirty threats to health, the public ranked industrial waste first—much higher than cigarettes, alcohol, or cholesterol (Yankelovich, Skelly, and White 1979). Later surveys (Roper 1990) confirmed the earlier ones. For example, 75 percent of Americans rated environmental contamination from chemical waste disposal as a serious problem. This compared to 32 percent for indoor air pollution, 51 percent for pesticide residues on foods, and 56 percent for worker exposure to toxic chemicals. Baxter's (1990) review of two decades of American public opinion polls indicates that Americans want more emphasis on environmental protection, look favorably on environmentalists but not industries, and want more regulation of emissions.

Polls commissioned by the Chemical Manufacturers Association (1991:2) show that the "public still regards the chemical industry with a great deal of suspicion and distrust; the only industry ranking worse than chemicals is tobacco." Communities with plants had only slightly better opinions of industry. Thirty percent of respondents in chemical plant communities rated the chemical industry very or generally favorable compared to 27 percent of the general public. Only 13 percent of respondents strongly or somewhat agreed with the statement that the chemical industry is honest, ethical, and is doing a good job of self-regulating to protect health and the environment.

Images of dread, mistrust, violation, immorality, and the absence of control associated with Bhopal, Chernobyl, Love Canal, Seveso, Three Mile Island, and Times Beach, among others, have been branded onto massive technology sites. These images seem impervious to intervention, in this generation at least. The combination of continuing contamination incidents, the growth of combative environmental organizations, the absence of trust of industry and often government officials, and extensive mass media coverage lead us to conclude that the image of massive technology sites as evil will continue to impress both insiders and outsiders.

Local Activity Spaces. Some bars, fast-food places, garages, gasoline stations, liquor stores, local roads, restaurants, waste-recycling sheds, and fire, police, and ambulance-dispatch stations are needed by neighborhoods but often disturb their neighbors. People living near these spaces sometimes suffer from noise pollution, carelessly discarded garbage, odors, and invasion of their space by rowdy, noisy people and their illegally parked boats, cars, and motorcycles. Clay and Hollister (1983) call them "nuisance" land uses and observe that developers tend to avoid them. While there is virtually no literature about local activity spaces as environmental hazards, it is not hard to imagine that these spaces appear relatively benign from the outside but may have a bigger impact on neighborhood quality for their neighbors than the more sinister-appearing massive technology sites.

Blight. Abandoned houses, factories, and businesses; occupied buildings in poor or dangerous condition; inadequate street lighting; streets, roads, and sidewalks badly in need of repair; open ditches, litter, or trash in streets and vacant lots are damning symbols of neighborhood decay. Hart and Associates observed: "The weaknesses of a neighborhood are . . . tangible—its crime, its robberies, its sanitation, litter and dust, its boarded up buildings, its delinquents, and most of all—property not maintained. People can spot a weak neighborhood—it is there for them to see" (Clay and Hollister 1983:141).

Blighted neighborhoods rarely attract large-scale private capital (Clay and Hollister 1983; Goetze 1976). Using data from four suburban neighborhoods, Heimstra and McFarling (1978) found that neighborhood maintenance was the strongest statistical correlate of neighborhood satisfaction—stronger than the populations' friendliness and homogeneity and stronger than noise level. Litter, in particular, symbolizes aesthetic wounds and physical hazard. Sanoff (1975) argued that the environment sends behavioral messages. Tables with people reading suggest silence, a closed door suggests caution, and litter in the streets suggests neighborhood death.

Gallagher (1993) linked blight to a feeling of loss of control. He argued that abandoned housing, litter-strewn streets, vacant lots, and alleys are where drug and crime occur—that is, they are places that the neighborhood cannot control. Like an army that has lost a battle, neighbors retreat before the physical and behavioral blight to try to protect smaller and more defensible parts of the neighborhood. Behavioral geographers have also summarized the image of neighborhood blight: "To live in a blighted environment is dispiriting, demeaning, and profoundly dehumanizing. Ugliness spreads, often because people flee before it, as people in the Middle Ages fled bubonic plagues, leaving wastelands behind them" (Lewis, Lowenthal and Tuan 1973:1, 4).

The feedback between violence and blight has been apparent for many decades and identified through many mechanisms. For example, the Kerner Commission's (1968) famous report on the origins of civil disorders listed the following associated "environmental problems": insufficient number of receptacles for garbage, bulk refuse dumped by people moving out, abandoned cars, rodents attracted to garbage, traffic congestion, and slow snow removal hindering garbage pickup. In other words, clearing municipal garbage from streets and houses, not toxins from nearby massive technology sites, was what the commission perceived as the solution to neighborhood environmental problems.

Kotlowitz (1991) portrayed decay and violence though the eyes of two children, Pharoah and Lafayette, trying to survive their inner-city Chicago neighborhood, located about a mile from the Sears Tower. Kotlowitz's book, which was turned into a movie, vividly captured the environment of the deteriorating neighborhood: "The two- and three-family tenements sag and lean like drunkards. Many of the buildings are vacant, their contents lying on the sidewalk. There were no banks, there were no public libraries, movie theaters, skating rinks, or bowling alleys to entertain the neighborhood's children. . . . And there was no rehabilitation center, though drug use was rampant" (Kotlowitz 1991:12).

In this environment, the two children routinely witnessed acts of violence, were subjected to threats of violence, and in a "neighborhood which hungrily devoured its children" (Kotlowitz 1991:10), they became involved in violence. Even though he lived in an environmentally devastated neighborhood, Lafayette and his friend James created an image of an excellent one, which they described to each other: " 'I'm gonna have my own condominium in Calumet Park. It's nice out there' [said James]. 'You could sit outside all night and nothing would happen. They have flowers this tall,' [said Lafayette,] holding his hand four feet off the ground" (Kotlowitz 1991:31–32).

Blighted neighborhoods like Lafayette and Pharoah's have been extensively studied. Jakle and Wilson (1992) provided a comprehensive and historical review of the relationship between abandonment, disinvestment, vacancy, decay, and crime and derelict American policies. Greenberg et al. (1992) and Greenberg, Popper, and West (1990) noted that blight, symbolized by the acronym TOADS (temporarily obsolete abandoned derelict sites), has always been a characteristic of American urban and rural places. Some spaces are always at the bottom of the land-use cycle because they no longer fit the most recent tastes for industrial, commercial, and residential space. However, TOADS and the social decay associated with TOADS have reached unprecedented levels in large U.S. cities, especially in the Northeast and Midwest. This is because big-city governments cannot control TOADS and the accompanying problems they create, such as lead and asbestos inhalation in many older neighborhoods (Silbergeld 1993a).

Wallace (1981, 1988, 1989) forcefully argued that government did more than fail to prevent neighborhood decay and violence. He charged that the South Bronx and parts of Brooklyn were deliberately abandoned by the government of New York City. Officials, argues Wallace, deliberately reduced fire and police protection. Landlords abandoned their properties to arsonists, the homeless, and waste dumpers. Some landlords commissioned arsonists to burn down their buildings for insurance payments. Each vacant building led to further fires as criminals vandalized plumbing and wiring. Poor residents, unable to find decent quarters outside their neighborhoods, moved into the homes of neighborhood friends and relatives. The resultant overcrowding led to more blight and abandonment, as well as to substantial jumps in assaultive violence, illicit sexual behavior, rodent bites, and the spread of AIDS and tuberculosis.

In summary, blight should be a key signal, perhaps the strongest signal, of a poor quality neighborhood.

Crime and Other Behavioral Hazards. Uncontrolled dogs, rats, and other animals, unfriendly neighbors, and violence, especially assaultive violence, are perceived as menacing environmental hazards. Uncontrolled dogs, rats, and other animals are a menace. The annual incidence of animal bites ranges from three hundred to one thousand per one hundred thousand people in the United States (Behrman and Vaughan 1987). In fact, animal bites are responsible for 1 percent of all emergency room visits, with dogs accounting for 50 to 95 percent of these injuries. The bite victims of rats are almost exclusively sleeping children. Bites can lead to physical and psychological scarring, as well as vaccination for rabies and other infectious diseases. Animals, especially rats, can also spread disease by contaminating food through their bite, their urine and feces, and by carrying fleas, lice, and mites. Birds, such as pigeons and starlings, mice, deer, rabbits, and raccoons can also present health and aesthetic problems in some neighborhoods.

Unfriendly neighbors can ruin a neighborhood. In a study of neighborhood satisfaction in the United States, Campbell, Converse, and Rodgers (1976) found that good neighbors were a better predictor of neighborhood satisfaction than housing upkeep, safety, and convenience to shopping, schools, and other services. Zehner (1972) reported that unfriendly, snobbish, and gossipy neighbors were a neighborhood detriment.

A Gallup poll (1977) reported that unfriendly neighbors were the fourth worst neighborhood characteristic. Only crime, poor housing, and blight were considered worse. Crime should be a dominant concern in some of our neighborhoods. Roper surveys during the period 1975–89 asked the public to prioritize eighteen problems for federal government intervention (Baxter 1990). Crime was the highest priority. An average of 80 percent of respondents rated crime and drugs as a high priority, compared to 58 percent for trying to solve the problems of ghettos, race, and poverty, and 56 percent for trying to improve environmental quality.

Slovic, Fischhoff, and Lichtenstein (1979) asked college students, risk experts, members of the League of Women's voters, and members of a business club who lived in Oregon to rate the risks of thirty activities and technologies. This research is often cited as evidence of the general public's fear of certain types of technological hazards, such as nuclear power. The survey showed that handguns, not nuclear power, and motor vehicles, smoking, motorcycles, or alcohol, were the greatest concern of nearly every group. Rogerson et al. (1989) reported on a national survey of twenty characteristics considered important to the quality of life in the United Kingdom. Violent crime ranked first and nonviolent crime ranked second.

The public's fear of violence has been fueled by a substantial reported increase in assaultive violence, especially homicide. In July 1992, the United States Public Health Service produced its first progress review of violence and abusive behavior (Mason 1992). The national goal was to reduce the homicide rate from 8.5 per 100,000 in 1987 to 7.2 by the year 2000. The report noted a failure to make progress toward this goal because of the increasing homicide rate among males, especially African American males. Numerous other federal government reports have made the same observation (see United States Department of Health and Human Services, 1985, 1990, 1991, 1992 for examples).

Some of the highest homicide rates and most marked increases in the number of homicides are in cities. For instance, McCord and Freeman (1990) found that black residents of Harlem in New York City had a homicide rate 14.2 times higher than the rate among United States whites. Findley and Ford (1993) repeated the Harlem study and found that Harlem males are dying at an earlier age than their black and nonblack counterparts elsewhere in the United States. In fact, Harlem's male mortality rate is among the highest in the world. Rodriguez-Trias (1993), formerly president of the American Public Health Association, labeled violence the greatest public health threat. This is an astonishing statement when we consider cancer, heart disease, AIDS, teenage pregnancy, and various other problems that face the public health community.

The media have taken these alarming national and local data and created frightening images. Network television shows featuring homicides, drug addicts, detectives, street police, vigilantes, lawyers, and judges are too numerous in both number and variety to even count. The news media are only a little less stingy with crime and violence coverage. For example, *USA Today,* the second most widely sold newspaper in the United States, started 1991 with this headline and story:

19 CITIES SET RECORDS FOR MURDER

More people were murdered during 1990 than any time in the USA's history—and by most projections this is just the start of the nation's most violent decade. (*USA Today,* 2 January 1991, p. 1)

Daily papers, magazines, and television routinely focus on violent crime, especially homicide committed by youths (Carnay 1986; Fedarko 1992; *Home News* 1990; *New York Times* 1992; Schwaneberg 1991; Stengel 1985; *Time* 1992a, 1992b; Traver 1992). Such violence has attracted the attention of political leaders. It is hard to conceive of circumstances that would stop an elected United States government official from placing crime reduction, more police, judges, and jails on the top of the priority list, along with reducing the size of government and not increasing taxes.

Prominent journalists have not ignored violence. For example, George Will's (1992) column "The Toughest Epidemic of All: Violence" describes the substantial increase in homicide. William Buckley's (1993) "Poverty, Racism Don't Explain Black Crime" focuses on the need for a more effective response from the criminal justice system.

A massive literature debates a host of primary and secondary causes of violence, such as alienation of youth, American's violent history, improved record keeping and reporting of violence, class hatred, envy, deterioration of the two-parent family and family values, drugs, frustration, lenient courts, loss of job opportunities for the unskilled, massive public-housing projects, neighborhood blight, oppressive police, poor public schools, professional criminals, poverty, racism, and welfare (see Harries 1992; Rose and McClain 1990; Rosenberg and Fenley 1991; and U.S. Department of Health and Human Services 1985 for discussions).

Each of these "causes" of violence is used in support of ideological causes and political positions. Opportunities to argue about the meaning of violence data abound, as do seemingly innumerable opportunities to blame individuals, groups, and society as a whole. In short, assaultive violence, like massive technology sites, is an amplified hazard—that is, a risk that is disproportionately of concern to Americans compared to the actual risk. For example, homicide and suicide rates in the United States are almost identical, but political officials pay relatively little attention to suicide, whereas political speeches are characteristically filled with concern about murderous criminals. Many Americans doubtless live in a general state of fear of being assaulted, robbed, and having their children, friends, and relatives assaulted and robbed. Fear, we assume, colors their whole lives, including their ability to learn, work, visit friends, trust officials, take care of their health, and enjoy their neighborhood.

Hazard Sensitivity and Insensitivity

Some people are so sensitive to environmental risks that they perceive risks that are not physically present. Others do not acknowledge the existence of risks that terrify the vast majority of Americans. For example, Weinstein (1988) compared the risk perceptions of New Jersey environmental officials with residents of selected towns. He found much greater concern among residents than state officials. Notably, some respondents perceived the existence of hazards in towns that were deliberately selected because those hazards did not exist in those towns. These unusually sensitive people presumably responded to hazards that they perceived as unfamiliar, uncontrollable, unfair, irreversible, dreaded, and artificial (Lowrance 1976; Slovic 1993). On the other hand, Douglas (1985) pointed out that some people interpret environmental disasters as omens or punishments that they cannot complain about. These people are unusually risk insensitive.

Meining (1979) recognizes the existence of people who view the landscape through ideological lenses. Some, he says, see blight, clutter, congestion, disorder, sprawl, and other problems; others see symbols of American competition, freedom, growth, power, and utility. We expected to find evidence of the most and least sensitive people in environmentally devastated neighborhoods. But we expected to find more evidence of insensitive than sensitive residents because of likelihood that residents of these neighborhoods would become inured to prominent hazards in order to survive psychologically in their difficult environments.

Amenities and Neighborhood Quality

Numerous national and local surveys show that a good neighborhood has good housing, friendly people, public safety and other services, and an attractive appearance (see Campbell, Converse, and Rodgers 1976; Clay and Hollister 1983; and Heimstra and McFarling 1978 for summaries). To most Americans, good housing means single family or condominium units. Neighborhoods that have high-valued and new housing are especially preferred.

"Friendly people" is a code that implies stable residents who are similar in age, class, culture, ethnicity, interests, race, religion, and other personal characteristics (Campbell, Converse, and Rodgers

1976; Clay and Hollister 1983). Similar people often form tight neighborhood social networks. For example, David Ward (1989) documented how poor nineteenth-century immigrant groups worked together to combat discrimination and to create jobs and services. Gans's (1962) classic description of insiders' perceptions of Boston's West End neighborhood exemplifies the importance of neighborliness. Insiders, most of whom were relatively poor Italian Americans, perceived the West End as a pleasant, low-rent, stable area. They focused their energies on building social networks, not on improving the physical appearance of buildings they did not own. The city government, the outsiders, had a different perception of the neighborhood environment and tore much of it down.

In urban areas, police services are usually essential for good neighborhood quality. Other desirable services and conveniences include good schools, fire protection, garbage collection, public transportation (in relatively poor areas), and medical services. Many of these neighborhood services were reduced during the 1980s because of fiscal problems. For example, Ginzberg, Berliner, and Ostow (1993) used Chicago, Houston, Los Angeles, and New York City to illustrate the rapid decline of health care services in the most economically stressed neighborhoods of economically stressed cities.

An attractive environment is an amenity. But what is attractive? Tod and Wheeler (1978) observed that utopian images of places to live have little in common. Three notable exceptions were the absence of lawyers, pure clear spring water, and green areas such as flowery meadows, beautiful woods, and trees that grow fruit. The absence of lawyers may indicate the desire for a noncontentious atmosphere. The importance of clean water is demonstrated by the billions of dollars spent to build water and sewerage treatment facilities and the extremely high priority given to protecting and remediating water supplies in hazardous-waste remediation programs (see chapter 6 for examples). A green environment has symbolic functions. Warner (1978) identified trees as part of the American democratic image. Detwyler and Marcus (1972) point to the therapeutic role of parks, cemeteries, greenbelts, railroad and utility lines, institutional properties, riverbanks, industrial sites, private lakes, gardens, and even closed dumps as the only source of routine contact between many urban Americans and the therapeutic natural environment, if one can accept the image of a closed dump as therapeutic.

Providing a green area in a neighborhood also creates jobs, often for neighborhood residents. Job creation through providing nature has a long history. For example, Callow (1965:126) described the development of New York City's Central Park: "The park was becoming less an oasis of Arcadian virtue and more a refuge of hungry job-seekers and unprincipled politicians." In short, Americans like neighborhoods that are comfortable, safe, stable, and natural.

Filters

Distance from potential hazards, physical barriers between people and hazards, and residents' personal experiences and characteristics change actual environments into perceived ones. Distance is a surrogate for sensual stimulation. Generally those who live close to an incinerator are more likely to see, hear, smell, read about, and otherwise experience the facility and react to it than those who live miles away. Yet their perception of danger is not always higher.

One reason is that linear distance is an imperfect measure. For example, Stoffle et al. (1991) studied public reaction to a proposed low-level radioactive waste facility in south-central Michigan and adjacent areas in Ohio and Indiana. Using a circular area with a radius of thirty-five miles as the area of potential perceptual impact, they found that public concern was concentrated within fifteen miles of the potential site. Yet the researchers also found "risk perception islands" twenty to seventy miles from the inner fifteen-mile area. Residents of these islands were concerned about transporting low-level radioactive waste through their communities. In other words, perceptual hot spots exist because of local conditions.

Physical barriers such as tall buildings, highways, and woods can partly or wholly filter out a nearby hazard. Conversely, the absence of visual barriers, the presence of prevailing winds, or a highway can stretch the area of concern, causing expanses of great hazard sensitivity.

Experience can increase or decrease residents' concerns. Those who have lived through hazard events become desensitized and stay or infuriated and try to leave. For example, Burton, Kates, and White (1978) reported that residents of areas that periodically flood experience flooding as part of their routine. Neighborhoods adjacent to noisy massive technology sites report the same result—that is, hazards become common everyday stresses that can be ignored, especially because the hazard is often a source of jobs and taxes (Douglas 1985; Greenberg 1979).

For instance, many of the residents of Oak Ridge, Tennessee have benefited from the nuclear research carried out in the area. Thompson (1992) described the community of Oak Ridge as one in which people live "happily near a nuclear trash heap." Residents are sometimes willing to tolerate an existing familiar hazard rather than risk the stigma associated with remediating it. In fact, Russell, Colglazier, and English (1991) reported that some communities with hazardous-waste sites do not want their site listed on a national hazard waste list because listing would further stress the local economy by frightening tourists away.

Neighborhood change is rarely uneventful to residents (Aitken 1990; Kaplan and Kaplan 1978; Palen 1987). Campbell, Converse, and Rodgers (1976) found that perception of neighborhood quality usually changed more rapidly than personal, work, and other life changes that influence quality of life. Some people experience change as improving quality of life. For example, higher socioeconomic status residents of recently gentrified areas report change as stimulating and positive. Conversely, neighborhood change sometimes produces a grief reaction similar to death or divorce (Freeman 1988; Folkman and Lazarus 1988; Gallagher 1993). Rapid, uncontrolled change can mean the in-migration of people who are considered undesirable, the loss of cherished friends who want to leave, the demolition of the local school, or the building of a noisy grocery store on what was a favorite open space.

Previous neighborhood experiences can powerfully effect perceptions of present neighborhood. A noisy and treeless neighborhood that distresses someone who previously lived in a quiet and heavily wooded area might please someone who just moved from an area where quiet and trees were associated with mugging.

Clay and Hollister's (1983) classification of neighborhood residents' propensity and reasons for relocating is a guidepost of what to expect in environmentally devastated neighborhoods. "Involuntary out-movers" leave because the neighborhood is changing in unsatisfactory ways, such as the development of gangs or the building of a sewerage treatment plant. This population possesses resources and the energy to leave. They are a headache for researchers because many will have moved out of the neighborhood by the time researchers arrive to obtain their views. In strong contrast, Clay and Hollister's "unwilling stayers" may be the angriest people in the environmentally devastated neighborhood. Lacking the resources or energy to relocate, they will probably rate their neighborhood as poor. "In-movers" who have taken advantage of housing bargains left by involuntary out-movers are likely to rate neighborhoods highly. Many recently lived in a worse neighborhood and may be willing to ignore the nearby factory and stray dogs for their new housing bargain.

Gender, age, race/ethnicity, and socioeconomic status are correlated with neighborhood perception (see Cutter 1993 and Van Liere and Dunlap 1980 for reviews). Studies of gender show that women are more concerned than men about physical and behavioral hazards (Blocker and Eckberg 1989; Douglas 1985; Hamilton 1985; Van Liere and Dunlap 1980). Younger people are more distressed by technological hazards, such as massive technology sites; older people are more anxious about crime (Buttel 1987; Ostman and Parker 1987). Van Liere and Dunlap (1980) speculate that younger people are willing to make the long-term investment to protect the environment, whereas older people are more concerned about their personal health and physical safety.

Generally, more educated and affluent people are more concerned with environmental protection than persons with less income and education. The former are assumed to have more time and resources to devote to the world environment; the latter are assumed to be concerned with shelter, food, and other necessities. The translation of this generalization into neighborhood quality is not clear. If illegal drugs move into a neighborhood, relatively affluent people can act on their feelings and leave. Poorer people may be equally distressed but may not be able to leave. A further complication is that low-income people are disproportionately likely to be happy with their neighborhood because it may be their sole sense of self-worth and control (Campbell, Converse, and Rodgers 1976; Gans 1962; Rapoport 1977).

Studies of ethnicity/nationality/racial/religious differences are inconclusive for some of the same reasons. For example, African Americans, in general, are less concerned with environmental protection than their counterparts in national polls. Yet some researchers have found greater concern among African Americans than others (Greenberg and Amer 1989; Lake 1983). These contradictory findings are consistent with the observation that people are more concerned with personal neighborhood threats than global and regional ones (Baldassare and Katz 1992). Sensitivity to personal threat also supports the strong reaction by minority populations against sitting massive technology sites in their neighborhoods and the slow remediation of existing ones (Bullard 1990; Commission for Racial Justice 1987).

Furthermore, ethnicity/nationality/racial/religious also become confounded by socioeconomic status (Taylor 1989). For instance, in a study of New York City college freshmen, Hinshaw and Allott (in Porteous 1977) observed that Jews and white Protestants were more satisfied with their neighborhoods than others. But these respondents tended to be affluent and live in desirable single-family structures.

In summary, residents' personal experiences and their experiences as part of their neighborhood influence how they perceive hazards and amenities. They will amplify the importance of some neighborhood attributes and attenuate the importance of others.

The Ethical Foundation

Considerable media, political, and environmental activist attention has been focused on distress felt by those who live near existing and proposed hazardous-waste sites and other LULUs. These LULUs have led to civil unrest, federal and state mandates to remediate sites, and efforts to prevent pollution through changing processes and recycling. As noted earlier in the chapter, setting priorities for remediating hazardous-waste sites initiated this project. But although we began our research in small cities, suburbs, and rural places with hazardous-waste sites, our strong sense was that much worse environmental devastation was to be found in multiple-hazard city neighborhoods. The research on TOADS described earlier in the chapter led us to believe that some central-city neighborhoods have become the dumping grounds for every land use and population that mainstream Americans do not want near them.

Central cities did not look like the major incubator of poor quality neighborhoods in the first half of the twentieth century. In 1950, measured by population size, wealth, jobs, and political power, American cities were juggernauts, and their neighborhoods were the pistons that drove them. According to Bureau of the Census data, the eighteen cities in the United States with populations of 500,000 or more in 1950 contained 18 percent of the national population. With a few exceptions, their populations were growing. After the Second World War, the federal government subsidized moderate-income housing in the suburbs and highways, which opened up tracts for suburban development. Between 1950 and 1990, seventeen of the eighteen big cities lost population, and their share of the national population declined from a high of 18 percent in 1950 to less than 10 percent in 1990.

The loss of personal wealth was even more marked. In 1949, the typical family in one of the eighteen big cities had an income 13 percent higher than the national average. In 1989, the typical big-city family's median family income was 17 percent lower than the national average. Most middle-class whites moved to the suburbs and were replaced by relatively poor southern blacks who migrated to the North and Hispanic immigrants. In 1950, for example, the black population comprised 13 percent of the population of the eighteen big cities; in 1990 it comprised 33 percent.

Jobs declined even more precipitously than population and personal wealth. In 1947, the eighteen biggest cities contained 38 percent of the wholesaling jobs, 26 percent of the manufacturing jobs, and 23 percent of the nation's retailing jobs. In 1987, the proportion of wholesaling, manufacturing, and retailing jobs were down to 9, 10, and 14 percent, respectively. New York City and Chicago combined lost about one million manufacturing jobs. Jobs moved to the suburbs, smaller cities, rural areas, and out of the United States.

The loss of people, wealth, and jobs has led to and been accelerated by the loss of political power. By delivering massive numbers of votes in support of Democratic Party candidates, big cities had tremendous political leverage, which they turned into jobs and social programs. In 1968, Republican Richard Nixon began to undermine the urban political agenda. His administration reallocated money from national programs focused on city social problems to state and local governments, which used the funds to operate and maintain their budgets rather than to address economic and social issues in cities.

Political scientist Dennis Judd (1988) concludes that by 1986, the federal government no longer had a serious urban policy. When asked about a policy to rebuild cities, President Ronald Reagan suggested that people should move to places with jobs rather than expect the government to rescue cities. Reagan won only one-third of the big-city vote in the presidential elections of 1980 and 1984. But he won almost 60 percent of the much larger suburban vote and was easily elected (Pomper 1984). In conclusion, central-city neighborhoods, once the locus of energies that incubated the United States economy, politics, and culture, are now viewed by many Americans as locusts devouring resources needed to compete in a global economy.

Before getting into the details of research design, it is essential that we directly tie the moral imperative of halting the rapid deterioration of once-prominent city neighborhoods to this design. In *A Theory of Justice,* Rawls (1971) argued for focusing on individuals at the bottom of the social and economic ladders. Our research questions and hypotheses target neighborhoods that seem to outsiders like us to exemplify Rawls's concept of worst-quality conditions. We believe that multiple-hazard neighborhoods are literally, as well as figuratively, high-hazard time bombs, which, unless addressed, will explode sooner than later into the kind of widespread civil unrest that characterized the 1960s. We believe there is a powerful moral imperative to prevent the kind of anger, violence, and racial and class tensions that such unrest would engender.

In addition to the acute health and political dangers associated with civil unrest, existing data already show higher levels of morbidity and mortality (United States Department of Health and Human Services 1991), which we are convinced will get worse if these neighborhoods continue to be neglected. There is, therefore, the additional moral imperative of preventing the slow-motion increase of chronic health hazards in these multiple-hazard neighborhoods.

Shrader-Frechette (1991b) provides ethical arguments against ignoring risks in Third World nations. This book describes some neighborhoods with hazards that rival or exceed those in Third World nations. We believe that the United States can less afford to isolate itself from wounded parts of its own cities than it can from Third World ones.

In other words, this book rejects an elitist ethical principle that funnels resources to neighborhoods inhabited by the population that already leads the nation in business, science, and culture. An elitist approach to environmentally devastated neighborhoods probably would call for moving the brightest young people from multiple-hazard neighborhoods to better places, or to level these neighborhoods for more productive land uses and activities. We also reject a utilitarian principle, which would maximize overall benefits to all the nation's neighborhoods. Utilitarian-based policies will not give priority to preventing improbable events, such as civil unrest in central-city neighborhoods.

In *Risk and Rationality,* Shrader-Frechette (1991a) describes and illustrates five ethically grounded dilemmas in risk evaluation. We faced these dilemmas, and a brief review of how they were resolved will help show how the research was designed to focus on addressing acute and chronic hazards in multiple-hazard neighborhoods. (See chapters 2, 8, and 9 for a more detailed presentation.)

The "fact/value" dilemma identifies the difficulty of balancing expert findings against public wishes. Most risk disputes in the United States involving neighborhoods center on a single risk, such as a hazardous-waste incinerator for chemicals, a disposal facility for radioactive wastes, or a prison. Experts can measure the existing environment, use mathematical models to predict the future environment, and focus on estimating the risk associated with each of these hazards. Their recommendations may be uncertain and are likely to be disputed by the potentially impacted public. At least the object of dispute is not disputed. It remains the LULU.

In multiple-hazard neighborhoods, the number and types of hazards and the risks they create are not apparent. We know of no method to estimate the cumulative risk of drug-related crime that poses acute and chronic risks, dilapidated buildings that pose a fire hazard and may or may not contain asbestos, lead, and various other dangerous chemicals, and a nearby manufacturing facility that emits small quantities of pollutants and poses the danger of explosion or transportation accidents. Law enforcement officials might rightfully argue that crime control is the highest priority for multiple-hazard neighborhoods because a good neighborhood must be safe. The housing department can argue that physical blight breeds crime, abandonment, and waste dumping. The sanitarian may argue that the stench from the local refinery and tank-farm complex needs to be addressed first because no one with any choices will invest in a neighborhood that stinks.

We cannot argue against any of these expert opinions. However, in today's political environment, in which comprehensive planning is not politically fashionable, we need to determine the relative importance of addressing different problems and solutions. One way of making a determination is to measure pollution, blight, arrests, mortality, and morbidity and to somehow figure out a credible method of comparing chronic and acute risks. Without these data there is no way to measure the total risk. While waiting for the data to be gathered and the integrative risk analysis methods to be developed, residents and local experts are the only feasible way of getting a sense of the relative importance of the variety of problems and solutions facing a neighborhood. Our emphasis is on residents, but we also rely on local experts to obtain an independent assessment of priorities.

Shrader-Frechette's second dilemma is "standardization." What should be the balance of using standardized methods of analysis and evaluation versus developing methods that allow for the special conditions of each neighborhood? We faced this problem twice. First, we wanted to measure neighborhood quality in devastated neighborhoods, but we needed both national and regional baselines to deal with the *de Minimis* dilemma (see below). Consequently, despite its limitations, we based our survey instrument on the United States Department of Commerce's instrument for the *American Housing Survey*. Second, each neighborhood had some unique features. We developed a standardized instrument and added a few stresses or amenities to reflect local circumstances. We also used the same method of delivering the instrument in each neighborhood, and the statistical methods were standardized as well to make sure that our evaluations were consistent across neighborhoods.

"Contributor's dilemma" is the third and perhaps the most challenging dilemma we had to confront. All our case-study neighborhoods, especially east Elizabeth and Marcus Hook, contain numerous hazards. Our approach was to allow respondents to tell us their perception of each neighborhood characteristic and to use multivariate statistical methods to determine the association of the characteristics with neighborhood quality. The policy proposals made in chapter 9 rest on these statistical evaluations and are tested against the judgments of local experts.

The issue of what constitutes *de Minimis* risk was Shrader-

Frechette's fourth evaluation dilemma. The focus of the national risk debate (where a specific geographical place is part of the debate) is over death or morbidity rates per million people at risk from nuclear generating stations and waste repositories, incinerators, hazardous-waste sites, and various other LULUs. As noted above, neither the data nor the methods currently exist to make calculations for all the hazards found in multiple-hazard neighborhoods. We use the proportion of Americans who rate their neighborhoods as "poor" quality as a measure of *de Minimis*. In other words, subject to convincing evidence to the contrary from local health, environmental, and planning officials, neighborhoods rated poor quality by a substantially larger proportion of their residents than national and regional populations are considered environmentally devastated.

"Consent" was the fifth dilemma. Despite statements to the contrary (see chapter 9), risk decisions that impact neighborhoods are frequently made with minimal input from and without the consent of the directly affected public. The most often cited reason is that the public worries too much about small risks and not enough about big ones, that is, the public does not know the science. In multiple-hazard neighborhoods, we believe that federal and state officials, companies, and academic scientists are normally the ones who are ill informed. These outsiders are assigned the job of risk assessment and often have the training to worry only about one kind of environmental risk. Rather than the public being risk-phobic and irrational, we feel certain that public perceptions of their own neighborhoods are a better reflection of the complicated package of risk in their multiple-hazard neighborhoods than the outside expert whose job focuses on only one problem.

Local experts, such as health officers and planners, should have good insights about neighborhood problems and solutions. Their views must be judged against public perception, so we compared the priorities of local health and planning officials with the public's concerns. We made no effort to determine federal and state experts' concerns about our study neighborhoods, because in our collective judgement, their responsibilities are too narrowly defined for them to accurately integrate the different kinds of hazards and amenities found in multiple-hazard neighborhoods. Rather, we suggest a policy that seeks their involvement in outsider and insider redevelopment and remediation projects. We propose taking advantage of politically mandated and private redevelopment projects proposed by "outsider" state and federal officials and outside private parties. These "targets of opportunity" would be joined to "insider" projects initiated by local and neighborhood interests. Outsider and insider projects are not going to work unless both parties consent to work with together. In short, our policy, described and evaluated in chapter 9, requires outsiders, such as the federal and state government, and outside business interests to cooperate with neighborhood resident insiders and insider-outsiders such as local health officers and city planners. In multiple-hazard neighborhoods, working together, or at least supporting one another's projects, makes more sense than fighting over who is wrong and who is right about environmental risk in the neighborhood. Our proposal, in essence, empowers national, federal, state, business, and local interests to effect hazard reduction.

Measuring Neighborhood Quality: Research Questions and Hypotheses

---

The moral imperative to address acute and chronic hazards in poor quality multiple-hazard neighborhoods led us to formulate hypotheses for testing in these environments.

Research Question 1: *How do people who live in the immediate vicinity of potentially hazardous land uses and activities rate their neighborhoods?*

Hypothesis 1.1: *Residents of environmentally devastated neighborhoods rate their neighborhoods as lower quality than Americans as a whole rate their neighborhoods.*

This hypothesis allows us to compare each neighborhood to national and regional *de Minimis* rates of poor quality.

Hypothesis 1.2: *People who live in stressed neighborhoods have an accurate perception of what potential hazards are actually present and not present in their neighborhood. In other words, there are relatively few respondents who are unusually sensitive or unusually insensitive to potential hazards.*

This hypothesis is one way of determining if respondents are out of touch with the reality of hazards in the immediate neighborhood.

Research Question 2: *What factors most influence neighborhood ratings, especially ratings of a neighborhood as poor quality?*

Hypothesis 2.1: *Massive technology sites are not as important as crime and blight, especially if the sites are being controlled, but are more important than local activity spaces and amenities.*

This hypothesis focuses on the relative importance of hazards that seize the attention of outsiders but may be less important to insiders, especially if the hazards are controlled.

Hypothesis 2.2: *Crime, other behavioral risks, and blight are the characteristics most likely to result in a poor quality rating.*

This hypothesis permits us to test the assumption that crime and physical decay create acute threats that undermine neighborhoods and frighten their residents.

Hypothesis 2.3: *Local activity spaces are an important stress to people who live immediately adjacent to them but are the least important of the four types of potential hazards.*

So little has been written about these land uses that this hypothesis permits us to evaluate them in the context of the more prominent land-use and behavioral hazards.

Hypothesis 2.4: *Personal experiences, especially previous neighborhood experiences and length of residence in the neighborhood, are important filters.*

This hypothesis allows us to analyze the confounding of local characteristics by the personal characteristics of our respondents.

Hypothesis 2.5: *Amenities are not important explanatory factors in environmentally devastated neighborhoods, except for the presence of friends and relatives.*

This hypothesis addresses the policy option of improving poor quality neighborhoods by adding amenities.

Hypothesis 2.6: *Residents use mental shortcuts—that is, heuristics —to help them integrate their perceptions into an overall neighborhood evaluation. We hypothesized and tested four heuristics: (1) outsider perception, (2) specific hazard type, (3) specific hazard type checkoff, and (4) aggregate hazard burden. We also had a baseline run. These heuristics should help explain neighborhood quality, especially poor neighborhood quality.*

This hypothesis was critically important because it required us to determine the extent to which multiple hazards, amenities, and personal characteristics are associated. Heuristics that can be consistently found in our neighborhoods and replicated elsewhere in the United States can provide guidance to policy makers trying to design neighborhood redevelopment programs that will satisfy local residents.

Cities and Neighborhoods

Chapters 4 to 7 describe our experiences in twenty neighborhoods. The ten neighborhoods surveyed in chapter 6 include three of the worst hazardous-waste Superfund sites in the United States as defined by EPA criteria. Yet the main focus of this book is south Chester (chapter 4), east Elizabeth (chapter 5), and east Camden (chapter 7). Camden, Chester, and Elizabeth, the three central cities in our case studies, illustrate both the decline of American cities and the concentration of problems in their neglected neighborhoods described earlier in the chapter for the largest cities. In 1950, the three cities had 303,000 people; in 1990 they had 236,000 people, a loss of 22 percent. In 1950, 13 percent of the population of these three small cities was "nonwhite." In 1990, 42 percent of their population was black and 31 percent Hispanic. Their residents are poorer, less educated, and much more likely to be unemployed, to be the victim of a serious crime, to die at a young age, and to receive welfare payments than residents of the rest of the nation. In 1991, the reported rate of violent crime (e.g., murder, nonnegligent manslaughter, forcible rape, robbery, aggravated assault, burglary, larceny, and motor vehicle theft) was 2.2 times higher in these three cities than in the United States as a whole; in 1988, the infant mortality rate was 1.75 times the national rate; and the proportion of income from public assistance was 3 times the national rate (Bureau of the Census 1994). Chapters 4, 5, and 7 provide data about the cities, the neighborhoods of interest, and especially their residents' perceptions of neighborhood quality.

    Chapter 2 describes the selection of neighborhoods with prominent environmental hazards, the overall design of the research, and its limitations. The third chapter describes how Americans as a whole rate their neighborhoods and initially tests hypotheses about the causes of their neighborhood ratings. Chapters 4 to 7 present case studies of neighborhoods with prominent environmental hazards. Chapters 4 and 5 focus on neighborhoods that have massive technology hazards (e.g., airports, incinerators, waste sites, refineries) and behavioral and blight hazards (e.g., crime, rats, abandoned buildings). Chapter 6 focuses on places that have a hazardous-waste site(s), and chapter 7 describes a place that has a major crime problem and serious blight. Chapter 8 summarizes the answers to the questions we posed, analyzes the limitations of the research, and suggests follow-up studies. In the last chapter, we argue for the numerous advantages as opposed to the few disadvantages of adopting a much broader definition of environmental risk and implementing it to aid poor quality, multiple-hazard neighborhoods.

Data and Methods

This chapter explains five decisions made to test our hypotheses: (1) elimination of economic-based, secondary data-based, and experimental psychometric approaches; (2) selection of a closed and fully scaled survey instrument; (3) selective application of an open-ended survey instrument; (4) selection of field study sites and distribution of the field surveys with follow-up phone calls; and (5) methods of testing the hypotheses. We also discuss the limitations of the data and methods we used.

Economic, Secondary Data, and Experimental Approaches

We initially considered economic-based methods that could have provided indirect answers to our hypotheses. For example, Hedonic models tie property values to the proximity of factories, air pollution, highway noise, and other stresses through mathematical equations. Coefficients in these equations are used to estimate the economic impact of the hazard on the neighborhood and the economic benefit of remediating the hazard. Using these methods, researchers have found that waste sites lower property values 5 to 10 percent within one-quarter mile of a site (Greenberg and Hughes 1993; Hoehn, Berger, and Blomquist 1987; McClelland, Shulze, and Hurd 1990; Skaburskis 1989). If the average value of two hundred properties located one-quarter mile from a waste site is $200,000, then all the properties are worth $40 million. Remediation of the site might be expected to raise the values of these properties by 5 to 10 percent, or $2 to $4 million.

Contingent valuation is a second economic method. It asks respondents to assign economic value to changes. In the case of a hazardous-waste site, an interviewer asks respondents how much they would be willing to pay for site remediation or would accept to allow a new facility. For instance, Kunreuther et al. (1990) surveyed 1,001 Nevada residents and 1,201 U.S. residents to determine if Nevada residents would be willing to accept compensation in exchange for the location of a high-level nuclear waste repository. Federal tax incentives of one to five thousand dollars for a twenty-year period did little to reduce opposition.

Hedonic and contingent valuation approaches provide useful insights when compensation is a policy option. However, both have major disadvantages for our purposes. Economic benefits and costs, at best, provide distorted views of the frustrations, jubilations, and other feelings residents really feel about their neighborhoods. Because equal levels of anger do not translate into equal options to leave a neighborhood (see chapter 1), property exchanges and property values lag behind people's perceptions. Furthermore, recent studies show that people are often more concerned about control and mitigation of impacts than they are about compensation (Himmelberger, Ratick, and White 1991; Kunreuther, Susskind, and Aarts 1991; Zeiss and Atwater 1987, 1989). In other words, economic benefits and costs are not necessarily residents' highest priorities.

Contingent valuation methods also require people to put a value on clean air, safe streets, and repairing buildings. This can cause respondents to become outraged by the method, much less the condition, of their neighborhood (see Randall, Hoehn, and Brookshire 1983 and Smith and Desvousges 1987). We were advised by people who know some of these neighborhoods not to use contingent valuation. Neither economic method was used. However, we did ask town planners and/or business managers to prioritize the expenditure of funds in multiple-hazard neighborhoods.

Ratings of nations, states, cities, and neighborhoods are routinely made with secondary data, such as air pollution, population density, and amount of recycling (see Cutter 1985 and Rogerson et al. 1989 for interesting discussions of the use of secondary data for rating places). States, cities, counties, provinces, shopping centers, restaurants, and resorts vie for high rankings and incorporate their high ranks into advertizing. Low rankings are often ignored, sometimes disputed, even in court.

Hall and Kerr's (1991) "green index" illustrates some of the advantages and disadvantages of using secondary data for our purposes (see Gould 1986:chap. 1 for another example). They used 256 indicators, including state policies (73), air pollution (18), water pollution (24), energy and auto use (38), toxic, hazardous, and solid waste (30), and others to compare the fifty American states. The database is comprehensive—that is, ratings do not depend on one or two indicators. Second, because much of the data are routinely collected, indices based on secondary data can be updated and reissued as trends in environmental ratings. Ideally, neighborhood ratings should be based on many neighborhood characteristics and should be replicated and updated.

Secondary data have two major limitations for our purposes. First, the vast majority of the indicators used to rate places are not available at the neighborhood scale. The second limitation is that recycling, energy use, and many other indicators used in studies that rate places, like economic data, are indirect measures of residents' perceptions. It is fallacious to assume that residents of an environmentally devastated neighborhood, or any other neighborhood, are individually cognizant of hundreds of indicators of pollution, pollution prevention, and environmental policy.

For instance, we use toxic release inventory data (TRI) in chapters 4 and 5 to provide context for the Elizabeth and Chester case studies. People in the street did not talk about TRI data. What they did talk about were smells, sights, and sounds, and sometimes what their local newspaper wrote. Overall, we used secondary data as context for our case studies, and along with expert opinions, we used secondary data as a way of choosing neighborhoods to study. But we did not use secondary data as information to rate neighborhoods. Instead, as a check on the results of the neighborhood surveys, we asked the health officers of each multiple-hazard neighborhood to prioritize environmental concerns.

Experimental psychologists and social scientists have studied risk perception in controlled laboratory settings. For example, Aitken (1990) used photos of actual structures to measure people's responses to neighborhood change. Geographers and many others have learned about neighborhood perception by having people draw mental maps (see Cutter 1993 and Thrill and Sui 1993 for recent discussions).

Experimental designs have general limitations for measuring risk perceptions (see Cutter 1993 for a summary). For purposes of our work, three limitations could not be overcome. Many of the neighborhoods we wanted to study had multiple stresses. We could not figure out how these could be realistically portrayed with photos, videotapes, sound equipment, and other technical devices for testing in a laboratory setting. Second, we had no ability or expectation that residents of environmentally devastated neighborhoods would be willing to meet with us in an experimental setting. Third, we wanted residents to respond to their own neighborhoods, not to representations of them.

Finally, actual environmental monitoring and health data are not available at the neighborhood scale. Chapter 8 discusses how monitoring and health data should be joined with expert opinion and the kind of data gathered as part of this research to develop a scientific database for neighborhood environmental risk analysis and management.

Closed and Fully Scaled Field Surveys

Field surveys were the only feasible way of conducting our research. Survey methods can directly measure residents' perception of neighborhood quality and the factors that contribute to it (see Clay and Hollister 1983 for examples).

Survey approaches do have disadvantages, the most important of which is access to respondents. Researchers must choose among telephone, written instruments with and without follow-up, and in-person interviews. Each of these has implications for response rate and bias.

Telephone interviews are a convenient way of obtaining quantitative data and images from respondents. Phone interviews, like surveys instruments, provide less reliable information than long personal interviews. U.S. Census data for 1990 showed that 10 to 15 percent of housing units in our poorer neighborhoods did not have telephones, a figure 3 to 8 percent higher than their surrounding counties (Department of Commerce 1992). Consequently, we initially did no phone interviewing to avoid this obvious bias. Respondents to our written survey were asked to indicate if they would be willing to be called on the phone. If so, they were asked to provide their names, phone number, and a convenient time to receive a call. Unfortunately, only about 20 percent were willing to be called, and many who provided their phone number were much less receptive to our follow-up questions when we did call. Frankly, whether due to our lack of skill, the unwillingness of respondents from these troubled neighborhoods to talk about their environments, or a combination of both, the telephone was not a productive data-gathering tool in this research. Chapter 8 describes the proposed use of the telephone to obtain information from groups that are particularly difficult to recruit into a survey.

In-person interviews can provide a great deal of meaningful data. Yet not everyone is willing to sit with an interviewer for twenty to ninety minutes. Furthermore, the interviewer must be trained to avoid biasing responses because of age, race/ethnicity, language ability, tone of voice, and other characteristics. We did a limited number of in-person interviews as a supplement to the formal closed-ended and fully scaled instrument used in all our neighborhoods (see the next section of this chapter and chapter 6). Appendix 2 is the instrument.

We chose the Department of Commerce's biannual *American Housing Survey for the United States* (AHS) (Department of Commerce 1983–91) to anchor our empirical field survey research. The AHS provided the only feasible baseline for testing our hypotheses with both national and regional data. The major purposes of the AHS are to determine the size and composition of U.S. housing, to characterize its occupants, and to monitor neighborhood quality. Begun in 1973 as the Annual Housing Survey, the name was changed to the American Housing Survey in 1984 because the national sample is now conducted every other year rather than annually.

The AHS provides some data on neighborhood quality, stresses, amenities, and personal characteristics. In this section, we discuss the strengths and weaknesses of the AHS for our purposes and how AHS questions were modified for our field surveys.

The AHS asks people to define their own neighborhood. We adopted the AHS approach to defining neighborhood, recognizing the limitation that neighbors may have different views of what constitutes their neighborhood. We attempted to control for varying definition of neighborhood in the statistical analyses by defining a neighborhood variable (see the last section of this chapter).

Prior to 1985, the AHS asked people to rate their neighborhood on a four-point scale: (1) "excellent," (2) "good," (3) "fair," and (4) "poor." In 1985, the AHS developed a ten-point scale, number 1 labeled the "worst" neighborhood, number 10 the "best." No consensus exists on the best form for a closed survey question. The closest to a consensus is that five- to seven-point scales work best, but not much better than other options (Diefenbach, Weinstein, and O'Reilly 1993; Dixon, Bobo, and Stevick 1984; McKelvie 1978; Rohrman 1985; Sutherland et al. 1991; Wallsten et al. 1986). Accordingly, we originally intended to use the AHS's ten-point scale, but we changed our minds after an informal pilot test. Some respondents who had not gone to college, many of whom were elderly, had difficulty with that scale. They wanted us to tell them where "okay," "satisfactory," "lousy," and various other ratings were on the scale. In fact, they strongly recommended the old form of the AHS neighborhood question, which was labeled with the four choices excellent, good, fair, and poor.

The use of the four-point scale, we thought, would make it difficult to compare our field results with the most recent AHS results, which are based on a ten-point scale. Yet an analysis of the 1981, 1983, 1985, 1987, 1989, and 1991 national AHS found a remarkable consistency when we used the scale number 10 to represent excellent, the scale numbers 6 to 9 to represent good, the scale numbers 3 to 5 to represent fair, and numbers 1 to 2 to represent poor. This finding corresponds to Campbell, Converse, and Rodgers's (1976) observation of consistently high public ratings of neighborhoods (see chapter 3 for further confirmation). The last section of this chapter discusses how the categorical scale was used to test the hypotheses stated in chapter 1.

The AHS asks about bothersome neighborhood conditions. Data on crime, noise, traffic, litter or housing deterioration, poor city/county services, undesirable nonresidential land uses, people in the neighborhood, and other bothersome features are available in recent surveys. Early surveys provided more options, very important ones for our work, such as odors and smoke.

Unfortunately, the AHS categories were too general for our neighborhood surveys. We added more specific categories, such as uncontrolled animals, utility towers and rights-of-way, petroleum refineries, gas tanks, and hazardous-waste sites. The total number of potentially distressing neighborhood characteristics in our field survey was twenty-six. Table 2.1 lists the four environmental hazard categories from chapter 1 and their corresponding physical and behavioral characteristics in our field survey and the AHS. We also included flooding, a natural hazard, which was a potential problem in several neighborhoods. The AHS sacrifices considerable detail in every category, especially massive technology sites. This is understandable, because few people have these facilities in their neighborhoods (see chapter 3). Because some of our neighborhoods were selected specifically near massive technology sites, we needed more detailed categories.

The AHS asks respondents if any of these bothersome conditions exist in their neighborhood. The earlier AHS posed questions with even finer distinctions. Respondents were asked if a condition was present. If it was present, they were asked if it was bothersome. If it was bothersome, they were asked if it was so bothersome that they would like to leave the neighborhood. These questions were precisely what we needed to test some of our hypotheses, so we used the old format of the AHS questions.

The AHS also asks why respondents picked their present neighborhood. It offers a series of attractions, such as convenience to work, friends, and shopping. With a few modifications, we used the AHS amenity and attraction categories listed in table 2.2. After visiting each neighborhood and talking to people in the street, the categories religious institution, convenience to shopping, and hospital were added. In addition, the AHS housing amenities question was changed because some people we spoke with were unsure about what the AHS meant by "house was most important consideration."

Our intended respondents for the amenities and attractions questions were all neighborhood residents. The AHS's intended respondents were recent movers, that is, people who had moved into their neighborhood during the prior twelve months. In other words, at the national scale, analysis of the importance of amenities and attractions was limited to recent migrants (see chapter 3), whereas the analyses in chapters 4 to 7 include all respondents.

The AHS provides data on respondents' age, race, tenure in the

Table 2.1. Potentially Distressing Neighborhood Characteristics

Hazard Category	Field Survey Characteristic	AHS Characteristic
Massive technology site	Airplane noises	Noise; nonresidential[a]
	Chemical plant	Nonresidential
	Hazardous-waste site, landfill	Nonresidential
	Incinerator	Nonresidential
	Metal or furniture factory	Nonresidential
	Natural gas tanks	Nonresidential
	Odors and smoke	Nonresidential
	Petroleum refinery and/or tank farm	Nonresidential
	Polluted water	Other
	Right-of-way for utility	Nonresidential
	Sewage plant	Nonresidential
	Train noise	Noise; nonresidential
	Water treatment plant	Nonresidential
Crime and other behavioral	High crime rate	Crime
	Dogs, cats, other uncontrolled animals	Other
	Unfriendly neighbors	People
Blight	Abandoned factories and businesses	Litter or housing deterioration
	Abandoned houses	Litter or housing deterioration
	Inadequate street lighting	Poor city or county services
	Litter and trash in the street, lots	Litter or housing deterioration
	Occupied buildings in poor condition	Litter or housing deterioration
	Streets, roads, and sidewalks in disrepair, open ditches	Poor city or county services
Local activity spaces	Junkyard, gasoline station, other local nonresidential	Nonresidential
	Recreational facilities that attract rowdy people	People
	Motor vehicle noise and heavy traffic	Noise; traffic
Natural hazard	Flooding	Other

Source: U.S. Bureau of the Census, American Housing Survey for 1991 (computer file).
[a]Nonresidential includes undesirable commercial, institutional, and industrial characteristics.

Table 2.2. Neighborhood Amenities and Attractions

Field Survey	AHS
Convenient to job	Convenient to job
Convenient to friends or relatives	Convenient to friends or relatives
Convenient to religious activities	Nothing
Convenient to leisure activities	Convenient to leisure activities
Convenient to public transportation	Convenient to public transportation
Good schools	Good schools
Other public services (police, fire, health)	Other public
Convenient to hospital	Nothing
Convenient to shopping	Nothing
Looks/design of neighborhood	Looks/design of neighborhood
House was inexpensive/inherited	House was most important consideration

dwelling unit, and the other personal characteristics we needed (table 2.3). It also asks respondents to compare their present and previous neighborhoods. Based on advice from people in the field, we used the same variables, but provided respondents with categories for the variables age, length of residence in the neighborhood, and education. We used the AHS categories for the other demographic variables. We did not ask respondents to indicate their racial/ethnic identification because we expected many potential respondents would be so distressed by the question that they would discard the survey (see Lee 1993 for a discussion of sensitive questions). Chapter 8 discusses an approach for obtaining data like ours for racial and ethnic groups.

The AHS restricted their request for a comparison of present and previous neighborhood to recent in-migrants. Like the amenity data, our analyses of neighborhood comparison in the United States data are limited to recent migrants (see chapter 3).

Open-Ended Questions

Ittelson (1974), Saarinen (1976), Pocock and Hudson (1978), and numerous others have described the great difficulty people have articulating their conscious and unconscious views and researchers have documenting these feelings. Although we relied on closed-ended, fully scaled questions for our field survey database, we recognized that closed-ended questions could too narrowly circumscribe what residents could tell us (Schuman and Scott 1987). Closed-

Table 2.3. Demographic Variables in AHS and Field Survey

Variable	Field Survey	AHS
Age	18–30 years 31–50 51–70 70+	Years
Sex	Male Female	Male Female
Tenure	Own Rent	Own Rent
Length of residence in the present neighborhood	0–6 months >6 months–2 years >2–5 years >5–10 years >10 years	Years
Formal education	1–8 years 9–11 Graduated high school Technical school Some college Graduated college	Years

Neighborhood comparison	Present neighborhood:
	  is better
	  is worse
	  is about the same
	  is the same
		Present neighborhood:
		  is better
		  is worse
		  is about the same
		  is the same

ended, Likert-scaled questions can accurately measure residents' intellectual recognition of their environment, but word associations might be a good method of determining if the information had penetrated beyond the conscious level to the subconscious.

Word associations have a distinguished history in psychoanalysis (Freud 1952; Galton 1880). Recently, Slovic et al. (1991) used word associations to determine Nevada residents' perceptions of a proposed high-level nuclear waste repository in Yucca Flats. The images showed the great depth of fear about nuclear facilities. Fischer et al. (1991) used open-ended questions to determine what risks really concern people.

We designed an open-ended survey instrument for use in our neighborhoods. It asked respondents to choose two neighborhoods. Neither had to be their own. The first neighborhood should be one they enjoy being in, and the second neighborhood one they hate being in. We asked them to imagine that they are walking, biking, or riding through the great neighborhood and to make a list of their feelings (e.g., jubilation, sense of openness, friendly, etc). Then we asked them to repeat the exercise with the terrible neighborhood, again noting their feelings (e.g., fear, anger). Third, respondents were told that we were particularly interested in their feelings about the terrible neighborhood. We asked them to close their eyes and tell us those things they see that make this neighborhood terrible. Fourth, they were asked to tell us how different distressing characteristics interact in the neighborhood. Fifth, we asked them to tell us how the terrible neighborhood could be improved. Finally, if the respondent did not mention the specific hazard in their own neighborhood, we asked them to comment about it. The next section describes how we used this instrument in selected areas.

Field Study Sites and Distribution of the Field Surveys

We "piggybacked" (Lee 1993) a test of our hypotheses about devastated neighborhoods onto the AHS national data set in order to be able to compare our field research results with a national database. In fact, the AHS was partly designed to rate neighborhoods. It has been used to examine some hypotheses, such as the relationship between neighborhood quality and population size (Dahmann 1983). The AHS data from 1981, 1983, 1985, 1987, 1989, and 1991 were used to obtain national estimates of neighborhood quality. Already published 1989 and 1991, aggregate data are used to obtain a general sense of the relationship among neighborhood quality, stresses, attractions, and personal characteristics. A tape of the raw data from the 1989 national survey data was obtained and all cases analyzed to test our hypotheses at the national scale. The last section of this chapter describes how these analyses were made, and chapter 3 presents the analyses.

The neighborhoods we chose for our neighborhood studies are what Lee (1976) calls "outcrops"—that is, places where we expected many ratings of poor quality. We used four criteria to select neighborhoods to survey. First, we wanted three types of neighborhoods: (1) one or more massive technology sites and some evidence of behavioral hazards and blight, (2) a well-known massive technology site, and (3) documented crime problems but no obvious massive technology sites. Second, we wanted neighborhoods that were located within one-half mile of a hazard. Third, we wanted locations that could be reached by automobile within three hours so that we could revisit the area to administer the open-ended survey and meet with local officials and citizens' groups. Fourth, we wanted to study some neighborhoods with differences in race/ethnicity, socioeconomic status, and behavioral risks.

After consulting with colleagues and officials and making numerous site visits, we chose twenty neighborhoods (table 2.4). The eastern area of Elizabeth, New Jersey (three neighborhoods) and the adjacent areas of Marcus Hook, Chester, and Lower Chichester, Pennsylvania (six neighborhoods) are the areas with multiple hazards. We picked ten areas immediately adjacent to hazardous-waste sites to study people's perceptions of a highly prominent form of a massive technology site. Seven of the ten were selected to pilot the entire research project. The other three were among the highest ranked hazardous-waste sites in the United States and were partly remediated. The eastern area of Camden, New Jersey, known for a variety of behavioral risks, was the final (twentieth) neighborhood. Each of these neighborhoods is described in detail in chapters 4 to 7.

The cover letter, survey instrument, and a stamped return envelope were inserted into a brown envelope. We attempted to place these in the door of every residence within one-quarter mile of a prominent hazard, such as an incinerator or a corner where drug sales occur. In areas where a forest, stream, or road intervened, we extended the sample area to approximately one-half mile. In other words, our intent was to saturate the residences in the area around the hazard with the survey instrument.

Our neighborhood surveys had seven limitations. Access was by far the biggest problem. Survey research literature shows that written surveys with no follow-up can expect about a 10 to 20 percent return (Drane 1991). People who are relatively affluent, more formally educated, and homeowners are the most likely to respond.

In our neighborhoods, access was particularly a problem in areas with apartments. In some of the low-income areas, residents told us that more people lived in units than any government database indicated. We had no way of knowing precisely how many families lived in each unit. We counted mailboxes and left one instrument for each. Yet another problem was vacant apartments. For instance, about 20 percent of the units in the Chester tracts were vacant. We

Table 2.4. Field Survey Neighborhoods and Their Most Apparent Hazards

Chapter	Municipality	Neighborhood	Most Apparent Hazards
4	Chester Marcus Hook Lower Chichester	Main, River, Park Center, Waterfront Linwood	Two petrochemical complexes, county incinerator, chemical plants, blight, crime-drugs
5	Elizabeth	Frog Hollow, Peterstown, Elizabethport	International airport, petrochemical complex, natural gas tanks, major interstate highway, blight, crime-drugs, hazardous-waste site
6	Mantua	Lipari Helen Kramer Landfill	Major Superfund hazardous-waste site Major Superfund hazardous-waste site
	Gloucester	GEMS	Major Superfund hazardous-waste site
	Bayonne	Industrial district	Chromium site
	Bound Brook	Off Main Street	Former pesticide plant
	Brick	Housing overlooking waste site	Brick Township landfill
	Bridgewater	Adjacent to American Cyanamid	Industrial lagoons
	Dover	Adjacent to chemical plant	Formerly Toms River Chemical Company
	Linden	Tremley Point	Numerous small waste sites and abandoned factories
	Sayreville	Housing overlooking waste site	Global Landfill
7	Camden	Eastern part of city	Crime and blight

asked people in the street and looked for physical evidence of occupation and abandonment. Doubtless, however, we placed surveys at the doors of vacant units. A related problem was houses with fences, locks, dogs, and other deterrents. In a few locations, we could not gain access to the door without jeopardizing our safety.

The instrument was prepared only in English. This decision was our second limitation, especially in east Elizabeth and Camden. For example, 39 percent of the east Elizabeth study area's population indicated in the 1990 U.S. Census that they "did not speak English very well." The non-English-speaking groups that constituted 10 percent or more of the population of the study area were Italian, Polish, Portuguese, and Spanish. It was infeasible to prepare the survey in five languages because of cost and the reality that a large multipage instrument would have substantially reduced our response rate. Consequently, we settled for a single-page instrument in English and expected a lower response rate from those residing in apartments and without a working knowledge of English. To a lesser extent, we had the same problem in Camden.

Our third problem was a modest response rate, less than 20 percent, in a few neighborhoods. Because each instrument was coded, we considered a second round of surveys. However, colleagues and people who were familiar with the areas strongly suggested that we would not do much better with a second round.

To assist in deciding about the generalizability of the results, we provide age, gender, education, length of residence, and tenure data about respondents compared to the census tract or small town in which the neighborhood is embedded. Even in those neighborhoods where the respondents were clearly not representative, we believe that the results provide considerable insight into factors driving neighborhood quality perceptions. Nevertheless, because of the modest response rate, it would be imprudent to generalize the results to entire populations of these neighborhoods. Chapter 8 discusses an approach for obtaining a higher response rate in neighborhoods with many apartments, with high vacancy rates, and where fluency in English is lacking.

The fact that all the neighborhoods are either in New Jersey or the Philadelphia metropolitan area was the fourth limitation. This is another reason to exercise caution about generalizing the case studies to other regions. The AHS conducted special surveys of northern New Jersey in 1987 and 1991 and of the Philadelphia metropolitan area in 1985 and 1989. All of our neighborhoods are included in those two special surveys. We provide data from these special surveys to gain further insight about quality in the neighborhoods we studied compared to their surrounding regions.

We had hoped to measure the impact of physical barriers and distance in attenuating hazard perception. This was to be done by sampling at progressively greater distances from the hazards. However, this was not possible in our study areas, and was the fifth limitation. Using census data, we found sharp demarcations in demographic characteristics among adjacent census tracts, often corresponding to the presence of highways, rivers, forests, factories, and farms, which act as barriers. There were no areas that could legitimately be claimed as controls for our neighborhoods—that is, we could not argue that the populations of adjacent areas were sufficiently similar to function as controls. In short, we cannot say much about distance attenuation of hazard perceptions.

The sixth limitation was that our open-ended survey instrument was restricted to two neighborhoods with hazardous-waste sites because of funding limitations. Unlike the closed-ended surveys, multiple trips were made to each neighborhood in order to find people who were willing to speak with us for a considerable length of time.

Our perceptions of the twenty neighborhoods was the seventh limitation. Our perceptions could bias the results. We consulted with state and local government officials, talked to people in the street, looked at census data, and visited every site before conducting surveys. Nevertheless, we are outsiders and our interpretations of the data could be biased by our perceptions of the neighborhoods. We begin each chapter with a personal description of the neighborhood supplemented with census data and newspaper stories. These introductions should provide context and help distinguish our perceptions from the survey results.

Methods of Testing the Hypotheses

We repeat the questions and hypotheses and then describe how they were tested at the neighborhood scale with the survey data. The case studies (chapters 4 to 7) provide unique circumstances about each area. The use of the open-ended survey questions is discussed in detail in chapter 6 (hazardous-waste sites), and the testing of the hypotheses with the national AHS data is described below.

Research Question (RQ) 1: *How do people who live in the immediate vicinity of potentially hazardous land uses and activities rate their neighborhoods?*

Hypothesis (H) 1.1: *Residents of environmentally devastated neighborhoods rate their neighborhoods as lower quality than Americans as a whole rate their neighborhoods.*

We used AHS surveys to provide neighborhood quality for the United States as a whole and for northern New Jersey and the Philadelphia metropolitan regions. We computed the proportion of respondents in our twenty neighborhoods who rated their neighborhood as excellent, good, fair, and poor and compared them to the United

States and the two regions. Ninety-five percent confidence limits were calculated to aid the comparisons.

The book chapters are ordered so that the neighborhoods with the most complex neighborhood environments are presented first and compared to the United States and two regions. In addition, each neighborhood is compared to an aggregate of all other neighborhoods (without that neighborhood included). For instance, the east Elizabeth study area consists of three neighborhoods. We compared each of the three neighborhood ratings to each other, to an aggregate of all the other seventeen study neighborhoods, as well as to the United States, Philadelphia, and northern New Jersey regions. Ninety-five percent confidence limits were calculated to help with the comparisons.

H1.2: *People who live in stressed neighborhoods have an accurate perception of what potential hazards are actually present and not present in the neighborhood. In other words, there are relatively few respondents who are unusually sensitive or unusually insensitive to potential hazards.*

We calculated the proportion of respondents who rated prominent and potential distressing characteristics as not present as an indicator of unusually insensitive people—that is, people who do not know or acknowledge that the hazard exists. We inserted at least one hazard into the survey in each neighborhood that really did not exist. Those who indicated that it was present and bothers them were considered unusually sensitive. Finally, we picked utility rights-of-way with towers and hanging lines as a potential threat because of electromagnetic fields (EMF), but also as a possible amenity because in some of our neighborhoods the right-of-way was the only sizable green space. In these neighborhoods, we did not expect much concern about EMF along rights-of-way.

RQ2: *What factors most influence neighborhood ratings, especially ratings of a neighborhood as poor quality?*

We used rotated and orthogonal stepwise multivariate discriminant analysis to test our hypotheses and enhance our understanding of the interrelationship of neighborhood quality, hazards, amenities, and personal characteristics. Discriminant analysis chooses the variables that most strongly differentiate among the categorical dependent variable of neighborhood quality. The categorical variable was respondent rating of neighborhood as excellent, good, fair, or poor.

Discriminant analysis allows the analyst to weight the dependent variable. In our case, we are most interested in the feelings and thinking that go into poor and fair neighborhood ratings. When each category of the dependent variable is weighted equally important, the analysis focuses equally on each category, even if some categories have five to ten times as many respondents. In fact, this is the case in many of our study areas, especially in the United States database. American people disproportionately rate their neighborhoods as excellent or good (see chapter 3 for the data). For purposes of discriminant analysis, by weighting each category as equal we drive the solution toward solving the puzzle of why people rate their neighborhoods as poor and fair. If we had weighted each respondent equally, the analysis would have focused on explaining the difference among the majority of respondents, that is, people who rated their neighborhood as excellent and good.

To further focus the discriminant analysis on poor and fair ratings, we combined the excellent and good ratings into a "good/excellent" rating. Discriminant analysis had to distinguish among only three categories, two of which, poor and fair, were our major concern. In other words, the dependent variable for the discriminant analysis was the categorical variable "neighborhood rating" with three categories: excellent-good, fair, and poor. We underscore the fact that these were deliberate decisions. It should also be noted that analyses were made with all four categories (excellent, good, fair, poor), and with two categories (excellent/good and fair/poor). The results are not markedly different, but the two- and four-category analyses are not as revealing about the relatively few who rated their neighborhood as poor. Because they are not, we only present the three-category analyses in the text.

The variables for the neighborhood studies were the twenty-six potentially distressing neighborhood characteristics (table 2.1), the eleven factors that might attract people to a neighborhood (table 2.2), the comparison of present and previous neighborhood, and the demographic characteristics (table 2.3). In addition, each respondent's census tract or small town was recorded as a dichotomous variable (1 or 0) to capture unique characteristics of the neighborhood. For example, Jane Doe lives in neighborhood A and Bill Green in neighborhood B. Jane Doe would get a 1 for A and 0 for B. Bill Green would get the opposite scores.

The variables for the national data set were the eight potentially distressing neighborhood characteristics, eight attractions, the comparison of present and previous neighborhood, and demographic characteristics (see tables 2.1 to 2.3). In the case of the national data set, we added region of the United States (Northeast, Midwest, South, and West) and regional description (central city, metropolitan suburb, other urban, and rural) as indicators analogous to the neighborhood variable in the neighborhood studies.

We briefly discuss how each of the RQ2 hypotheses were tested with discriminant analysis.

H2.1: *Massive technology sites are not as important as crime and blight, especially if the sites are being controlled, but are more important than local activity spaces and amenities.*

If massive technology sites are major stressors, then they ought to be among the most prominent discriminators—that is, the statistical analysis should show that respondents who classified their neighborhoods as poor and fair should consistently choose massive technology sites as stressors.

There was no massive technology site indicator in the AHS national data set. The closest approximations are nonresidential land use, noise, and traffic. But these could be associated with local activity spaces, a limitation of the analysis of the AHS data found in chapter 3.

H2.2: *Crime, other behavioral risks, and blight are the characteristics most likely to result in a poor quality rating.*

If crime is a major problem, then it ought to be a prominent discriminator of poor neighborhoods. We were particularly interested in determining if respondents differentiated between blight and crime, and if blight and uncontrolled animals appeared as an important factor in neighborhoods that had little, if any, crime.

Crime and litter or housing deterioration are variables in the AHS national data set, so that it was possible to determine how often these were part of respondents' perceptual images.

H2.3: *Local activity spaces are an important stress to people who live immediately adjacent to them but are the least important of the four types of potential hazards.*

If local bars, hotels, and other land uses are distressing, the discriminant analysis should identify these land uses as prominent discriminators. Unfortunately, as noted above, the AHS national data set does not include a variable for this category. Nonresidential land use, noise, traffic, and other could be massive technology sites, local activity spaces, or both.

H2.4: *Personal experiences, especially previous neighborhood experiences and length of residence in the neighborhood, are important filters.*

We expected personal experiences to be important in neighborhoods that have undergone marked changes in hazards. Poor quality should be associated with long-term residents who experience the neighborhood as worse than their previous one because of new unwelcome hazards. Recent migrants who experience their present neighborhood as an improvement should rate the neighborhood as higher quality. In particular, we expected strong evidence of the personal experience factor at hazardous-waste sites that have been partly remediated (e.g., no longer imminent danger, no obvious odors, covered with a cap, grass, shrubs and other barriers added to buffer the site). The discriminant analysis should manifest strong statistical associations by length of residence and relative neighborhood quality. Long-term residents should continue to be encumbered by the legacy of sites, smells, and sounds at these waste sites, whereas newcomers should not.

The neighborhood and national databases use the same variables. However, in the AHS data set the neighborhood comparison variable is only available for recent migrants, which was a major limitation.

H2.5: *Amenities are not important explanatory factors in environmentally devastated neighborhoods, except for the presence of friends and relatives.*

Only friends or relatives should be a strong discriminator of neighborhood quality. The AHS survey included almost the same set of variables, but only for recent migrants.

H2.6: *Residents use mental shortcuts—that is, heuristics—to help them integrate their perceptions into an overall neighborhood evaluation. We hypothesized and tested four heuristics: (1) outsider perception, (2) specific hazard type, (3) specific hazard type checkoff, and (4) aggregate hazard burden. We also had a baseline run. These heuristics should help explain neighborhood quality, especially poor neighborhood quality.*

The heuristics were tested with multiple discriminant analysis runs. To guide the reader through the hypotheses and tests of the heuristics, we will use two fictitious people, Smith and Jones, in a hypothetical neighborhood called Washington (table 2.5). The first run is the baseline. We insert all of the massive technology sites, crime, and other behavioral hazards, local activity spaces, and blight, amenities, and personal experience variables to determine their relative statistical strength. Smith is extremely distressed by seven different hazards, Jones by four. Smith is attracted by five amenities, Jones by four. Smith is a thirty-one to fifty-year-old female who rents, has lived in the area two to five years, did not graduate high school, and feels the present neighborhood is better. Jones is a fifty-one to sixty-four-year-old male who owns a house, has lived in the neighborhood for more than a decade, had some college education, and thinks the neighborhood is worse than his previous neighborhood. All of these variables would be included in the baseline discriminant analysis.

The second run is the outsider perception. It determines the discriminating ability of the hazard or hazards that outsiders see. In the case of the Washington neighborhood, we determined the statistical ability of respondents' distress with an incinerator to predict neighborhood rating. Table 2.5 shows that Smith is troubled by the incinerator but Jones is not. Smith gets a 1, Jones a 0.

In the third run, we test the specific hazard type hypothesis. Five aggregate variables are created: massive technology sites, behavioral hazards, blight, local activity spaces, and amenities (nonhazards). These aggregates were computed by adding each respondents' scores by category. Smith, for instance, gets a 3 for massive technology sites, 2 for behavioral hazards, 2 for blight, 0 for local activity space hazards, and 5 for amenities. Jones gets a 1 for each of the four hazard categories and a 4 for amenities.

The fourth run is the specific hazard type checkoff heuristic. Each respondent focuses on each of the four hazard categories. Any extremely distressed designation within a category results in a score of 1 for that entire category. Then a total aggregate score is obtained by adding the 0 or 1 scores for all four hazards. The maximum score is a 4, the minimum is a 0. Smith gets a 3, Jones a 4.

The fifth run, fourth heuristic, is that the aggregate number of hazards and amenities is more important than any specific one or

Table 2.5. Hypothetical Responses by Smith and Jones to Survey Questions

	Response	
Question	Smith	Jones
Massive technology site:		
Hazardous-waste site, landfill	1	1
Petroleum refinery and tank farm	1	0
Incinerator	1	0
Behavioral hazards:		
High crime rate	1	1
Uncontrolled animals	1	0
Blight:		
Abandoned factories and businesses	1	1
Inadequate street lighting	1	0
Local activity spaces:		
Junkyard, gasoline station	0	1
Amenities:		
Convenient to job	0	1
Convenient to friends or relatives	1	1
Convenient to leisure activities	1	0
Good schools	1	1
Other public services	0	1
Convenient to shopping	1	0
Looks/design of neighborhood	1	0
Demographic characteristics:		
Age	31–50	51–64
Sex	Female	Male
Tenure	Rent	Own
Length of residence (years)	2–5	10+
Education (grade)	9–11	Some college
Neighborhood comparison:		
Present is	Better	Worse

Note: A response of 0 indicates not distressed; 1 indicates distressed.

specific type. All of the individual hazards and amenities are replaced by an aggregate score. Smith gets a 7 for hazards and a 5 for amenities. Jones gets a 4 for hazards and a 4 for amenities.

It was possible to test only the baseline and aggregate burden hypotheses with the AHS national data because of the limited number of hazard categories.

Discriminant analysis provides a variety of clues that allow the analyst to judge their hypotheses (See Kachigan 1991 for a longer and readable treatment). Each independent variable's absolute and relative strength can be assessed by F-values and P-values. A high F-value means that the among-group variance is greater than the within-group variance, which means that the independent variable significantly discriminates among one or more groups. A low P-value provides corroboration of significance.

Even if a variable is a strong discriminator, it may covary with other discriminators. We must establish if its discrimination is independent of the other independent variables or covaries with them. Discriminant analysis creates functions, which are multivariate linear combinations of all the independent variables. The strongest independent variables that are part of a discriminant function are the keys to understanding respondents' neighborhood ratings. For example, suppose the discriminant analysis of the hypothetical Washington neighborhood finds two discriminant functions. The first we call poor versus excellent/good neighborhood because the average standardized score (Z-score) for respondents who rated Washington as excellent/good was −1.5 and the average standardized score for respondents who rated Washington as poor was 1.2.

The neighborhood characteristics associated with this function are indicated by correlation coefficients between the independent variables and the mathematically created function that we called poor versus excellent/good. In the case of Washington, we observe correlation coefficients of 0.725 with the variable blight, 0.550 with the variable hazardous-waste site, and 0.509 with the variable age. These correlations mean that respondents in Washington who rated it as excellent are not distressed by blight and the hazardous-waste site and tend to be relatively young. Older residents who are distressed by blight and the hazardous-waste site tend to rate the neighborhood as poor.

Other correlations between the independent variables and the function are lower and do not play a key role in explaining the difference between excellent/good and poor ratings. The distinction between important and less important correlations can be evaluated with standard statistical tests that establish correlations that are significantly different from a correlation coefficient of 0.0 at a P-value of .05 or another value selected by the analyst.

In addition to the strength of each independent variable, the strength of each function is evaluated by examining the canonical correlations—that is, the correlations between the functions and the dependent variable. In the case of Washington neighborhood, the canonical correlation between the mathematically created function that we have labeled excellent/good versus poor was .7. This means that about 50 percent of the variance of the dependent variable, neighborhood quality, is associated with this single function. The statistical significance of each function is also judged by a P-value.

Finally, the overall success of the discriminant analysis is judged by noting what proportion of the actual respondents' neighborhood quality ratings were accurately predicted by the mathematical model created by the discriminant analysis. For instance, let us assume that Smith actually rated Washington neighborhood as fair and Jones rated it as poor. Discriminant analysis calculates a set of mathematical equations that use the input data from each respondent to predict a hypothetical neighborhood quality group. This prediction is then compared to their actual group. Suppose the model predicts that Smith and Jones both rate their neighborhood as fair. Smith's prediction is correct, Jones's is not, and the model's success is 50 percent. The higher the proportion of accurately predicted respondents, the better the discriminant analysis result. The accurately predicted proportions can be compared to the null hypothesis.

Although we rely on discriminant analysis because it can simultaneously analyze all the variables, we compare proportions of respondents who rated their neighborhood as poor to show how each independent variable relates directly to neighborhood quality.

We made a deliberate decision to limit the presentation of the statistical results in the text because too many numbers can divert attention from the key findings. For example, the canonical correlations and standardized Z-scores are reported in tables, not in the text.

3

Snapshots of Neighborhood Satisfaction

The purpose of this chapter is to examine how Americans rate their neighborhoods. Using data from the American Housing Survey (AHS), we focus on associations between poor quality ratings, neighborhood characteristics, and characteristics of respondents. These data, associations, and text serve as the national context. They show that the overwhelming majority of Americans like their neighborhoods. We will compare the considerably less favorable opinions expressed in our neighborhood surveys (chapters 4 to 7) to the rosy numbers in this chapter.

Neighborhood Quality

During the period 1981–91, an average of 35 percent of those responding to the AHS rated their neighborhood as excellent. An additional 50 percent felt they lived in a good neighborhood. Only 12 percent felt their neighborhood was fair, and less than 3 percent rated it poor. Table 3.1 also shows that residents of northern New Jersey and the Philadelphia region fit the national pattern. Few rated their neighborhood as fair or poor.

We were concerned that our collapsing of the ten-point neighborhood rating scale to a four-point one (see chapter 2) might have inadvertently created spurious results. Specifically, we noted a slight trend toward more good and fewer excellent ratings after 1985. To make sure that this trend was not an artifact, we analyzed the 1

Table 3.1. Neighborhood Quality Ratings for Northern New Jersey, Philadelphia, and the United States, 1981–1991

| Area | Year | Percentage Rating Neighborhood Quality | | | |
		Excellent	Good	Fair	Poor
Northern New Jersey[a]	1987	37.1	50.6	9.7	2.6
	1991	32.9	54.7	9.7	2.7
Philadelphia[b]	1985	34.8	51.0	11.1	3.1
	1989	34.8	49.7	11.7	3.8
United States	1981	33.3	49.1	15.4	2.2
	1983	34.9	48.1	14.8	2.2
	1985	39.1	46.0	12.1	2.8
	1987	35.5	50.3	11.6	2.6
	1989	34.9	51.2	11.0	2.9
	1991	33.6	52.6	11.2	2.6

Source: U.S. Bureau of the Census, Annual Housing Survey for the United States for 1981, 1983, and 1985 and American Housing Survey for 1987, 1989, and 1991. Percentages computed for occupied units that reported a response. For the years 1985–91, the scale 1–10 in the survey was converted so that "excellent" was 10, "good" was 6–9, "fair" was 3–5, and "poor" was 1–2.
[a]Northern New Jersey includes Bergen, Essex, Hudson, Hunterdon, Middlesex, Monmouth, Morris, Ocean, Passaic, Somerset, Sussex, and Union Counties, New Jersey.
[b]Philadelphia includes Bucks, Chester, Delaware, Montgomery, and Philadelphia Counties, Pennsylvania, and Burlington, Camden, and Gloucester Counties, New Jersey.

(worst) to 10 (best) scale used by the AHS since 1985. The proportion who rated their neighborhood as good (e.g., scale numbers 6, 7, 8, and 9) increased from 4.8, 9.8, 19.4, and 12. percent in 1985 to 5.3, 11, 22.1, and 14.2 in 1991, respectively. Furthermore, each rate increased during each time period, that is, 1985 to 1987, 1987 to 1989, and 1989 to 1991. In other words, there is a small but consistent trend in the good and excellent categories. No such trend was demonstrated for the fair and poor ones.

Before examining the association between neighborhood quality and neighborhood and respondent attributes, we describe two characteristics of the AHS that required us to patch together different data sets to answer the research questions. The most recently published AHS is of data collected in 1991. Unfortunately, the raw data from the 1991 AHS were not available on computer tape at the time this research was done. Consequently, nearly all of the analyses made from the AHS data in the chapter are from the 1989 AHS. Data for 1991 are presented when they were available.

The second characteristic, initially discussed in chapter 2, is that the AHS asks everyone about problems and their personal characteristics. But only people who have resided in the neighborhood for less than twelve months are asked about attractions and previous neighborhoods. The result is that some of the tables mix results from all respondents and recent migrants. Source notes for each table in this chapter serve as a reminder of this need to combine two different data sets in the same table. In the text we inserted the words *recent migrants* or other language to signal that we are writing about residents who have lived in the neighborhood for twelve months or less.

Problems, Attractions, and Comparisons with Previous Neighborhoods

Table 3.2 reports neighborhood characteristics for the 1989 and 1991 AHS data. Thirty-eight percent of Americans reported at least one problem in their neighborhoods. Bad people in the neighborhood was the most often cited problem: 12.5 percent. Traffic, noise, crime, and a nonspecific "other" problem category were reported as problems by 6 to 10 percent of respondents. Litter and housing deterioration, undesirable nonresidential land uses, and poor services were noted by less than 5 percent.

Convenience to work, friends, and relatives, characteristics of the house, appearance of the neighborhood, and a general "other" category were considered attractions by 16 to 35 percent of respondents who moved during the last year prior to the survey. Good schools and convenient leisure activities, public transportation, and other public services were important attractions to less than 9 percent of these recent migrants.

Forty percent of Americans (recent migrants) rated their neighborhood as better than their previous one, compared to only 17 percent who rated it is worse. The remaining 43 percent of Americans considered the new neighborhood the same quality, or have always lived in the neighborhood.

Using the 1989 AHS data tapes, table 3.3 ties neighborhood characteristics to a poor quality rating. It shows a striking association between number of problems and poor quality. Sixty-two percent of the 44,933 respondents reported no problems. Only .4 percent of these respondents (111 out of almost 28,000) rated their neighborhood as poor quality. Twenty-seven percent reported one problem,

Table 3.2. Prevalence of Neighborhood Characteristics in the United States, 1989 and 1991

	Percentage of Respondents	
Characteristic	1989	1991
Problems:	38.7	38.0
Bad people in the neighborhood	12.5	12.5
Other neighborhood characteristic	9.9	9.2
Traffic	7.7	7.3
Noise	7.4	7.7
Crime	6.4	7.4
Litter or housing deterioration	4.9	4.6
Undesirable commercial, institutional, industrial activities	1.8	1.7
Poor city or county services	1.6	1.6
Attractions:		
Other characteristics	34.7	35.5
Convenient to job	25.1	24.5
House was most important consideration	25.7	24.4
Looks/design of neighborhood	20.8	19.6
Convenient to friends or relatives	16.7	17.6
Good schools	8.1	8.7
Convenient to leisure activities	4.9	4.3
Convenient to public transportation	3.5	3.1
Other public services	2.4	2.1
Neighborhood comparison:		
Present neighborhood is better	40.4	39.1
Present neighborhood is the same or same neighborhood	42.7	44.3
Present neighborhood is worse	16.9	16.6

Source: U.S. Bureau of the Census, American Housing Survey for 1989 and 1991. Percentages computed for occupied units that reported a response. Percentages for problems were calculated from all respondents to the survey, whereas the responses to the attractions and neighborhood comparisons were from people moving into the neighborhood during the last twelve months.

and 3.8 percent of these respondents rated their neighborhood as poor.

The proportion of poor quality ratings sharply increased as the number of perceived problems increased. Two problems were associated with 11 percent rating their neighborhood as poor, three problems with 19 percent poor quality, four to five problems with 32 percent, and six to eight problems with 52 percent rating their neighborhood as poor quality.

What specific problems were most associated with poor neighborhood quality? To help answer this question, we labeled the data in

Table 3.3. Neighborhood Characteristics/Variables Associated with Poor Neighborhood Quality Rating, United States, 1989

Characteristic/Variable	Respondents Who Rated Neighborhood as Poor	
	Percent	95% Confidence Limits
All respondents	2.8	2.7, 2.9
Problems:		
Number of problems:		
0	0.4	0.3, 0.5
1	3.8	3.5, 4.1
2	11.3	10.3, 12.3
3	19.1	16.6, 21.6
4–5	32.2	26.4, 38.0
6–8	52.2	31.8, 72.6
Specific problems:		
Crime	18.0	16.6, 19.4
Bad people in the neighborhood	11.5	10.7, 12.3
Litter or housing deterioration	10.9	9.6, 12.2
Noise	9.1	8.1, 11.0
Poor city or county services	8.9	6.8, 11.0
Undesirable commercial, institutional, industrial activities	8.0	6.2, 9.8
Other distressing features	4.8	4.2, 5.4
Traffic	4.7	4.0, 5.4
Attractions:		
Number of attractions:		
6–8	0.0	0.0, 0.0
3–5	1.2	0.5, 1.9
2	2.2	1.7, 2.7
1	4.5	4.1, 5.0
0	3.5	2.3, 4.7
Specific attractions:		
Looks/design of neighborhood	0.6	0.3, 0.9
Convenient to leisure activities	1.0	0.2, 1.8
Good schools	2.3	1.3, 3.3
Convenient to job	2.4	1.8, 3.0
Other public services	2.6	0.7, 4.5
Convenient to friends or relatives	3.2	2.4, 4.0
House was most important consideration	3.9	3.2, 4.6
Convenient to public transportation	4.6	2.5, 6.7
Other reasons	5.4	4.7, 6.1

Source: U.S. Bureau of the Census, American Housing Survey for 1989 (computer file). Percentages computed for occupied units that reported a response. Percentages for problems were calculated from all respondents to the survey (44,933), whereas the responses to the attractions and neighborhood comparisons were from people moving into the neighborhood during the last twelve months (12,432).

table 3.2 "prevalence" of the problem and the data in table 3.3 "association" of the problem with a poor quality rating. A high association compared to prevalence suggests that the problem was strongly associated with a poor neighborhood quality rating. For example, noise had a prevalence of 7.4 percent in 1989, that is, 7.4 percent of respondents said it was a problem (table 3.2). If its association was 20 percent, then noise doubtless was a major cause of the poor rating because those who identified it as a problem disproportionately rated their neighborhood as poor. Conversely, if only 2 percent of those who said noise was a problem rated their neighborhood as poor, it follows that noise by itself was probably not sufficiently stressful to cause a poor neighborhood quality rating.

Crime, litter, and housing deterioration stand out as problems with high prevalence and even stronger association. Six percent of Americans identified crime as a problem, and 18 percent of them rated their neighborhood as poor. About 5 percent said litter or housing deterioration was a problem, and almost 11 percent who said it was a problem rated their neighborhood as poor. Traffic and the "other" category were among the most prevalent problems but were not strongly associated with poor quality. Eight and 10 percent of respondents rated these as problems, respectively, but only 5 percent of them also rated their neighborhoods as poor quality.

Attractions should reduce the likelihood of a neighborhood being labeled poor quality. Table 3.3 shows inconsistent evidence of the expected inverse association. No respondent (recent migrant) who was attracted by six to eight attributes rated their neighborhood as poor. As the number of positive attributes dropped from three to five to two, the proportion rating their neighborhood as poor increased from 2.2 to 4.5 percent. Yet the association between poor quality and attractions is not as striking as it was for problems, that is, the association between attractions and poor quality shows a less marked change. Furthermore, there is an exception in the attraction data. Seven percent of respondents reported no attractions. Yet only 3.5 percent of them rated their neighborhood as poor. This compares to the respondents who reported only one attraction. A total of 4.5 percent rated their neighborhood as poor.

With respect to preventing a low quality rating, table 3.3 suggests that an attractive neighborhood appearance, convenience to leisure activities, good schools, and convenience to work were the most

Table 3.4. Respondent Characteristics/Responses Associated with Poor Neighborhood Quality Rating, United States, 1989

Characteristic/Response	Respondents Who Rated Neighborhood as Poor	
	Percent	95% Confidence Limits
All respondents	2.8	2.7, 2.9
Comparison of present and previous neighborhood:		
Present neighborhood is better	1.1	0.8, 1.4
Present neighborhood is the same or same neighborhood	2.3	1.9, 2.7
Present neighborhood is worse	14.3	12.8, 15.9
Age:		
18–30	4.2	3.8, 4.7
31–50	2.9	2.7, 3.1
51+	2.2	1.9, 2.5
Sex:		
Male	2.1	1.9, 2.3
Female	4.2	3.9, 4.5
Tenure:		
Owner	1.5	1.4, 1.6
Renter	5.5	5.1, 5.9
Length of residence (years):		
0–2	3.8	3.5, 4.1
>2–5	3.0	2.6, 3.4
>5–10	2.4	2.0, 2.8
10+	2.0	1.8, 2.2
Education:		
Grades 1–11	5.1	4.7, 5.5
High school graduate	2.9	2.6, 3.2
Some college	2.3	2.0, 2.6
College graduate	1.0	0.8, 1.2

important attractions. Each of these was associated with about 2 percent or less low quality ratings. Conversely, convenience to public transportation, an inexpensive dwelling unit, and convenience to friends or relatives seemed to be less protective against a poor quality rating. Three to five percent of respondents who noted these as attractions nevertheless rated their neighborhood as poor quality. Because these respondents were restricted to recent migrants, we cannot generalize the same result to all Americans.

Table 3.4. Continued

Characteristic/Response	Respondents Who Rated Neighborhood as Poor	
	Percent	95% Confidence Limits
Race/ethnicity:		
Black	7.5	6.8, 8.2
Hispanic	5.1	4.3, 5.9
Other	3.5	2.5, 4.5
White	2.2	2.1, 2.4
Marital status:		
Divorced	4.9	4.4, 5.4
Never married	4.0	3.5, 4.5
Widowed	2.6	2.2, 3.0
Married	1.9	1.7, 2.1
Region of residence:		
Northeast	3.0	2.7, 3.3
West	2.9	2.6, 3.2
Midwest	2.7	2.4, 3.0
South	2.7	2.4, 3.0
Metropolitan location:		
Central city	4.7	4.4, 5.0
Suburb of central city	1.9	1.7, 2.1
Other urban	2.2	1.7, 2.7
Rural	1.5	1.3, 1.7

Source: U.S. Bureau of the Census, American Housing Survey for 1989 (computer file). Percentages computed for occupied units that reported a response. All respondents were included in the survey.

Personal Filters

Table 3.4 lists ten categories of respondent characteristics. Some of these characteristics were expected to filter perception of neighborhood problems and attractions. Chapter 1 discussed these characteristics. Briefly recapitulating, we expected that those respondents who have a less powerful position in society because they suffered from segregation, were less educated, were divorced, and/or were young would be less tolerant of problems than those who had acquired more prestige and material goods.

The results are striking for the neighborhood comparison variables. Fourteen percent of Americans who perceived that their present neighborhood was worse than their previous one rated their neighborhood as poor. This compared with only 1 percent of respondents who rated their neighborhood as better than their previous one.

In order of their likelihood to rate their neighborhood as poor quality, the other six respondent characteristics most strongly associated with a poor neighborhood quality rating were as follows: being a black respondent (7.5 percent), a renter (5.5 percent), a Hispanic respondent (5.1 percent), having a formal education up to and including the eleventh grade (5.1 percent), being a divorced respondent (4.9 percent), and being a resident of a central city (4.7 percent).

Summarizing, the bivariate comparisons of poor neighborhood quality, problems, attractions, previous neighborhood, and personal characteristics identified behavioral and blight-related hazards, total number of hazards, absence of any attractions, perception that the present neighborhood is worse than the previous one, and black respondents as most strongly associated with a poor quality neighborhood rating. All of these were expected.

Discriminant Analysis of Neighborhood Quality

Using the 1989 AHS data tapes, two sets of discriminant analyses were done to determine which characteristics and answers to questions on the AHS best predict neighborhood quality ratings (excellent/good, fair, poor). The first set utilized the responses of all 45,000 respondents. The second set used only responses from the 12,500 persons who moved into their dwelling unit within the past year. We expected the first set of analyses to be less valuable than the second because the 45,000 data set did not include information about attractions and responses to the neighborhood comparison question. In other words, the first set was attempting to predict neighborhood quality ratings in the absence of important information people should use to rate their neighborhoods.

We were correct in our expectations. The predictive performance of the first set of analyses was poorer, by far, than that of the second. Specifically, the canonical correlations with the neighborhood quality variable were lower; the ability to predict respondents into the proper categories was less accurate; and the results provided less insight about the correlates of poor neighborhood quality. In contrast, the second set of analyses yielded far stronger and more complete results because they included more variables. We present those results in detail below, results based on all the problems, attractions,

Table 3.5. Discriminant Analysis: United States, 1989

| | | Correlation of Variable with Function | |
| | | General Poor Quality Function | Behavioral Hazard Function |
Variable	F-value	Function 1	Function 2
Present neighborhood is worse	544	.626	
Noise problem	138	.478	
Bad persons in the neighborhood	536	.453	.284
Neighborhood is attractive	104	−.373	
Crime problem	588		.613
Black respondent	42		.401
Educational achievement	61		−.377
Litter or housing deterioration problem	191		.352
White respondent	37		−.330
Male respondent	15		−.278
Public housing project	31		.271
Canonical correlation with neighborhood quality dependent variable (P-value)		.577 (.0001)	.122 (.001)
Average standardized Z score with poor quality responses		1.32	1.79

Source: U.S. Bureau of the Census, American Housing Survey for 1989 (machine-readable file).
Note: Variables with a correlation of >0.25 with one of the two functions are shown. All correlations shown were statistically significant discriminators at P < .0001.

neighborhood comparisons, and respondent characteristics found in the 12,500 recent-mover data set.

Baseline Run

Table 3.5 presents two functions that help interpret the interrelationships among the discriminating variables. Both focus on poor neighborhood quality ratings. The first identifies respondents who perceived the present neighborhood as worse than the previous one (r = .626). They were troubled by noise (r = .478) and bad people in their neighborhood (r = .453), and they found the neighborhood to be unattractive (r = −.373 with neighborhood attractiveness/design).

We labeled function 1 "general poor quality." It contained bad people, noise, an unattractive appearance, and was considered less desirable than respondents' previous neighborhood. All of these are elements commonly associated with an undesirable neighborhood (see chapter 1).

The second function identified eight characteristics also strongly associated with a poor neighborhood quality rating. It focuses on people who were troubled by crime (r = .613), litter and deteriorated housing (r = .352), and bad people in their neighborhood (r = .284). These respondents tended to be black (r = .401), not white (r = −.330), had less formal education (r = −.377), were more likely to have been female (r = −.278 with male), and lived in a public housing project (r = .271). We labeled this the "behavioral hazard" function.

Overall, the variables strongly identified by the baseline discriminant analysis included five problems, one attraction, the neighborhood comparison variable, and four of the respondent characteristic variables. The metropolitan location and region of residence variables did not strongly identify with either of these functions.

Aggregate Hazard Heuristic Run

The second discriminant analysis presents the total hazard heuristic hypothesis described in chapter 2, that is, the greater the number of perceived hazards, the greater the likelihood of a poor quality rating. We added all the problems to form a total hazards variable and all the attractions to form a total attractions variable. The results in table 3.6 are similar to those in table 3.5. The general poor quality neighborhood function (function 1) of table 3.5 is even more general, that is, it focuses solely on total hazards (r = .687) and neighborhood comparison (r = .686).

The second function in table 3.6 is similar to the behavioral hazard function found in the first discriminant analysis (table 3.5). The respondents tended to be black (r = .595), not white (r = −.482), not highly educated (r = −.540), were likely to be female (r = −.480 with male), lived in a public housing project (r = .390), were troubled by hazards (r = .348), and were likely to be divorced (r = .250).

The only noteworthy differences between this second function and the one in the first discriminant analysis is the loss of information about what hazard(s) troubled the respondents, crime and bad persons in the baseline run, and the addition of the divorced variable to the explanation in the heuristic. In other words, function 1 remains a general neighborhood dissatisfaction one and function 2 is

Table 3.6. Discriminant Analysis of Aggregate Hazard Heuristic, United States, 1989

Variable	F-value	General Poor Quality Function Function 1	Behavioral Hazard Function Function 2
Aggregate number of problems	972	.687	.348
Present neighborhood is worse	544	.686	
Black respondent	42		.595
Educational achievement	61		−.540
White respondent	37		−.482
Male respondent	15		−.480
Public housing project	31		.390
Divorced respondent	11		−.250
Canonical correlation with neighborhood quality dependent variable (P-value)		.543 (<.001)	.092 (.001)
Average standardized Z score with poor quality responses		1.58	1.19

Source: U.S. Bureau of the Census, American Housing Survey for 1989 (computer file).
Note: Variables with a correlation of >0.25 with one of the two functions are shown. All correlations shown were statistically significant discriminators at P < .0001.

more narrowly defined around behavioral hazards faced disproportionately by African Americans who live in and around public housing projects.

The aggregate attractions variable is notable by its absence as an important discriminator of poor quality ratings. It had an F-value of 30 compared to 972 for the aggregate hazard variable and was weakly correlated (r = −.189) with the general poor quality function.

This first discriminant analysis correctly classified 74 percent of all respondents and the second correctly classified 71 percent. Yet only 66 percent of those who rated their neighborhoods as poor quality were correctly classified by the first discriminant analysis and 63 percent by the second. This result is attributable to the difficulty in distinguishing poor from fair quality neighborhoods. Seventy-two percent of the misclassifications of those who actually rated their neighborhood as poor quality were placed in the fair quality designation. We attribute this inability to accurately predict more poor quality respondents to the paucity of site-specific hazards data available in the AHS database.

Summary of Findings

RQ1: *How do people who live in the immediate vicinity of potentially hazardous land uses and activities rate their neighborhoods?*

Throughout the 1980s and early 1990s, less than three percent of Americans surveyed by the AHS rated their neighborhoods as poor. The northern New Jersey and Philadelphia metropolitan areas, which contain all twenty of our study neighborhoods, fit this national pattern.

RQ2: *What factors most influence neighborhood ratings, especially rating of a neighborhood as poor quality?*

As expected, crime, bad people in the neighborhood, and litter or housing deterioration were prominent variables in the bivariate and discriminant analyses. The neighborhood comparison variable was a strong discriminating variable. In addition, respondents who were black and had relatively less formal education identified disproportionately with poor neighborhood quality.

Massive technology sites and local activity spaces cannot be distinguished in the AHS data set. The variable of undesirable non-residential land use was seventh out of eight in prevalence among neighborhood problems (1.8 percent) and sixth in association with poor neighborhood quality (8 percent). It was not a prominent variable in the discriminant analyses. Although the AHS data provide little support for the hypothesis that massive technology sites are prominent concerns of residents, this observation must be tempered by the limitations of the data. In addition, it is plausible that the noise and traffic variables are surrogates for massive technology sites, as well as local activity spaces.

Neighborhood appearance was the strongest discriminator among the eight attraction variables, but attractions were not among the strongest correlates of neighborhood quality.

Because of the limitations of the AHS data, only one heuristic, aggregate hazard burden, could be tested. It was a powerful discriminator in the bivariate analyses. Along with the neighborhood quality comparison, the aggregate total number of problems variable correctly predicted more than 70 percent of respondent ratings of their neighborhoods.

4

Hazards and Environmental Inequity

The two-and-a-half-hour Metroliner train ride from Washington, D.C., to central New Jersey is for reading, thinking, and working. At eighty to ninety miles an hour, the backs of buildings and litter-strewn alleys of cities, suburban housing and shopping developments, and plowed fields and forested strips that look like they lost the war with acid rain do not promote gazing through the windows. But there is an exception. The twenty-eight-mile ride between Wilmington, Delaware, and Philadelphia is remarkable for its transformation from a relaxing to a tensing landscape.

Images of the Marcus Hook Area

After leaving Wilmington, the Metroliner train seems to descend northward into Delaware Bay. The rider is taken through a therapeutic landscape of sail boats, small towns hanging on cliffs, fishing boats and their yards, large birds circling and then diving for fish. All of this takes place in a context dominated by clear, soft blue water. Although the train rider can see an occasional chemical barge and tanker, for five to eight minutes the environment outside the speeding train seems like a snapshot of eastern salt marsh and bay ecology taken two hundred years ago (Teal and Teal 1969). You can feel your face muscles relax.

Therapeutic Delaware Bay ecology is interrupted by a tongue of flame to the northeast, signaling the approach of Sun Oil's Marcus

Hook refinery. At first, the Marcus Hook flare is a minor annoyance, but as the train approaches the Delaware-Pennsylvania border, the flare becomes the dominant image, like an approaching tornado.

The deteriorating Phoenix Steel Mill in Delaware quickly appears to the west, capturing the rider's attention for a few moments. But as the train crosses from Delaware into Pennsylvania, the refinery complex surrounds the train, engulfing it in a maze of towers, turrets, pipes, tanks, and flares. The refinery causes us to look out the window in every direction at the same time. Time seems to freeze and you can feel your face muscles again tense. Are there any signs of malfunctions? How many flares? Any signs of oil spills? Are there any collapsed tanks? Are they making any changes at the refinery? Even at eighty to ninety miles an hour, the short trip through the Sun Oil refinery seems to take at least a full minute.

The refinery abruptly ends, and the train speeds through the small towns of Lower Chichester, Marcus Hook, and Trainer. The BP oil refinery in Trainer appears suddenly, giving the impression that the Sun refinery complex never really ended. After the BP refinery, for thirty seconds the landscape becomes houses, schools, a few parks, churches, and streets.

Then out to the east appears the plume of the Delaware County trash-to-steam incinerator followed by its enormous stack and flashing light to warn off airplanes from nearby Philadelphia airport. The incinerator is the dominant image until the train reaches the Commodore John Barry Bridge. At that point, riders' attention returns to the movement of people inside the train preparing to disembark in Philadelphia. The abrupt transition from the therapeutic bay to the tension of the refineries and incinerator lingers. It is indelible, more powerful than others we have seen along the east coast of the United States because of the stark contrast.

The Sun and BP refineries each produce about 170,000 barrels of oil a day, about 55 percent of the amount produced by the EXXON/Tosco refinery that borders east Elizabeth (see chapter 5). On paper, the Marcus Hook refineries appear to be major polluters. According to Toxic Release Inventory (TRI) data, the Sun refinery was the fourth largest emitter of toxic chemicals in Pennsylvania in 1991. This is misleading, because at the time of this writing the TRI data considered any waste that is transferred off site to be an emission. In fact, 95 percent of Sun's almost 87 million pounds of pollution is sulfuric acid, which is sent to a sewage plant for treatment. BP Oil's Marcus Hook refinery was listed as the seventh largest water polluter in Pennsylvania in 1991. Nearly all of the 2.5 million pounds were ammonia. In fact, more than 95 percent of the ammonia is treated.

Like the former EXXON/Tosco refinery in east Elizabeth, both Sun and BP have invested considerable resources to reduce their refinery emissions to a small fraction of what they were a decade ago. The sheer size of the two refineries make them the dominant images in Marcus Hook, Trainer, and the Linwood area of Lower Chichester. Periodic incidents reinforce the image of the massive technology site hazard. Respondents provided some examples of incidents. One recalled the overfilling of a butane cavern, which led to a fire. While this chapter was being written, on March 21, 1994, a 420,000-gallon tank at the Sun refinery filled with sludge, an oil and water mixture, and sediment collapsed after an explosion. Nineteen workers were hospitalized with injuries ranging from multiple fractures to smoke inhalation. A small amount of oily substance was observed on Middle Creek, a stream that runs through the refinery (Hart 1994; Taylor and Hart 1994).

Although the two refineries are the dominant manufacturing facilities in the Marcus Hook area, the area between the Sun refinery and the Commodore John Barry Bridge contains numerous other manufacturing facilities. The town of Marcus Hook contains a large Congoleum factory, K. S. Processing (including an incinerator), a facility of the General Chemical Corporation, Air Products and Chemicals, a former, partly collapsed FMC facility, the Tubular Steel Company, and a few abandoned factories. Trainer, a one-square-mile municipality located between Chester and Marcus Hook, contains a Witco Chemical plant as well as the BP refinery. The area south of the Commodore John Barry Bridge in Chester has an iron and scrap-metal yard, brick firing and seafood processing plants, Fischer Tank, a Teledyne facility, and the Delcora sewage treatment plant. Scores of abandoned and boarded-up buildings in various stages of deterioration and collapse cluster along the riverfront and assorted other places in Chester. We saw small junkyards, abandoned gasoline stations, and many abandoned houses. Locked mailboxes and people in the streets testify to the presence of drugs and crime in the area east of the Conrail line.

Opened in 1991 over the protests of its residential neighbors, the massive Westinghouse incinerator, handling twenty-seven hundred tons per day, has a sleek elegance when viewed from the train at a distance of more than one-half mile at eighty miles an hour. But the area around the incinerator, the southeast corner of Chester, has a beleaguered look about it. Turning onto Thurlow Street gave us anything but a feeling of elegance. Most of the attached houses on both sides of the narrow street were completely or partly abandoned and deteriorating. Litter was all over the street. We did not have much time to study the blight because a garbage truck came racing toward us. Because we unwittingly were in the driver's glide path to the incinerator gate, the driver beeped angrily on his horn.

After parking our car as far away from the path of the garbage trucks as possible, we stopped to talk with neighborhood residents. They immediately pointed to a huge trash pile, which was described with great emotion as a source of terrible odors and ferocious rats. One woman said that she no longer let her cats out because one had been killed by rats. Eight people in this small neighborhood wrote that rats were a major problem (see presentation later in the chapter). Some also complained about dirt, soot, garbage spills, and even cracked foundations caused by the massive trucks rumbling down their streets (see also Stranahan 1993).

Residents of the Thurlow Street area have fought against the Westinghouse incinerator in their neighborhood. The fifth largest in the United States, the plant draws about two hundred trucks a day (Stranahan 1993). In 1993, it was fined by the state of Pennsylvania for violating its emission limits (Hardy 1993). The host municipality agreement between Chester and Westinghouse yields more than $2 million a year in revenues to Chester, but there was no evidence that any of the money has been spent around Thurlow Street. Although public pressure led to the construction of a road that removed trucks from Thurlow Street, residents complained that noise and odors were merely relocated to the back of their houses (Stranahan 1993).

At the time of our survey, plans were being considered to redevelop additional lands adjacent to the Delaware River in Chester. Biomedical Waste Systems, Inc. of Boston received a permit from the Pennsylvania Department of Environmental Resources (DER) to open what would be the largest infectious-waste treatment facility in the United States. The facility was to be operated on property immediately adjacent to the incinerator. Up to three hundred tons of waste plastic and paper from hospitals in the Northeast would be neutralized and turned into pellets in a steam-sterilization unit. The medical-waste facility was deemed completely safe by state officials, but it was opposed by the Chester Residents Concerned for Quality Living, which charged the city, county, state, and industry with environmental racism (Stranahan 1993).

Plans also existed to construct a facility along the riverfront that would remediate contaminated soil from gasoline stations. A risk assessment of the incinerator, proposed medical, and gasoline station waste facilities might show little health risk, but it is impossible to ignore the psychological impact of siting these LULUs in this poor, mostly black community.

We observed little that could soften the impact of the incinerator in Chester. There was no forested strip, no parks, and no highway barriers to block the view. Houses were literally pressed against the gate of the incineration facility and were close to the huge trash pile.

In contrast to those living near the incinerator, most of those living west of the north-south Conrail line could not even see the incinerator. A large park, hospital, schools, and other buildings blocked their view. Parks, stores, and other factories provided some buffering of the two refineries to some Marcus Hook residents.

Choice of Neighborhoods

We divided the study area into six neighborhoods (fig. 4.1). Each had a different physical orientation to the two refineries and the incinerator. The names we chose for these six areas are convenient labels and do not necessarily have official political status.

The southern section of Lower Chichester (known as Linwood) overlooks the larger of the two petroleum refineries. Anyone who left their home to go shopping, visit a friend, or go to work would drive by the massive refinery and its expansive tank farm. Housing in the area varied from older row housing facing directly towards the Sun refinery and the tank farm to new row housing situated uphill and overlooking the refinery. The population of Linwood had the highest socioeconomic status within the study area and suffered no other obvious distressing neighborhood characteristics. Our expectation

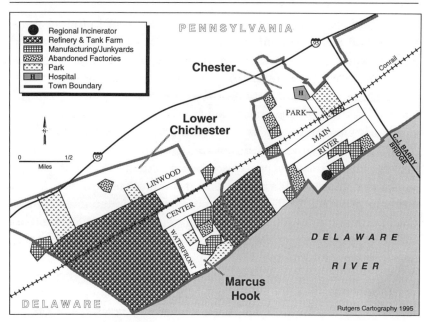

Figure 4.1. Marcus Hook Area

was that the massive old refinery would become the dominant hazard image of Linwood's population. There would be no cluster of hazards, and the area would have a relatively high neighborhood quality rating.

The residents of Marcus Hook Center were surrounded on all four sides by a variety of technological hazards. One refinery lies directly to the west and the other to the southeast. Other manufacturing facilities lie to the south. The main Conrail line is the northern border of the zone. Remarkably, the town's main street bisects Center along its horizontal axis. Small shops, restaurants, city hall, and other service establishments line both sides of the street. The dominant image along this axis is of a pleasant, small town. We expected that residents of Center would be distressed by the refinery complexes and other manufacturing facilities on the edges but would consider the neighborhood as a whole to be a good place to live.

The Waterfront area of Marcus Hook presents sharply contrasting images. The riverfront contains a medium-sized park with a pleasant unobscured view of the Delaware River. The road that heads north from the park to the town center is broad and gives the impression of open space. A second park sits adjacent to the road. Yet two major petroleum refineries and other manufacturing facilities give a counter-impression of running a gauntlet through industrial facilities. During our second visit, loud disturbing vibrations made by machinery at one of the refineries could easily be heard 150 feet away from the refinery gates near homes we were surveying. We expected that some respondents would be pleased by the parks and spacious feeling, but many also would be affected by the noises and smells of local industry.

The small town of Trainer (we did not sample in Trainer) and the BP refinery are a buffer between the towns of Marcus Hook and Chester. The River area of Chester is bordered by the BP petroleum refinery and active and abandoned factories to the southwest. There is no river view. The waterfront is dominated by the Delaware County waste-to-energy incinerator. Without doubt, the Chester River area is severely perceptually impacted by a wide variety of technological hazards. It appears to be an area disproportionately burdened with massive technology sites, a real on-the-street example of a neighborhood suffering from environmental inequity.

Industries in the River area are located about one-quarter mile from the Main area of Chester. But some of the facilities in the River area cannot be seen from the Main neighborhood because of buildings. This shielding, we expected, might reduce reaction in the Main area to the incinerator, sewage plant, and other manufacturing facilities. On the other hand, based on the limited number of outdoor mailboxes observed in this zone and on conversations with some residents, we suspected that the Main and River areas had serious crime and vandalism problems. The River and Main areas were expected to have the lowest neighborhood quality rating because of the combination of behavioral, blight, local activity, and massive technology site hazards.

The Park area of south Chester was chosen because it was distinct. First, it contains no large technological hazards. Although the River zone is less than one-half mile away, the elevated railroad bed of the main Conrail line and housing units block residents' view of the facilities, except in a few spots where the incinerator stack and plume are visible. Second, the Park area is bordered on the east by a large and heavily used park and on the north by an attractive-appearing hospital. We expected that Park area residents would not focus on technological hazards as the primary determinant of neighborhood quality.

United States census data for 1990 (Department of Commerce 1992) showed differences among Delaware County as a whole and the three municipalities. Delaware County's population included 11 percent blacks and Hispanics. Less than 5 percent of Marcus Hook's population of twenty-five hundred and Lower Chichester's population of thirty-four hundred was black or Hispanic. In strong contrast, almost 90 percent of south Chester's population was black and 4 percent was Hispanic. The 1989 per capita income of county residents exceeded $17,000. The figures for the Linwood area of Lower Chichester, Marcus Hook, and the southern part of Chester were $11,700, $10,000 and $7,000, respectively. Twenty-six percent of south Chester's population was below the official government poverty designation compared to 9 percent of Marcus Hook's, 6 percent of Lower Chichester's, and 5 percent of Delaware County's. Twenty-five percent of the county's population were college graduates, compared to 4 percent of the residents of the study area. Finally, 30 percent of Marcus Hook's employed population worked in manufacturing and construction compared to 37 percent of Lower Chichester's, 21 percent for the county as a whole, and only 15 percent of south Chester's. We reviewed local newspapers and noted they carried stories about drug problems in Chester. Overall, the study area appeared to have densely packed behavioral, blight, and massive technology hazards. Its population was relatively poor and quite varied in race/ethnicity and type of employment.

Survey Questions, Methods, Problems, and Returns

Ten attractions, seven personal characteristics, and twenty-one hazards were included in our survey instrument. Twenty of the twenty-one hazards were obvious in at least one of the six neighborhoods. An old steel mill can be seen from Lower Chichester. But we knew of no other massive and dangerous-appearing metal or furniture plant in the area. We used the steel plant and furniture plants to identify unusually sensitive people. In other words, few people should identify them as a problem because they are not present.

We used the refineries and incinerator to identify the proportion of respondents who were insensitive to an obvious potential hazard. No one living in Marcus Hook or Linwood should indicate that a refinery or tank farm was not present. No one living in the River area of Chester should indicate that an incinerator was not present. Utility rights-of-way with towers and hanging lines were present, but frankly seemed to be located among pleasant green areas. In addition, they were obscured by numerous other land uses. Consequently, we did not expect many respondents to be stressed by utility lines and towers.

The cover letter, survey instrument, and a stamped return envelope were inserted into a brown envelope. We attempted to place an instrument in every occupied dwelling unit within one-quarter mile of the two refineries and the incinerator.

Chapter 2 described generic problems associated with distributing the instrument. Vacant apartments in the Main and River areas of Chester were a particular local problem. In several places, we asked people if someone lived in a unit that appeared to be vacant. Such opportunities, however, were rare. In the Main area of Chester, several children were observed removing the survey instruments immediately after we left. A resident stopped them, which allowed us to return the surveys. However, it is possible that these children returned to their game of picking up our instruments as soon as we and the neighbor left.

We distributed 1,142 surveys on March 12, 1993. A total of 286 useful responses (25 percent) were received by May 12, 1993. A total of 284 were complete, that is, they were missing no data. The response rate was 25 to 29 percent from Linwood, Marcus Hook, and the River and Park areas of Chester. It was only 16 percent in the Main Chester area. The lower response rate in the Main area was not surprising given the problems of vacant apartments and children noted above.

As expected, respondents were not representative of all 13,500 residents of the Marcus Hook area. Eighty percent of respondents graduated high school, compared to 57 percent of area residents ($P < .01$); 67 percent were female, compared to 57 percent of residents ($P < .01$); and 75 percent were homeowners, compared to 54 percent of area residents ($P < .01$). Fourteen percent of respondents and 13 percent of residents were more than seventy years old. Fifteen percent of respondents and 26 percent of residents were eighteen to thirty years old (P < .01). Finally, we note that 67 percent of area residents had lived in the same house and 95 percent in the same county for at least five years, compared to 69 percent of respondents who had lived in the neighborhood for at least five years. Overall, our respondents were more likely to be female, educated at least through high school, homeowners, and probably short-term residents of the neighborhood than the population of the area as a whole.

Neighborhood Quality

Almost 17 percent of Marcus Hook area respondents rated their neighborhood as poor quality (table 4.1). Another 41 percent rated their neighborhood as fair, 37 percent as good, and only 6 percent rated it as excellent. Marcus Hook area respondents clearly were less satisfied with their neighborhoods than Americans as a whole, respondents to the most recent northern New Jersey and Philadelphia metropolitan region surveys, and our other neighborhood survey respondents as a whole. But the 17 percent poor, 41 percent fair, 37 percent good, and 6 percent excellent ratings for the Marcus Hook area were similar to the ratings for east Elizabeth (17 percent poor, 44 percent fair, 35 percent good, and 4 percent excellent; see chapter 5).

Like east Elizabeth, we found wide variations by neighborhood. The Chester Main and River areas had a much higher proportion of poor quality ratings (44 percent and 34 percent, respectively) than the four other neighborhoods. The Marcus Hook Center neighborhood, located less than a mile away, had no poor quality ratings, a remarkable difference.

Problems, Attractions, and Comparisons with Previous Neighborhoods

Eighty-nine percent of Marcus Hook area respondents reported at least one characteristic that was so distressing that they wanted to leave. Odors or smoke was identified by 43 percent of respondents. A petroleum refinery or tank farm, chemical plants, motor vehicle noise and heavy traffic, and the incinerator were distressing to more than 25 percent (table 4.2).

Table 4.1. Neighborhood Quality in Marcus Hook Area with Selected Comparisons

Year	Neigborhood	Percentage Rating Neighborhood Quality and 95% Confidence Limits			
		Excellent	Good	Fair	Poor
1993	Total Marcus Hook area	5.6	37.1	40.6	16.8
	(n = 286)	(2.9, 8.3)	(31.5, 42.7)	(34.9, 46.3)	(12.5, 21.1)
	Lower Chichester	8.0	40.9	43.2	8.0
	(n = 88)	(2.3, 13.7)	(30.6, 51.2)	(32.9, 53.6)	(2.3, 13.7)
	Marcus Hook Center	18.5	51.9	29.6	0.0
	(n = 27)	(3.9, 33.2)	(33.1, 70.8)	(12.4, 46.8)	(0, 0)
	Marcus Hook Waterfront	2.6	53.8	41.0	2.6
	(n = 39)	(–2.4, 7.6)	(38.2, 69.5)	(25.6, 56.4)	(–2.4, 7.6)
	Chester River	1.5	24.6	40.0	33.8
	(n = 65)	(–1.5, 4.5)	(14.1, 35.1)	(28.1, 51.9)	(22.3, 45.3)
	Chester Main	0	20.5	35.9	43.6
	(n = 39)	(0, 0)	(7.8, 33.2)	(20.8, 51.0)	(28.0, 59.2)
	Chester Park	7.1	39.3	50.0	3.6
	(n = 28)	(–2.4, 16.6)	(21.2, 57.4)	(31.5, 68.5)	(–3.3, 10.5)
1992–94	Other fourteen study neighborhoods	16.6	44.0	29.3	10.1
	(n = 1,132)	(14.4, 18.8)	(41.1, 46.9)	(26.7, 32.0)	(8.3, 11.9)
1991	Northern New Jersey[a]	32.9	54.7	9.7	2.7
1989	Philadelphia[b]	34.8	49.7	11.7	3.8
1991	United States	33.6	52.6	11.2	2.6

Source: Marcus Hook area results are based on 286 valid respondents.
Note: 95 percent confidence limits figures in parentheses.
[a]Northern New Jersey includes Bergen, Essex, Hudson, Hunterdon, Middlesex, Monmouth, Morris, Ocean, Passaic, Somerset, Sussex, and Union Counties, New Jersey.
[b]Philadelphia includes Bucks, Chester, Delaware, Montgomery, and Philadelphia Counties, Pennsylvania, and Burlington, Camden, and Gloucester Counties, New Jersey.

One Linwood (Lower Chichester) respondent was distressed by the sight of the "old [Phoenix] steel milling falling apart" across the state line in Delaware. Yet, in general, metal or furniture plants and utility rights-of-way were major problems for less than 10 percent of respondents. The minimal attention to these land uses seemed appropriate to us in this geographical context.

Table 4.3 further confirmed the initial evidence that relatively few unusually risk-sensitive people responded to the survey. Real characteristics, distance, and physical barriers rather than imaginary hazards appear to have shaped perceptions. For example, more than 40 percent of respondents from Linwood, Marcus Hook, and the Chester River area were greatly disturbed by one of the two refineries. Less than 20 percent of Chester Main and Park respondents

Table 4.2. Prevalence of Neighborhood Characteristics, Marcus Hook Area, 1993

Characteristic	Percentage of Respondents
Problems:[a]	88.8
Odors or smoke	43.4
Petroleum refinery or tank farm	35.3
Chemical plant	32.5
Motor vehicle noise and heavy traffic	26.2
Incinerator	25.5
Litter or trash in the streets, elsewhere	24.5
Sites with hazardous waste	24.1
Abandoned houses	22.4
Dogs, cats, uncontrolled animals	21.7
Occupied buildings in poor or dangerous condition	21.0
High crime rate	20.3
Junkyard, gasoline station, other nonresidential	17.1
Unfriendly neighbors	16.8
Streets, roads, sidewalks in disrepair	14.7
Recreational facilities that attract rowdy people	14.0
Abandoned factories and businesses	14.0
Inadequate street lighting	12.2
Airplane noise	11.9
Train noise	11.5
Right-of-way for a utility	8.0
Metal or furniture plant	7.7
Attractions:[b]	
Convenient to hospital	72.7
Convenient friends/relatives	66.8
House was inexpensive	66.8
Convenient to shopping	66.1
Convenient to public transport	61.5
Convenient to job	57.0
Good schools	49.0
Convenient to leisure activities	40.9
Other public services	39.2
House was inherited	15.0
Neighborhood comparison:	
Present neighborhood is better	25.5
Present neighborhood is same	46.9
Present neighborhood is worse	27.6

Source: Based on 286 responses.
[a]Percentage who found condition so disturbing that they wanted to leave.
[b]Percentage who gave these as reasons they live in the neighborhood.

were similarly distressed. Distance and physical barriers logically explain this attenuation of distress.

Distance and barriers also appear to explain the perception of the incinerator. The facility is located in the Chester River area. Forty-nine percent of Chester River respondents wanted to leave as a re-

Table 4.3. Neighborhood Problems Causing Residents to Want to Leave, 1993: Six Neighborhoods in the Marcus Hook Area

| | Percentage of Respondents | | | | | |
| | South Chester | | | Lower Chichester | Marcus Hook | |
Problem	River	Main	Park	Linwood	Center	Waterfront
Odors or smoke	54	41	21	42	48	44
Petroleum refinery or tank farm	46	18	11	39	44	39
Chemical plant	43	26	4	32	44	36
Motor vehicle noise and heavy traffic	46	49	11	19	7	10
Abandoned houses	40	60	18	6	0	10
Abandoned factories and businesses	34	23	7	2	4	10
Occupied buildings in poor or dangerous condition	40	31	7	14	7	15
Inadequate street lighting	26	18	11	7	0	5
Streets, roads, sidewalks in disrepair	29	26	11	8	0	8
Airplane noise	19	21	11	10	7	0
Train noise	22	13	14	5	15	5
Litter or trash in streets and elsewhere	48	33	21	15	7	13
Incinerator	49	31	7	9	30	28
Metal or furniture plant	15	15	0	5	7	0
Junkyard, gasoline station, other nonresidential	40	28	4	6	15	5
Hazardous-waste sites	46	26	4	10	33	26
Recreational facilities that attract rowdy people	26	37	11	5	0	8
Right-of-way for utility	15	15	4	6	0	3
Unfriendly neighbors	29	21	7	16	4	10
Crime	40	46	25	5	4	5
Dogs, cats, uncontrolled animals	42	36	11	15	0	13

Source: Based on 286 valid responses.
Note: The percentages are those respondents who found condition so disturbing that they wanted to leave.

sult of the trash-to-steam plant. This proportion dropped to about 30 percent in the Chester Main area and Marcus Hook, which are the immediately adjacent areas. Less than 10 percent of respondents from the Chester Park and Linwood neighborhoods, which are buffered from the incinerator by physical barriers and distance, were so distressed by the incinerator that they wanted to leave. Based on our observations of the Marcus Hook area, distance and physical barriers appear to account for the greater sensitivity of Chester River and Main areas to behavioral, blight, and local activity hazards.

The Park area of Chester was the only neighborhood in the study area without at least a single characteristic causing more than one-quarter of respondents to want to move. This observation also agreed with our own perceptions. The barrier of the north-south Conrail line, factories, main street, and a river to the west block the direct view of massive technology sites in all directions.

With respect to risk insensitivity, the data suggest that relatively few respondents were oblivious to the refinery. Only 7 of 154 (4.5 percent) Marcus Hook and Lower Chichester respondents indicated that a petroleum refinery or tank farm were not in their neighborhood. In comparison, 59 of Chester's 132 respondents (45 percent) indicated a refinery was not present. In fact, refineries are located on the edge of these two neighborhoods, not in them.

There was less recognition of the incinerator. Eighteen of 65 (28 percent) of Chester River respondents did not acknowledge the facility's existence in their neighborhood. The proportion increased to 50 percent in Marcus Hook and the Main area of Chester, and to more than 70 percent in Lower Chichester and the Chester Park area. As expected, acknowledgment of the facility decreased with distance and barriers. But the lack of acknowledgment appeared to be unusually high in the Chester River area.

We examined the responses of the sixty-five Chester Main respondents. Those who acknowledged the incinerator were not significantly different from those who did not in age, gender, length of residence in the neighborhood, tenure, or formal education. They were different in location. We found that sixteen of the eighteen were clustered in the southwestern most tip of the River area. Although they were within one-half mile of the site, their view of the incinerator was partly obscured by housing, abandoned factories, junkyards, and other nonresidential land uses. In addition, they were close to the smaller of the two petroleum refineries. In other words, we think that these respondents did not acknowledge the existence of the incinerator in their neighborhood because they have a more restricted definition of their neighborhood than the one we used. This possibility was supported by the observation that almost all the respondents who did not acknowledge the existence of the incinerator did acknowledge the existence of the refinery and junkyards in their neighborhood.

Returning to table 4.2, we see that convenience to the hospital, friends and relatives, shopping, pubic transportation, and inexpensive housing were attractions to more than 60 percent of respondents. Leisure activities and other public services, which were important to Americans as a whole (see chapter 3), were less important attractions in the Marcus Hook area and were about as prevalent as in east Elizabeth. Only 26 percent of area respondents rated their neighborhood as better than their previous one, compared to 39, 44, 54, and 24 percent of Americans, residents of northern New Jersey, the Philadelphia region, and east Elizabeth, respectively. Twenty-eight percent of Marcus Hook area respondents felt their neighborhood was worse. This was the highest proportion on any of our study areas.

The association between a given problem or attraction and a poor neighborhood quality rating is measured by the proportion of respondents who rated the neighborhood as poor quality out of all those who identified the characteristic. Excluding metal or furniture facilities and utility rights-of-way because they were mentioned as problems by less than 10 percent of respondents, table 4.4 shows a marked association between number of problems and poor neighborhood quality rating. The proportion of poor quality ratings increased as the number of perceived problems increased. No problems were associated with less than 2 percent rating their neighborhood as poor quality; one to five problems were associated with 9 percent of respondents rating their neighborhood as poor; six to nine problems with a 31 percent poor quality rating; and ten or more problems with 58 percent rating their neighborhood as poor quality.

What specific problems were most likely to be associated with poor neighborhood quality? Respondents who were distressed by behaviors and blight tended to rate their neighborhood as poor quality. Ten of the fourteen strongest associations were with behavioral- and blight-related hazards. Sixty percent of those who identified recreational facilities that attract rowdy people as a major problem also rated their neighborhood as poor quality. Rowdy children was a common complaint. For instance, a female aged fifty-one to seventy remarked that "since we have a dead end, warm weather attracts boys

Table 4.4. Neighborhood Characteristics/Variables Associated with Poor Neighborhood Quality Rating, Marcus Hook Area, 1993

Characteristic/Variable	Percent	95% Confidence Limits
All respondents	16.8	12.5, 21.1
Problems:[a]		
Number of problems:		
0	1.7	−0.6, 4.0
1–5	8.5	2.5, 14.5
6–9	30.6	15.6, 45.7
10+	58.3	44.4, 72.3
Specific problems:		
Recreational facilities that attract rowdy people	60.0	44.8, 75.2
Abandoned factories and businesses	57.5	42.2, 72.8
Inadequate street lighting	57.1	40.7, 73.5
High crime rates	56.9	44.2, 69.6
Streets, roads, sidewalks in disrepair or open ditches	54.8	39.8, 69.9
Abandoned houses	54.7	42.5, 66.9
Unfriendly neighbors	52.1	38.0, 66.2
Train noise	51.5	34.5, 68.6
Occupied buildings in poor or dangerous conditions	50.0	37.4, 62.7
Airplane noise	50.0	33.2, 66.8
Dogs, cats, or other uncontrolled animals	48.4	36.0, 60.8
Litter or trash in streets, empty lots, or properties	47.1	35.4, 58.8
Junkyard, gasoline station, other nonresidential	46.9	32.9, 60.9
Motor vehicle noise and heavy traffic	45.3	34.0, 56.6
Incinerator	37.0	25.9, 48.1
Sites with hazardous waste	36.2	24.9, 47.5
Odors or smoke	27.4	19.6, 35.3
Chemical plant	25.8	16.9, 34.7
Petroleum refinery or tank farm	25.7	17.2, 34.2

who don't live in the neighborhood to play basketball. They consistently use foul language."

Abandoned factories and businesses (58 percent), inadequate street lighting (57 percent), high crime rates (57 percent), abandoned houses (55 percent), and streets and roads in disrepair (55 percent) also were strongly associated with poor quality neighborhood ratings. Local activity spaces, such as junkyards, gasoline stations, and other nonresidential land uses (47 percent), and motor vehicle noise and heavy traffic (45 percent) were a little less likely to be associated with a poor quality rating. Some respondents tied behaviors

Table 4.4. Continued

Characteristic/Variable	Percent	95% Confidence Limits
Attractions:[b]		
Number of attractions:		
6–10	6.8	2.7, 10.9
1–5	24.4	16.8, 32.0
0	50.0	25.5, 74.5
Specific attractions:		
Convenient to leisure activities	4.3	0.6, 8.0
Good schools	5.0	1.4, 8.6
Other public services	8.9	3.6, 14.2
Convenient shopping	10.6	6.2, 15.0
Convenient to friends/relatives	11.0	6.6, 15.4
Convenient to jobs	12.3	7.3, 17.3
Convenient to hospitals	13.5	8.9, 18.1
House was inexpensive	13.6	8.7, 18.5
Convenient to public transportation	14.2	9.0, 19.4
House was inherited	27.9	14.5, 41.3

Source: Based on 286 valid responses.
[a]Percentage who rated their neighborhood as poor quality of those who found condition so disturbing that they wanted to leave. Only problems noted by at least 10 percent of respondents are listed. Metal or furniture plants and right-of-way for a utility were not included.
[b]Percentage who rated their neighborhood as poor quality of those who found condition an attraction.

and local activity spaces together. One resident of Lower Chichester who rated her neighborhood as fair was offended by "persons (who) use the phone at the gas station and are very loud and curse. You can hear everything, even with the windows closed." A female aged thirty-one to fifty was distressed by the "liquor stores down the street [that] bring in drunks who drive out of control. We have a lot of houses and children, which makes it very dangerous."

Compared to crime and blight, prominent massive technology sites were the least likely to be associated with a poor quality rating: petroleum refinery and tank farm (26 percent), chemical plant (26 percent), odors or smoke (27 percent), hazardous-waste sites (36 percent), and incinerator (37 percent). Respondents were distressed by these facilities, but few rated their neighborhood as poor because of them.

Respondents' written comments illustrate the quantitative disassociation of poor quality and massive technology sites and the association with a worse neighborhood. For example, one resident of

Lower Chichester wrote that "refineries are ruining our environment." Yet she rated her neighborhood as good. Her neighbor two houses away was also distressed by the refinery but rated the neighborhood as good and wrote that the neighborhood "was rated the third safest in the tristate area. Nice community activity for our children, nice place to raise a family." A third resident of Lower Chichester who rated the neighborhood as excellent wrote that "the problem with Sun Oil letting out harmful fumes and gases is the only problem in this neighborhood." A resident who lived near the second refinery wanted the "sludge pits that leak into the stream cleaned up." Yet he rated his neighborhood as excellent.

Airplane and train noise were the only two massive technology sites with an association above 50 percent. Though both are present in the area, the discriminant analyses presented below and written comments suggest that the disturbance they cause are secondary elements of great frustration felt by some respondents. For instance, one fifty-one to seventy-year-old female resident wrote that "the airplanes come over our bedroom like (they were) going to fall in it, and the trains come by all the time—day and night—like it was coming through your living room." This woman, in fact, was distressed by sixteen of the twenty-one potential problems. Yet her perceptions do not appear to us to be those of a hysterical person imagining things that do not exist. The train line was very close to her home. Other people in her immediate neighborhood also identified noise from airplanes and trains as a problem. Furthermore, the five problems she did not identify as troublesome in her neighborhood were chemical plants, high crime rate, the incinerator, junkyard and other nonresidential activities, and a petroleum refinery or tank farm. In fact, these five were not in her neighborhood.

Overall, these data suggest that behavioral hazards and blight are strongly associated with poor quality neighborhood ratings in the Marcus Hook area, and the prominent massive technology sites usually do not, by themselves, lead to a poor quality rating but are associated with a worse neighborhood.

Attractions should reduce the likelihood of a neighborhood being labeled poor quality. Table 4.3 shows evidence of the expected inverse association in the Marcus Hook area. Seven percent of respondents who were attracted by six to eight attributes rated their neighborhood as poor. As the number of positive attributes dropped from one to five to zero, the proportion rating their neighborhood poor increased from 24 to 50 percent.

With respect to preventing a low quality rating, table 4.3 suggests that convenience to leisure activities and good schools were the most protective attractions. Only 4 percent of those who were attracted by leisure activities rated their neighborhood as poor quality and only 5 percent who rated their school as an attraction also rated their neighborhood as poor quality. These data were supported by respondents' written notes. For example, a fifty-one to seventy-year-old female resident of Lower Chichester was stressed by the refinery, its odors and smoke, and by litter and trash left in the street. Yet she noted the existence of nine of the ten possible attractions, rated the neighborhood as good, and described it as follows: "It is a nice area with a good mix of young, middle aged and elderly residents. I intend to stay here the rest of my life." Another respondent who rated her neighborhood as good was stressed by the nearby refinery. Yet she also rated her neighborhood as good and described it as follows: "I live in a very good area because [near] where I live is located transportation, good schools, post offices, and convenient stores."

Conversely, table 4.4 showed that 28 percent of those who had inherited their homes rated their neighborhood as poor quality. Some of the most poignant written comments we received were from people who perceived that the neighborhoods they have lived in their entire lives have declined. For instance, a female aged thirty-one to fifty who lived with her elderly parents rated her neighborhood as poor and described it as follows: "We are highly taxed, yet services are poor. We rarely see patrol cars and when we call to complain because youths are loitering/sitting on top of cars—you must tell your name. The police tell the loiterers who called and then they vandalize your car more. Our street was not cleaned during the recent snow storm and driving through the city was poor for five days. There were pot holes in the street for 6+ weeks."

A male aged thirty-one to fifty indicated that his "mother still lives in the neighborhood and refuses to leave." He crossed out our "poor"—our worst neighborhood quality designation—and wrote next to it "pitiful." His description of the neighborhood reflects the sense of powerlessness expressed by neighborhood residents: "Since 1975, this neighborhood has deteriorated everywhere. There are over 1,000 houses abandoned. Graffiti everywhere. It wasn't like this before. You can't go out at night. That's a fact."

Personal Filters

Table 4.5 lists seven respondent characteristic variables. Some of these characteristics were expected to and did filter perception of neighborhood problems and attractions. In order of their likelihood to rate their neighborhood as poor quality, the four characteristics most strongly associated with a poor neighborhood quality rating were: Chester Main respondent (44 percent), Chester River respondent (34 percent), present neighborhood is worse (32 percent), and male respondent (25 percent).

Two of these differences were particularly notable. The higher proportion of low quality ratings among males (25 percent) than females (13 percent) was surprising because the literature suggests that women are more sensitive than men to pollution and physical violence (see chapter 1). In fact, the discriminant analyses found that the discriminating power of the gender variable was covariant with more statistically powerful variables, such as absence of good schools, and presence of abandoned factories and businesses, and the incinerator. We cannot say with certainty if this unusual finding was a case of confounding—that is, we do not know if males were more risk sensitive than females or if males were more likely to be located in places with these problems.

The difference between Marcus Hook respondents and Chester Main and River respondents is striking given the proximity of the two municipalities and the fact that both populations are surrounded by massive technology sites. Chester Main and River residents were blunt about the characteristics that led 39 percent of them to rate their neighborhoods as poor quality. Four who rated their neighborhood as poor illustrate some of the underlying anger and perceptions. A thirty-one to fifty-year-old female resident of the Chester Main area who was distressed by eighteen of the twenty-one problems in our list wrote, "The whole place sucks. Drugs, beer, bars, bad people, smell of trash and human waste everyday. It used to be nice to walk the streets, not anymore." A second respondent, a male aged fifty-one to seventy, was also suffering as a result of the perceived deterioration of his Chester Main neighborhood: "In recent years this neighborhood has caused me personal pain, illness and cause for alarm everyday. Watching the children playing with death in the streets. My grandchildren also. The trucks are a continuous terror to us all."

Table 4.5. Respondent Characteristics/Responses Associated with Poor Neighborhood Quality Rating, Marcus Hook Area, 1993

Characteristic/Response	Respondents Who Rated Neighborhood as Poor	
	Percent	95% Confidence Limits
All respondents	16.8	12.5, 21.1
Neighborhood comparison:		
Present neighborhood is better	5.5	0.3, 10.7
Present neighborhood is the same or same		
neighborhood	14.2	8.3, 20.1
Present neighborhood is worse	31.6	21.4, 41.9
Age:		
18–30	14.0	3.6, 24.4
31–50	15.0	8.8, 21.2
51+	19.8	12.6, 27.1
Sex:		
Male	25.0	16.2, 33.9
Female	13.0	8.2, 17.8
Tenure:[a]		
Owner	15.8	10.9, 20.7
Renter	15.3	6.1, 24.5
Length of residence (years):		
0–2	18.2	5.0, 31.4
>2–10	11.1	5.4, 16.8
>10	21.3	14.4, 28.2
Education:		
Grades 1–11	20.7	10.3, 31.1
High school graduate	9.7	4.2, 15.2
Some college or college	21.9	14.3, 29.5
Neighborhood of Residence:		
Linwood	8.0	2.3, 13.7
Marcus Hook Center	0.0	0, 0
Marcus Hook Waterfront	2.6	−2.4, 7.6
Chester River	33.8	22.3, 45.3
Chester Main	43.6	28.0, 59.2
Chester Park	3.6	−3.3, 10.5

Source: Based on 286 responses.
[a]Some respondents neither rented nor owned.

Two respondents from the Chester River area focused on deterioration associated with the incinerator. The following quotes from two respondents are typical of what we heard in the street: "It is a health hazard with the new plant at the end of the street. We can't breathe" and "We do not like the trash burning plant practically in our backyard. Too close to our home—the noise and odors."

Marcus Hook, like south Chester, has prominent massive technology sites. Yet, unlike the incinerator that was imposed on the area during the last few years, the refineries were begun in the 1920s. Furthermore, the town has provided a sense of neighborhood for many of its residents. One wrote, "I consider the town a good place to live. It has many activities for the children, and we take care of our own. We still have parades and riverfront celebrations that other towns have given in on." A second noted, "It may be a low income neighborhood, but it's filled with good people and good intentions."

Other residents of Marcus Hook were frank about local problems but rated their neighborhood as excellent or good. For example, one female aged thirty-one to fifty rated her neighborhood as good, yet she wrote the following in large print on her survey: "On my street alone 18 people had bouts with cancer out of 22 homes. 12 died from it!"

Another thirty-one to fifty-year-old female respondent wrote a list of positive and negative characteristics of her Marcus Hook neighborhood: "Positive: public library, excellent and affordable pre-school day-care facility, good public elementary school, two playground/picnic areas minutes away from us, trauma center and burn unit. Negative: air pollution worsens health—two children—have asthma, three of us have moderate to severe allergies. The DER was called in several years ago when the pollution was so bad they had to close the elementary school. Air pollution monitors installed at the school." This thoughtful respondent rated her neighborhood as good, but noted that "if we could afford to move, we would, only because of the heavy industrial pollution."

Discriminant Analysis of Neighborhood Quality

To explore potential associations among the explanatory variables, five stepwise discriminant analyses were done. They identified factors that discriminate among excellent/good, fair, and poor ratings by the 284 respondents. We first present the baseline run, then the results of the four heuristic runs.

Baseline Run

The baseline run contained twenty-one problems, ten attractions, as well as age, gender, tenure, length of residence, education, six neigh-

Table 4.6. Discriminant Analysis: Marcus Hook Area, Baseline Run

Variable	F-value	Multiple-Hazard Poor Quality Function 1	Better Neighborhood Function 2
Crime	68.2	.640	
Abandoned houses	69.2	.629	
Recreational facilities that attract rowdy people	40.1	.526	
Litter or trash in the street	47.2	.491	
Uncontrolled animals	41.0	.485	
Abandoned factories and businesses	35.9	.478	
Unfriendly neighbors	38.8	.452	
Streets, roads, sidewalks in disrepair	33.6	.448	
Occupied buildings in poor or dangerous condition	44.0	.437	
Inadequate street lighting	33.4	.433	
Junkyard, gasoline station, other nonresidential	25.6	.429	
Motor vehicle noise and heavy traffic	44.5	.429	
Train noise	18.9	.348	
Airplane noise	21.4	.316	
Good schools	22.9	−.290	
Respondent from Chester River area	10.9	.277	
Incinerator	20.1	.264	
Convenient to leisure activities	17.4	−.260	
Present neighborhood is better	36.4		.564
Odors or smoke	22.7		−.364
Petroleum refinery or tank farm	14.4		−.342
Chemical plant	11.6		−.263
Canonical correlation with neighborhood quality dependent variable (P-value)		.749 (.001)	.493 (.001)
Average standardized Z score with poor quality respondents		2.27	0.78

Correlation of Variable with Function

Source: Based on 284 responses.
Note: Variables with a correlation of >0.25 with one of the two functions are shown. All correlations shown were statistically significant discriminators at P < .05.

borhoods of residence, and comparison of present and previous neighborhood. Thirty-five of the forty-three potentially discriminating variables were statistically significant discriminators at P < .05 (table 4.6). Only two would have been expected to be statistically significant by chance.

Two discriminant functions help unravel the interrelationships

Table 4.7. Summary of Discriminant Analysis Runs, Marcus Hook Area, 1993

Run	Canonical Correlation Function		Percentage Correctly Classified	
	1	2	Total	Poor
Baseline (table 4.6)	.749	.493	74	79
Heuristic:				
Outsider perception	.369	.162	51	56
Specific hazard type (table 4.8)	.726	.435	71	88
Specific hazard type checkoff	.703	.344	70	85
Aggregate hazard burden	.715	.360	72	81

Source: Based on 284 responses.

among the discriminating variables in the baseline run. The first identified behavioral and blight-related hazards. The ten strongest correlates of the first function were all distressing behaviors or signs of blight: crime ($r = .640$), abandoned housing ($r = .629$), recreational facilities that attract rowdy people ($r = .526$), litter or trash ($r = .491$), uncontrolled animals ($r = .485$), abandoned factories and businesses ($r = .478$), unfriendly neighbors ($r = .452$), streets in disrepair ($r = .448$), occupied buildings in poor or dangerous condition ($r = .437$), and inadequate street lighting ($r = .433$). Local activity spaces, train and airplane noise, the incinerator, residence in the River area of Chester, and absence of good schools and leisure activities also identified with the function. We labeled this the multiple-hazard, poor quality neighborhood function. It is the prototype for this book.

The second function identified people who perceived that the quality of the their neighborhood had improved. We called it the better neighborhood function. It focused on people who perceived their present neighborhood as better ($r = .564$) and were not troubled by odors or smoke ($r = -.364$), petroleum refinery or tank farm ($r = -.342$), and chemical plant ($r = -.263$).

Heuristic Runs

The four heuristics attempt to model people's thinking about their neighborhoods. Table 4.7 compares the canonical correlations and accuracy of the classification produced by the baseline and four heuristics. The baseline analysis had slightly higher canonical correlations than any of the heuristics, was slightly better at classifying all respondents than the heuristics, but not as successful in correctly categorizing poor quality ratings.

The outsider perception heuristic assumes that Marcus Hook area respondents focus on the incinerator and two petrochemical complexes. It was the worst model. Its canonical correlations and ability to correctly classify respondents were significantly lower than the baseline (P < .001). It correctly classified only 51 percent of respondents compared to 74 percent for the baseline. In other words, knowing that someone is distressed by a refinery and incinerator in the Marcus Hook area is insufficient information to accurately predict how they will classify their neighborhood.

The two specific and aggregate hazard models are based on three different assumptions about people's decision-making processes. The specific hazard type aggregated the twenty-one problems into behavioral, blight, local activity space, and massive technology site variables. This was done by adding each score to form four aggregate scores. These four variables replaced the twenty-one problems. The aggregate hazard burden model assumes that people do not care about categories of problems. Rather, the greater the number of problems of any kind, the more likely they are to rate their neighborhood as poor quality. The specific hazard type checkoff remolds the four specific hazard variables. It assumes that people filter information by the four hazard categories of behavior, blight, local activity space, and massive technology site. One stress in a category is sufficient to cause great stress.

Table 4.7 shows that except for the outsider perception model the heuristics performed as well or better than the baseline model. The specific hazard type heuristic correctly classified 71 percent of respondents, and the aggregate hazard burden model 72 percent, compared to 74 percent for the baseline model. Notably, these heuristics were more effective at classifying respondents who rated their neighborhoods as poor quality. The difference between the baseline and the specific hazard type model (79 percent vs. 88 percent) was statistically significant at P < .01, and the difference between the baseline and aggregate burden (79 percent vs. 85 percent) was statistically significant at P < .08.

Table 4.8 presents the discriminant analysis run for the specific hazard type heuristic. The first function resembles the multiple-hazard, poor quality neighborhood function described above. It identified respondents who were distressed by behavioral (r = .791), blight (r = .765), and local activity space hazards (r = .684). These respondents were also distressed by massive technology sites (r = .404), did not perceive their neighborhood as providing attractions ($r = -.297$), and the respondents tended to be residents of the Chester Main (r = .308) and River areas (r = .273).

The association of behavioral, blight, local activity, and massive machine-site hazards in the Chester Main and River areas is daunting. Respondents' written notes helped us understand the interrelated problems they encounter. For instance, eight respondents described the association of the incinerator and rats in their written notes. One wrote, "We have rats the size of rabbits because of the trash steam plant. They attack our cats." A second resident of these neighborhoods focused on the transportation-industry-incinerator association: "Tractor trailers driving down residential streets, and speeding garbage trucks in residential areas speeding through back alleys with kids playing." A third pointed to a multiplicity of associations: "Drive by shootings, car thefts, young and older children destroying property, not enough lights, unruly patrons from local bars. Drug dealers, loud noise, rowdy people."

Perhaps the most poignant written note came from a female homeowner aged eighteen to thirty who was distressed by twenty of the twenty-one problems: "I live in the worst neighborhood anyone could live in. There are drugs, trash, and odors that no one should have to live in. Our property value is $0.00. This neighborhood is a health hazard and none of the residents deserve it."

The second function resembles the better neighborhood function of the baseline run. Respondents perceived that the present neighborhood is better (r = .647), and they were not troubled by massive technology sites ($r = -.264$). They tended to be shorter-term residents of the area ($r = -.263$) and had relatively less formal education ($r = -.252$).

We use the written comments and ratings of two respondents to further illustrate the critical link of neighborhood change and neighborhood quality. Both respondents rated their new neighborhood as good and better than their previous neighborhood. One was a young adult male who did not graduate from high school; the second was a thirty-one to fifty-year-old female who graduated college. Both were homeowners. The first said, "I think we live in a nice neighborhood." The second said, "A trash-to-steam plant is in my neighborhood, but I still rated the neighborhood as good." The remarkable fact about

Table 4.8. Discriminant Analysis of Specific Hazard Type Heuristic, Marcus Hook Area, 1993

		Correlation of Variable with Function	
Variable	F-value	Multiple-Hazard Poor Quality Function 1	Better Neighborhood Function 2
Behavioral hazards	94.6	.791	
Blight hazards	86.8	.765	
Local activity space hazards	67.2	.684	
Massive technology site hazards	35.4	.404	−.264
Respondent from Chester Main area	13.3	.308	
Aggregate attractions	17.8	−.297	
Respondent from Chester River area	10.9	.273	
Present neighborhood is better	36.4		.647
Length of residence in neighborhood	2.7		−.263
Formal education	2.4		−.252
Canonical correlation with neighborhood quality dependent variable (P-value)		.726 (.001)	.435 (.001)
Average standardized Z score with poor quality respondents		2.14	0.65

Source: Based on 284 surveys.
Note: Variables with a correlation of >0.25 with one of the two functions are shown. All correlations shown were statistically significant discriminators at P < .05.

these two respondents is that they lived in the River area, close to the incinerator, abandoned houses, and factories, and within two hundred feet of the respondent who was quoted above as indicating that this neighborhood was "the worst neighborhood anyone could live in."

Table 4.9 provides additional support for the specific hazard type and aggregate hazard burden heuristic models. It shows that neighborhood quality decreases as aggregate stresses mount. For example, the petroleum refinery and gas tanks were identified as a major stress by 19 percent of respondents who rated their neighborhood as excellent/good quality, 45 percent of those who rated their neighborhood as fair, and 54 percent who rated it as poor. Judged by the 95 percent confidence limits around the mean, stress related to a petrochemical facility was unable to clearly distinguish between a rating of fair and poor. That is, the 95 percent confidence limits overlap. Likewise, concern about the incinerator barely discriminated the

27 percent who rated their neighborhood as fair from the 12 percent who rated it as excellent/good. In contrast, judged by the confidence limits, the behavioral, blight, specific hazard type, and aggregate hazard heuristics were able to distinguish all three categories of neighborhood quality.

The aggregate hazard variable, by far, was the best at distinguishing among the three quality groups of poor, fair, excellent/good. An average of 1.5 problems were identified as distressing by respondents who rated their neighborhood as excellent or good, compared to 4.3 who rated their neighborhood as fair and 11.1 who rated their neighborhood as poor quality. In other words, in the Marcus Hook area, those who rated their neighborhood as poor typically identified 9 to 13 major stresses in their neighborhoods, or about seven times as many as those few who rated their neighborhoods as excellent or good.

Summary of Findings

RQ1: *How do people who live in the immediate vicinity of potentially hazardous land uses and activities rate their neighborhoods?*

Forty-four percent of Chester Main and 34 percent of Chester River respondents rated their neighborhood as poor quality. These extremely high proportions compare to 8 percent of Lower Chichester's, less than 4 percent of Marcus Hook's and Chester Park's respondents, and to 3 to 4 percent of their counterparts in the United States as a whole, northern New Jersey, and the Philadelphia metropolitan area.

Using the petroleum refineries and incinerator to identify unusually insensitive people, we observed no more than 4 percent of respondents who could be labeled insensitive. An exception was observed in the Chester River area, where 28 percent of respondents did not acknowledge the presence of the incinerator in their neighborhood. Rather than this being a cluster of unusually insensitive people, we believe it is the case that these people have a different definition of their neighborhood than the one we used. Using furniture and metal factories to identify hazard sensitive respondents, no more than 8 percent of respondents could be considered unusually sensitive.

Table 4.9. Neighborhood Characteristics and Neighborhood Quality, Marcus Hook Area

Neighborhood Quality	Total Number of Hazards (maximum is 21)	Specific Hazard Type (maximum is 4)	Incinerator (1 = yes)	Petroleum Refinery (1 = yes)	Behavioral Hazards (1 = yes)	Blight Hazards (1 = yes)
Excellent/good	1.5 (1.0, 2.0)	0.6 (0.4, 0.8)[a]	.12 (.06, .18)	.19 (.12, .26)	.11 (.05, .16)	.11 (.06, .17)
Fair	4.3 (3.5, 5.2)	1.7 (1.5, 2.0)	.27 (.19, .35)	.45 (.36, .54)	.36 (.27, .45)	.41 (.32, .50)
Poor	11.1 (9.3, 12.8)	3.4 (3.1, 3.7)	.56 (.42, .71)	.54 (.40, .69)	.88 (.78, .97)	.90 (.81, .99)

Source: Based on 286 responses.
[a]Respondent gets a score of 1 for noting great distress with one indicator of a behavioral risk, blight, local activity space, and massive technology sites. For example, a respondent who expresses a desire to leave as a result of crime (behavioral risk), and airplane noise (massive technology site) would receive a score of 2.

RQ2: *What factors most influence neighborhood ratings, especially rating of a neighborhood as poor?*

Blight and behavioral risks clearly were the characteristics most consistently associated with poor neighborhood quality ratings. Present neighborhood quality compared to previous neighborhood quality was an extremely important filter.

Massive technology sites were less strongly associated with poor neighborhood quality than behavioral-, blight-, and local activity space-related hazards. Even in the neighborhood that hosts the incinerator, crime and blight were more likely to be associated with poor neighborhood quality than the trash-to-steam plant. Furthermore, Marcus Hook area respondents were no more likely to rate their neighborhoods as poor quality than Americans as a whole, despite the presence of petrochemical and other massive technology sites around them. But these massive landscape features were associated with a worse neighborhood.

Absence of leisure activities and poor schools were strongly associated with poor quality neighborhoods. The presence of friends and relatives, although noted in some written comments, did not protect against a poor quality rating. Persons who inherited their homes were disproportionately stressed.

The outsider perception model, which assumes that neighborhood residents focus on the kinds of hazards that outsiders see, was a relatively poor predictor of neighborhood quality ratings. The aggregate burden heuristic was almost as successful in predicting neighborhood classification as the baseline model, and it was actually better at predicting poor quality ratings.

5

Multiple-Hazard
Neighborhoods

The New Jersey Turnpike, the most heavily traveled road in the United States, runs directly through east Elizabeth. Houses, schools, and churches should be visible to the tens of thousands of people who drive to Newark Airport, northern New Jersey, New York City, Philadelphia, Washington, D.C., and all points north and south. Yet, like the yard of a prison surrounded by high walls and guard towers, east Elizabeth's neighborhoods are invisible.

Images of East Elizabeth

The New Jersey Turnpike is elevated fifty or more feet over east Elizabeth, and noise barriers have been constructed along much of the highway. Because of the noise barriers, it is easier to see the twin towers of the World Trade Center six and a half miles away than it is to see houses one hundred yards away from the New Jersey Turnpike.

The twin towers do not dominate the east Elizabeth landscape. East Elizabeth is surrounded by many prominent massive technology sites. Newark Airport, with an average of 1,255 flights a day, is the tenth most used airport in the United States (Davis 1993). Aircraft taking off or landing on the main north-south runway fly directly over the northern part of east Elizabeth, located less than one mile away. The sound is deafening. On the ground you feel as if you need to hold on to something to keep your balance. We had to stop conversing with residents because it was impossible to hear them. One fleeting thought was that people in this area ought to learn sign language. Protests against Newark Airport's flight paths have raged for well over a decade (Schwab 1993). We clearly expected east Elizabeth residents to be greatly distressed by airplane noise.

The largest petrochemical complex on the east coast of the United States is the southwest boundary of the study area. The Bayway refinery was recently sold by EXXON to Tosco, a New Jersey petrochemical producer. According to toxic release inventory data supplied under federal regulations, the Bayway facility is the seventh largest waste-producing site and eighth largest emitter of toxins in New Jersey (Citizen Fund of New Jersey 1993).

Although the toxic inventory data imply that the refinery complex is a major polluter, Bayway's emissions were once even more obvious. Bayway was one of the first petrochemical complexes to build a sophisticated sewage treatment facility, one of the first to build an enormous scrubber to remove sulfur, and one of the first to adopt a program to reduce evaporation from its tank farm. Residents no longer routinely feel rain showers directly over the microenvironment of the refinery or read technical reports that the stream that runs through the complex had to be assigned a unique classification appropriate to a severely polluted water body.

Chronic emissions are much lower than they were in the 1970s and 1980s, but the refinery's image as a hazard endures because of accidents. For example, the year 1994 began with a front-page story in the *Newark Star-Ledger* announcing the most recent accident (Wyckoff 1994). A valve malfunctioned allowing about one hundred gallons of a smelly oil and steam mixture into the air. The New Jersey Turnpike interchange and ramps to the Goethals Bridge (to Staten Island, New York City) were closed for several hours and seventeen toll workers were taken to a local hospital with respiratory symptoms. The newspaper reporter reminded readers that similar problems had occurred three and six years ago. The incident three years ago was called the "Valentine's Day Massacre."

Recent newspaper stories about hazards associated with Bayway actually understate the perceptual impact of this facility in New Jersey and the east Elizabeth area in particular. For instance, there was a controversy about cancer rates in New Jersey for more than two decades. In the mid-1970s, newspaper stories about New Jersey's supposed cancer epidemic routinely featured background pictures of the Bayway complex.

To the outsider, the refinery complex is the most visible massive technology site surrounding east Elizabeth. It continues to periodically call attention to itself with odoriferous releases. Yet despite its size and reputation, we did not expect Bayway to be the most powerful massive technology image in the area because it is buffered by the Elizabeth River, the New Jersey Turnpike, parks, and other natural barriers. The Elizabeth River is a particularly effective buffer. The river's floodplain is covered with high grass and walking paths. We observed people jogging, strolling, walking their dogs, sunbathing, and playing catch alongside the river.

Two massive natural gas tanks form the southeast boundary of east Elizabeth. Although they have attracted little attention compared to the refinery, we expected the gas tanks to attract considerable attention because they tower over houses located directly across a narrow street and cast a large shadow over part of one neighborhood.

The site of the former Chemical Control Corporation neither smells nor is visible to residents. Nevertheless, we expected anyone who has lived in east Elizabeth for a decade or more to have mental scars related to the former hazardous-waste incinerator. Chemical Control made national headlines when it exploded in 1980, sending flames hundreds of feet into the air and threatening the gas tanks, the ramps to the Goethals Bridge, and the study area. Michael Brown, the prize-winning journalist, described the scene in his book *Laying Waste* (1981:159): "330-foot mushroom cloud with a brilliant fireball at its epicenter . . . bursting like Independence Day mortars, into colorful cascades." The cover of the June 1980 *EPA Journal* memorialized the fireball enveloping thirty-five thousand fifty-five-gallon drums containing biological, chemical, and physical toxins. The adjacent Elizabeth River turned a blood red color as materials flowed from the site. In "We Almost Lost Elizabeth," Weinberg (1980) described the near destruction of east Elizabeth. In December 1993, Peet reported that the Chemical Control cleanup was completed at a cost of about $41 million. The 2.2-acre site is surrounded by an eight-foot-high chain link fence. Contaminated soils are trapped within the site covered by an impermeable mass and three feet of crushed stone. The site will be monitored.

East Elizabeth also contains other manufacturing facilities and businesses and railroad lines that surround and cross the neighborhoods. We observed clusters of abandoned housing, some streets badly in need of repair, numerous littered lots, locks on mailboxes and Beware of Dog signs. We were warned by the police not to survey people living near the public housing projects located in the center of east Elizabeth because the area was said to be the epicenter of illegal drug activity. This public-housing project is a long-standing symbol of violence and crime in the area. For example, during the July 1967 national civil disturbances, Elizabeth police concentrated patrols near the housing project, leading residents to charge that the projects were being turned into a "concentration camp" (Kerner Commission 1968).

Choice of Neighborhoods

We chose three census tracts in east Elizabeth corresponding to three neighborhoods: Elizabethport, Frog Hollow, and Peterstown (fig. 5.1). Elizabethport is directly adjacent to Newark Airport and is bounded on the west by the New Jersey Turnpike. Factories, some abandoned, others operating, form the northern border. Elizabethport had the most obvious signs of physical blight in east Elizabeth and is closest to the public housing project.

Frog Hollow's southern border is the gas tanks and a chemical plant. Chemical Control was just south of these massive sites. Jets fly directly over Frog Hollow, but not as close to the ground as they do over Elizabethport. The southern border of Peterstown is composed of large parks and the Elizabeth River. Behind them are the refinery and ramps for the New Jersey Turnpike. Peterstown is furthest removed from the jet aircraft and is screened from the public housing project by the New Jersey Turnpike. The residential area adjacent to the park has small, pleasant-appearing, single-family houses, with few fences and little evidence of locked mailboxes.

All three study areas are relatively poor. The 1989 per capita income of New Jersey's population was $18,714 (Department of Commerce 1992). The comparable figures for the Elizabethport, Frog

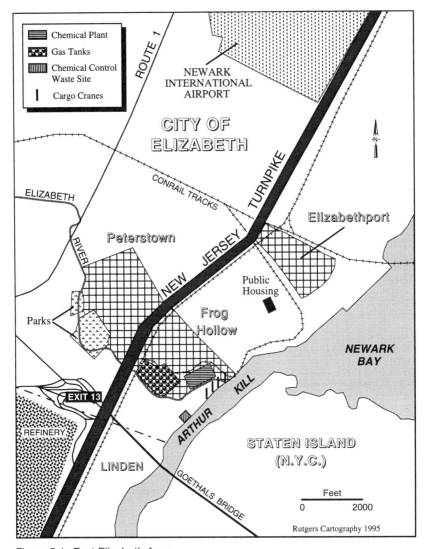

Figure 5.1. East Elizabeth Area

Hollow, and Peterstown areas were only $9,600, $10,900, and $11,800, respectively. Twenty-five percent of the state's population graduated college, compared to only 4 percent in the study area. The area work force remains concentrated in production. Forty percent of the area's employed population worked in manufacturing and construction, compared to only 13 percent of New Jersey's.

The study area contains a wide variety of ethnic/racial groups. In 1990, 49 percent of the population was foreign born, compared to 13 percent of New Jersey's population. The major populations were black, Italian, Polish, Portuguese, and other Hispanic. Each of these ethnic/racial populations comprised more than 10 percent of the study area's population. Overall, the Elizabeth study area had the desired characteristics, that is, massive technology sites, local distressing land uses, blight, perceived behavioral risks, and a mix of relatively poor ethnic/racial groups.

Survey Questions, Methods, Problems, and Returns

Ten attractions, seven personal characteristics, and twenty-one hazards were included in our survey instrument. Eighteen of the twenty-one clearly were present in at least one of the three census tracts. Three were not. Train noise sometimes was present in Frog Hollow, but not elsewhere. We did not observe a metal or furniture plant in east Elizabeth. We used these two land uses to identify unusually sensitive people. In other words, these three should not be identified as problems by many people. We used airplane noise to identify the proportion of respondents who were insensitive to an obvious stress. That is, no one should indicate that airplane noise was not present. Utility rights-of-way with towers and hanging lines were present, but frankly, like the Marcus Hook area, seemed among the more pleasant pockets of green in the area.

We attempted to place an instrument in every occupied dwelling unit within one-quarter mile of the gas tanks, refinery, airport, and New Jersey Turnpike. Generic problems associated with distributing the instrument were described in detail in chapter 2. Two problems particularly complicated the task in east Elizabeth. First, it was not possible to get a representative sample in areas where there were more people than mailboxes. One respondent, pointing to the apartment across the street from his house, described the problem: "Twelve or more families live in that small apartment house for 4 or 5." Second, 39 percent of the study area's population indicated in the 1990 U.S. Census that they "did not speak English very well." These problems doubtless reduced the response rate.

We distributed fifteen hundred surveys on three week days during July 1993. A total of 295 useful responses (19.7 percent) were received by September 30, 1993. A total of 293 were complete, that is, they were missing no data.

As expected, respondents were not representative of all 12,100 residents of east Elizabeth. Seventy-seven percent of respondents graduated high school, compared to 47 percent of area residents (P < .01); 58 percent were female compared to 52 percent of residents (P < .05); and 66 percent were homeowners, compared to 34 percent of area residents (P <.01). Eleven percent of both respondents and residents were more than seventy years old. Thirty-six percent of respondents and 26 percent of residents were eighteen to thirty years old (P < .01). Finally, we note that 56 percent of area residents had lived in the same house and 81 percent in the same county for at least five years compared to 75 percent of respondents who had lived in the neighborhood for at least five years. Overall, our respondents were more likely to be female, educated at least through high school, homeowners, and probably long-term residents of the neighborhood than the population of the area as a whole.

Neighborhood Quality

East Elizabeth shared with Camden (see chapter 7) the unenviable distinction of having more than one-half of respondents rate their neighborhood as poor or fair. More than 17 percent of east Elizabeth respondents rated their neighborhood as poor quality (table 5.1). Another 44 percent rated their neighborhood as fair, 35 percent as good, and only 4 percent rated it as excellent. The 95 percent confidence limits of these rates suggest that these low ratings were unlikely to have occurred by chance. East Elizabeth respondents clearly were less satisfied with their neighborhoods than Americans as a whole, respondents to the most recent northern New Jersey and Philadelphia metropolitan region surveys, and our other neighborhood survey respondents in the aggregate.

Within east Elizabeth, Elizabethport had a much higher proportion of poor quality ratings (43 percent) than Peterstown (8 percent) and Frog Hollow (15 percent). In fact, Elizabethport was one of two neighborhoods in our study without a single excellent rating.

Table 5.1. Neighborhood Quality in East Elizabeth with Selected Comparisons

Year	Neigboorhood	Percentage Rating Neighborhood Quality and 95% Confidence Limits			
		Excellent	Good	Fair	Poor
1993	Total east Elizabeth	4.1	34.8	43.7	17.4
	(n = 295)	(1.8, 6.4)	(29.4, 40.3)	(38.0, 49.4)	(13.1, 21.7)
	Elizabethport	0.0	26.2	31.1	42.7
	(n = 61)	(0, 0)	(14.6, 37.8)	(19.1, 43.2)	(29.8, 55.6)
	Frog Hollow	3.0	36.0	46.0	15.0
	(n = 100)	(0.0, 6.0)	(26.4, 45.6)	(36.0, 56.0)	(7.9, 22.1)
	Peterstown	6.1	37.9	48.5	7.6
	(n = 132)	(1.8, 10.4)	(29.1, 46.7)	(39.4, 57.6)	(2.7, 12.5)
1992–94	Other seventeen study neighboorhoods	17.1	44.5	28.4	10.0
	(n = 1,125)	(14.9, 19.3)	(41.6, 47.4)	(25.8, 31.0)	(8.3, 11.8)
1991	United States	33.6	52.6	11.2	2.6
1991	Northern New Jersey[a]	32.9	54.7	9.7	2.7
1989	Philadelphia[b]	34.8	49.7	11.7	3.8

Source: East Elizabeth ratings based on 295 respondents; 2 did not provide their neighborhood.
Note: 95 percent confidence limits figures in parentheses.
[a]Northern New Jersey includes Bergen, Essex, Hudson, Hunterdon, Middlesex, Monmouth, Morris, Ocean, Passaic, Somerset, Sussex, and Union Counties, New Jersey.
[b]Philadelphia includes Bucks, Chester, Delaware, Montgomery, and Philadelphia Counties (PA) and Burlington, Camden, and Gloucester Counties, New Jersey.

Problems, Attractions, and Comparisons with Previous Neighborhoods

More than 60 percent of east Elizabeth respondents reported at least one characteristic that was so distressing that they wanted to leave. Airplane noise was identified by 42 percent. Odors or smoke, crime, motor vehicle noise and heavy traffic, litter or trash, and the petroleum refinery and tank farm were distressing to more than 20 percent of respondents (table 5.2). Only a utility right-of-way, metal or furniture plant, and train noise were major problems for less than 5 percent of respondents. The minimal attention to these three land uses is notable because these were the three selected to signal the presence of unusually sensitive respondents.

Table 5.3 further confirms the evidence that relatively few unusually sensitive people responded to survey. Distance and physical barriers rather than imaginary hazards appear to have helped shape perceptions. Elizabethport had the highest level of distress from air-

Table 5.2 Prevalence of Neighborhood Characteristics, East Elizabeth, 1993

Characteristic	Percentage of Respondents
Problems:[a]	62.5
Airplane noise	42.0
Odors or smoke	31.1
High crime rate	27.3
Motor vehicle noise and heavy traffic	24.2
Litter or trash in the street, elsewhere	23.9
Petroleum refinery or tank farm	22.2
Recreational facilities that attract rowdy people	19.4
Occupied buildings in poor or dangerous condition	18.4
Chemical plant	17.4
Natural gas tanks	17.1
Junkyard, gasoline station, other nonresidential	15.3
Unfriendly neighbors	14.3
Abandoned houses	14.0
Streets, roads, sidewalks in disrepair	14.0
Dogs, cats, uncontrolled animals	13.7
Hazardous-waste sites	13.3
Inadequate street lighting	10.2
Abandoned factories and businesses	9.2
Train noise	4.4
Metal or furniture plant	4.1
Right-of-way for a utility	2.0
Attractions:[b]	
Convenient to friends/relatives	60.3
Convenient to hospital	59.3
House was inexpensive or inherited	57.5
Convenient to religious activity	56.3
Convenient to job	51.2
Convenient to public transport	49.2
Convenient to shopping	47.1
Good schools	37.6
Other public services	36.6
Convenient to leisure activities	28.5
Neighborhood comparison:	
Present neighborhood is better	24.2
Present neighborhood is same	54.9
Present neighborhood is worse	20.8

Source: Based on 293 responses.
[a]Percentage who found condition so disturbing that they wanted to leave.
[b]Percentage who gave these as reasons they live in the neighborhood.

plane noise. Only 23 percent of Elizabethport respondents said airplane noise did not distress them, and 59 percent said it disturbed them so much that they wanted to leave. One resident summarized the impact as follows: "The planes fly low, you can't hear TV or the phone ringing." Another added: "Airplane traffic really ruins the whole neighborhood." In contrast, 50 percent of Peterstown respondents were not disturbed by airplane noise and 25 percent wanted to leave as a result of it. Our experiences in the neighborhoods suggest that the fact that the aircraft fly approximately one-third mile to the east of Peterstown and directly over Elizabethport and Frog Hollow accounts for this reduced sensitivity in Peterstown.

Elizabethport respondents were also much more sensitive to crime, litter or trash, unfriendly neighbors, and occupied buildings in poor condition than their counterparts in Peterstown and Frog Hollow. These responses agree with our observations of the increased prevalence of these hazards in this neighborhood.

Respondents of Peterstown and Frog Hollow were more disturbed by the petroleum refinery, gas tanks, chemical plant, former hazardous-waste site and associated smoke and odors than residents of Elizabethport. Elizabethport residents live about eight-tenths of a mile to the north of these massive technology sites and are buffered from some of the activity by the wall of the New Jersey Turnpike. Twenty-five percent of Frog Hollow and Peterstown respondents were distressed by the refinery complex. One wrote: "The air pollution it causes is horrendous." Only 5 percent of Elizabethport respondents considered the refinery a major problem. About 20 percent of Frog Hollow and Peterstown respondents compared to only 7 percent of Elizabethport ones considered the gas plant a major problem. One wrote: "a horrible smell comes from the plant on certain days." A second wrote: "I hate the smell of the gas plant."

Respondents' perceptions of crime and blight also seemed to us to reflect the effects of distance and barriers. For instance, 57 percent of Elizabethport respondents were greatly distressed by crime, compared to 24 percent of Frog Hollow's. Peterstown's lower rate of stress about crime, 16 percent, reflects, we believe, the New Jersey Turnpike barrier, which limits east-west access in east Elizabeth. This, in effect, buffers the neighborhood from the criminal activity on the other side of the twelve-lane road.

Table 5.2 shows that convenience to friends and relatives, the lo-

Table 5.3. Neighborhood Problems Causing Residents to Want to Leave: Elizabethport, Frog Hollow, and Peterstown, 1993

	Percentage of Respondents		
Characteristic	Elizabethport	Frog Hollow	Peterstown
Airplane noise	59	53	25
Odors or smoke	21	35	30
High crime rate	57	24	16
Motor vehicle noise and heavy traffic	30	28	18
Litter or trash in the street and elsewhere	38	26	16
Petroleum refinery and tank farm	5	24	26
Recreational facilities that attract rowdy people	21	21	16
Occupied buildings in poor or dangerous condition	30	19	10
Chemical plant	7	19	22
Natural gas tanks	7	22	16
Junkyard, gasoline station, other nonresidential	23	16	12
Unfriendly neighbors	34	10	8
Abandoned houses	27	16	4
Streets, roads, sidewalks in disrepair	27	16	6
Dogs, cats, or other uncontrolled animals	21	12	11
Hazardous-waste sites	11	18	10
Inadequate street lighting	25	7	4
Abandoned factories and businesses	23	6	2
Train noise	0	11	1
Metal or furniture plant	2	7	2
Right-of-way for a utility	4	4	1

Source: Based on 293 valid responses.
Note: The percentages are those respondents who found condition so disturbing that they wanted to leave.

cal hospital, religious activity, and work, and inexpensive housing were considered attractions by more than half of respondents. Leisure activities and other public services, which were important to Americans as a whole (see chapter 3), were less important attractions in east Elizabeth.

Twenty-four percent of east Elizabeth respondents rated their neighborhood as better than their previous one, compared to 21 percent who rated it is worse. These data compared to 39, 44, and 54 percent of Americans, residents of northern New Jersey, and the Philadelphia region who rated their neighborhood as an improvement, respectively.

The association between a given problem or attraction and a poor

Table 5.4. Neighborhood Characteristics/Variables Associated with Poor Neighborhood Quality Rating, East Elizabeth, 1993

Characteristic/Variable	Percentage	95% Confidence Limits
All respondents	17.4	13.1, 21.7
Problems:[a]		
Number of problems:		
0	9.1	3.7, 14.5
1–4	6.7	1.5, 11.9
5–9	22.3	12.3, 32.3
10+	74.1	57.6, 90.6
Specific problems:		
Inadequate street lighting	66.7	49.8, 83.6
Streets, roads, sidewalks in disrepair or open ditches	55.0	39.6, 70.4
Occupied buildings in poor or dangerous conditions	49.1	35.6, 62.6
Abandoned houses	48.8	33.5, 64.1
Unfriendly neighbors	47.6	32.5, 62.7
Junkyard, gasoline station, other nonresidential	46.7	32.1, 61.2
Sites with hazardous waste	43.6	28.0, 59.2
Dogs, cats, or other uncontrolled animals	42.5	27.2, 57.8
High crime rates	41.3	30.5, 52.1
Litter or trash in streets, empty lots, or properties	40.0	28.5, 51.5
Motor vehicle noise and heavy traffic	38.9	27.6, 50.2
Recreational facilities that attract rowdy people	38.6	26.0, 51.2
Chemical plant	33.3	20.4, 46.2
Odors or smoke	30.0	20.5, 39.5
Natural gas tanks	30.0	17.3, 42.7
Airplane noise	29.8	21.8, 37.9
Petroleum refinery or tank farm	26.2	15.5, 36.9

neighborhood quality rating is measured by the proportion of respondents who rated the neighborhood as poor quality out of all those who identified the characteristic. For example, if one hundred respondents were distressed by airplane noise and twenty-five of them rated the neighborhood as poor quality, the association is 25 percent.

Table 5.4 shows a strong association between number of problems and poor quality. The proportion of poor quality ratings increased as the number of perceived problems increased. No problems and one to four problems were associated with less than 10 percent of respondents rating their neighborhood as poor; five to nine problems with a 22 percent poor quality rating; and ten or more problems with 74 percent rating their neighborhood as poor quality.

Table 5.4. Continued

Characteristic/Variable	Percentage	95% Confidence Limits
Attractions:[b]		
Number of attractions:		
6–8	10.0	4.8, 15.2
1–5	22.7	15.8, 29.6
0	18.2	2.1, 34.3
Specific attractions:		
Good schools	8.1	3.0, 13.2
Convenient to leisure activities	10.7	4.1, 17.3
Convenient to job	11.9	6.7, 17.1
Convenient to shopping	13.0	7.4, 18.6
Other public services	13.1	6.7, 19.5
Convenient to friends/relatives	15.2	9.9, 20.5
Convenient to religious activities	15.2	9.7, 20.7
Convenient to public transportation	15.2	9.4, 21.2
Convenient to hospital	15.5	10.1, 20.9
House was inexpensive or inherited	19.6	13.6, 25.6

Source: Based on 293 valid responses.
[a]Percentage who rated their neighborhood as poor quality of those who found condition so disturbing that they wanted to leave. Only problems noted by at least 10 percent of respondents are listed. Abandoned factories and businesses, right-of-way for a utility, metal or furniture plant, and noise from trains were not included.
[b]Percentage who rated their neighborhood as poor quality of those who found condition an attraction.

What specific problems were most likely to be associated with poor neighborhood quality? Respondents who were distressed by signs of blight tended to rate their neighborhood as poor quality. For instance, 67 percent of those who identified inadequate street lighting as a major problem also rated their neighborhood as poor quality. Streets in need in repair (55 percent), buildings in poor condition (49 percent), and abandoned housing (49 percent) also were strongly associated with poor quality neighborhood ratings.

Behavioral problems were a little less likely to be consistently associated with poor quality. Unfriendly neighbors (48 percent) was the most distressing characteristic. Uncontrolled animals (43 percent), crime (41 percent), and recreational facilities that attract rowdy people (39 percent) were also prominent behavioral problems in east Elizabeth.

Local activity spaces, such as junkyards, gasoline stations, and other nonresidential land uses (47 percent) and motor vehicle noise and heavy traffic unrelated to the New Jersey Turnpike (39 percent) were as likely as behavioral characteristics to be listed as problems. Several respondents tied behaviors and local activity spaces together. For example, one respondent noted: "There [are] too many drugs in the neighborhood related to the clubs." Another wrote: "There is a rundown motel that attracts transients and prostitutes." A third added: "A disturbing business operates on my corner bringing dangerous people and dangerous conditions. Nothing is done about it."

Massive technology sites were the least likely to be associated with a poor quality rating: petroleum refinery (26 percent), airplane noise (30 percent), the natural gas tanks, odors or smoke (30 percent), and a chemical plant (33 percent). These data suggest that blight appears to be strongly associated with poor quality neighborhood rating in east Elizabeth, and the prominent massive technology sites usually do not by themselves lead to a poor quality rating.

Attractions should reduce the likelihood of a neighborhood being labeled poor quality. Table 5.4 shows little evidence of the expected inverse association. Ten percent of respondents who were attracted by six to eight attributes rated their neighborhood as poor. Yet as the number of positive attributes dropped from one to five to zero, the proportion rating their neighborhood poor decreased from 23 to 18 percent rather than increased.

With respect to preventing a low quality rating, table 5.4 suggests that good schools seemed to be the most protective attraction. Only 8 percent of those who rated their school as an attraction also rated their neighborhood as poor quality. Conversely, 20 percent of those who were attracted by inexpensive housing still rated their neighborhood as poor quality. In other words, housing is not protective of neighborhood quality in east Elizabeth. One respondent who rated the neighborhood as poor quality stated what we had heard from some residents on the street: "We are still here because it is familiar, and we know some nice people, and it is inexpensive."

Personal Filters

Table 5.5 lists seven respondent characteristic variables. Some of these characteristics were expected to filter perception of neighborhood problems and attractions. Elizabethport respondent (42.9 percent) and present neighborhood is worse (29.5 percent) were the two characteristics most strongly associated with a poor quality neighborhood.

Table 5.5. Respondent Characteristics/Responses Associated with Poor Neighborhood Quality Rating, East Elizabeth, 1993

Characteristic/Response	Respondents Who Rated Neighborhood as Poor	
	Percentage	95% Confidence Limits
All respondents	17.4	13.1, 21.7
Neighborhood comparison:		
Present neighborhood is better	8.7	2.1, 15.4
Present neighborhood is the same		
or same neighborhood	16.4	10.6, 22.2
Present neighborhood is worse	29.5	18.1, 40.9
Age:		
18–30	23.6	15.5, 31.7
31–50	14.6	7.8, 21.4
51+	11.0	5.6, 16.4
Sex:		
Male	17.1	10.5, 23.8
Female	17.8	12.0, 23.6
Tenure:		
Owner	15.7	10.5, 20.9
Renter	18.4	10.7, 26.1
Length of residence (years):		
0–2	15.6	3.0, 28.2
>2–10	19.4	11.8, 27.0
>10	16.5	10.7, 22.3
Education:		
Grades 1–11	15.2	6.5, 23.9
High school graduate	15.4	8.0, 22.8
Some college or college	20.0	13.3, 26.8
Neighborhood of Residence:		
Elizabethport	42.9	30.0, 55.8
Frog Hollow	14.7	7.6, 21.8
Peterstown	7.8	2.9, 12.7

Source: Based on 293 responses.

Discriminant Analysis of Neighborhood Quality

The results reported in tables 5.2 to 5.5 are clues about the relationship among neighborhood quality, perceived environmental hazards and attractions, and respondent characteristics. The clues may be misleading, however, because they did not integrate all the neighborhood and personal characteristics into patterns that model people's perceptions. To investigate potential integrations, five stepwise discriminant analyses were done. They identified factors that discriminate among excellent/good, fair, and poor ratings by the 293 respondents. We first present the baseline run, then the results of the four heuristic runs.

Baseline Run

The baseline run contained twenty-one problems, ten attractions, as well as age, gender, tenure, length of residence, education, three neighborhoods of residence, and comparison of present and previous neighborhood. Thirty-one of the forty potentially discriminating variables were statistically significant discriminators at $P < .05$ (table 5.6). Only two would have been expected to be statistically significant by chance.

Two functions help interpret the interrelationships or integrations among the discriminating variables in the baseline run. The first function identifies the blighted Elizabethport area and the second describes a worse quality neighborhood.

Six of the seven strongest correlates of the first function were as follows: inadequate street lighting ($r = .660$), streets in need of repair ($r = .503$), abandoned factories and businesses ($r = .451$), occupied buildings in poor condition ($r = .438$), abandoned houses ($r = .351$), and litter or trash in the street ($r = .346$). The exception was the Elizabethport respondent variable ($r = .548$). The strong correlation of Elizabethport respondents with this function led us to label it "Elizabethport blight."

In addition to the blight variables, table 5.6 shows that the Elizabethport function incorporates behavioral problems (crime, unfriendly neighbors, uncontrolled animals), local activity spaces (junkyard, gasoline station, and other nonresidential; motor vehicle noise and heavy traffic), and massive technology sites (hazardous-waste sites). A thirty-one to fifty-year-old male resident of Elizabethport testified to the multiplicity of problems in the neighborhood: "We need to clean up our street. Animals are all over the place. Heavy airplane noise, drugs! You name it, this neighborhood has got it. I can't sell my house."

The problems in Elizabethport are both unusual and interrelated. For instance, one exasperated resident asked us this rhetorical question? "Why are some people permitted to have chickens and roosters running loose in the city?" After asking the question he proceeded

Table 5.6. Discriminant Analysis: East Elizabeth, Baseline Run

		Correlation of Variable with Function	
Variable	F-value	Elizabethport Blight Function 1	Worse Neighborhood Quality Function 2
Inadequate street lighting	37.4	.660	
Elizabethport respondent	24.1	.548	
Streets, roads, sidewalks in disrepair	31.8	.503	
Abandoned factories and businesses	26.0	.451	
Occupied buildings in poor or dangerous condition	36.5	.438	.277
Abandoned houses	22.7	.351	
Litter or trash in the street	32.0	.346	.344
Crime	39.9	.342	.418
Junkyard, gasoline station, other nonresidential	24.7	.293	.263
Unfriendly neighbors	21.0	.288	
Uncontrolled animals	15.2	.275	
Hazardous-waste sites	13.0	.264	
Motor vehicle noise and heavy traffic	26.3	.262	.252
Present neighborhood is worse	21.8		.573
Airplane noise	24.7		.431
Good schools	16.3		−.421
Recreational facilities that attract rowdy people	21.5		.389
Odors or smoke	16.9		.298
Canonical correlation with neighborhood quality dependent variable (P-value)		.705 (.001)	.418 (.01)
Average standardized Z score with poor quality respondents		1.75	0.91

Source: Based on 293 responses.
Note: Variables with a correlation of >0.25 with one of the two functions are shown. All correlations shown were statistically significant discriminators at P < .05.

to tell us that the roosters are used for cock fights. Another linked two problems in the neighborhood: "Since the Turnpike started their expansion, we have been invaded by very huge rats."

The second function identified ten characteristics also strongly associated with a poor quality in the three neighborhoods as a whole. It focuses on people who perceived their present neighborhood as worse ($r = .573$) and were troubled by airplane noise ($r = .431$), absence of good schools ($r = −.421$), crime ($r = .418$), rowdy people attracted to recreational facilities (r = .389), litter or trash (r = .344), odors or smoke (r = .298), occupied buildings in poor condition (r = .277), junkyards, gasoline stations, and other nonresidential land uses (r = .263), and motor vehicle noise and heavy traffic (r = .252). We labeled this the "worse neighborhood quality" function because it contains characteristics of behavioral, blight, local activity space, and massive technology site problems, the neighborhood comparison variable, and the absence of good schools.

The importance of previous neighborhood experiences in the general poor quality function cannot be understated. Two respondents illustrate the influence of previous neighborhood quality. The first was from a female who rated the neighborhood as poor and her previous neighborhood as better: "There are too many robberies around here. They have robbed my house once, my car 5 times for our radio, and our garage 3–4 times for my kids bike." The second response is from a female aged thirty-one to fifty who rated her present neighborhood as fair and her previous neighborhood as worse: "I lived in a neighborhood which was drug-infested—violence all over. I got sick of it and I feared for my 13 year old son. I had no other choice but to move here. I needed a safer place to live until I can save more money." The first respondent moved into a worse neighborhood that was less safe, the second into a better neighborhood that was safer. These contrasting views are remarkable because these respondents live within one hundred feet of each other in Elizabethport.

Heuristic Runs

The four heuristics attempt to model people's thinking about their neighborhoods. The logic behind each is briefly restated and the results are presented. The outsider perception heuristic assumes that insiders, like outsiders, focus on massive landscape features, such as noisy aircraft, the refinery complex, and gas tanks. Table 5.7 compares the canonical correlations and accuracy of the classification produced by the baseline and four heuristics. The baseline analysis had slightly higher canonical correlations than any of the heuristics, was slightly better at classifying all respondents than the heuristics, but not as successful in correctly categorizing poor quality ratings.

The outsider perception heuristic was the worst model. Its canonical correlations and ability to correctly classify respondents were sig-

Table 5.7. Summary of Discriminant Analysis Runs, East Elizabeth, 1993

	Canonical Correlation Function		Percentage Correctly Classified	
Run	1	2	Total	Poor
Baseline (table 5.6)	.705	.418	68	59
Heuristic:				
Outsider perception	.401	.038	44	73
Specific hazard type	.667	.339	65	69
Specific hazard type checkoff	.618	.310	65	65
Aggregate hazard burden				
(table 5.8)	.660	.298	63	74

Source: Based on 293 responses.

nificantly lower than the baseline (P < .01). It correctly classified only 44 percent of respondents. In other words, knowing that someone is distressed by a massive technology site in east Elizabeth is insufficient information to accurately predict how they will classify their neighborhood.

Even though the three heuristics sacrifice information about specific variables, table 5.7 shows that they performed as well or better than the baseline model. The two specific hazard heuristics each correctly classified 65 percent of respondents, and the aggregate hazard burden model 63 percent, compared to 68 percent for the baseline model. Notably, all three were more effective at classifying respondents who rated their neighborhoods as poor quality. The difference between the baseline and the aggregate model (74 percent vs. 59 percent) was significant at (P = .16).

Table 5.8 presents the discriminant analysis results for the aggregate hazard burden model. The two functions resemble the functions of the baseline run. The first identified people who were stressed by multiple problems (r = .714). They were likely to be residents of Elizabethport (r = .617) and not Peterstown (r = −.274). We called it "poor quality Elizabethport." The second function resembles the worse neighborhood quality function of the baseline analysis. Respondents perceive that their present neighborhood is worse than their previous one (r = .796), total number of problems is high (r = .315), and attractions are few (r = −.302). The respondents tended to be residents of Elizabethport (r = .383).

Table 5.9 provides additional support for the aggregate hazard burden heuristic model. It shows that stress increases as neighbor-

Table 5.8. Discriminant Analysis of Aggregate Hazard Burden Heuristic, East Elizabeth, 1993

		Correlation of Variable with Function	
Variable	F-value	Poor Quality Elizabethport	General Poor Neighborhood
Aggregate number of problems	66.0	.714	.315
Elizabethport respondents	24.1	.617	.383
Peterstown respondent	10.4	−.274	
Present neighborhood is worse	21.8		.796
Aggregate attractions	7.1		−.302
Canonical correlation with neighborhood quality dependent variable (P-value)		.660 (.001)	.298 (.001)
Average standardized Z score with poor quality responses		1.69	0.55

Source: Based on 293 surveys.
Note: Variables with a correlation of >0.25 with one of the two functions are shown. All correlations shown were statistically significant discriminators at P < .05.

hood quality decreases. For example, the petroleum refinery and gas tanks were identified as a major stress by 33 and 29 percent of respondents who rated their neighborhood as poor quality, respectively. This compared to 27 and 22 percent who rated their neighborhood as fair, and 12 and 6 percent who rated it as excellent or good. The 95 percent confidence limits show that the refinery and gas tanks were unable to clearly distinguish between the fair and poor quality rating. The specific hazard type heuristic was also unable to distinguish between fair and poor ratings. Measured by their 95 percent confidence limits, airplane noise was a better discriminator, that is, the 95 percent confidence limits do not overlap. But the excellent/good and fair confidence limits overlap.

In contrast, none of the confidence limits for crime and blight (measured by litter) overlap. The aggregate hazard variable, by far, was the best at distinguishing among the three quality groups of poor, fair, excellent/good. An average of 1.1 problems were identified as distressing by respondents who rated their neighborhood as excellent or good compared to 3.9 who rated their neighborhood as fair and 8.2 who rated their neighborhood as poor quality. In other words, in east Elizabeth, those who rated their neighborhood as poor typically identified 6 to 10 major stresses in their neighborhoods.

Table 5.9. Neighborhood Characteristics and Neighborhood Quality, East Elizabeth

Quality	Total Number of Hazards (maximum is 21)	Airplane (1 = yes)	Petroleum Refinery (1 = yes)	Gas Tanks (1 = yes)	Hazardous Waste Site (1 = yes)	Crime (1 = yes)	Litter or Trash (1 = yes)	Total Number of Amenities (maximum is 10)
Excellent/good	1.1	.21	.12	.06	.04	.06	.05	5.6
	(0.8, 1.5)	(.13, .29)	(.06, .18)	(.02, .11)	(.01, .08)	(.02, .11)	(.01, .09)	(5.0, 6.2)
Fair	3.9	.49	.27	.22	.13	.31	.28	4.5
	(3.2, 4.5)	(.19, .34)	(.19, .34)	(.15, .29)	(.07, .19)	(.23, .39)	(.20, .36)	(4.0, 5.0)
Poor	8.2	.73	.33	.29	.33	.65	.55	3.9
	(6.5, 9.9)	(.60, .85)	(.20, .47)	(.16, .42)	(.20, .47)	(.51, .78)	(.41, .69)	(3.1, 4.7)

Source: Based on 293 responses.

Summary of Findings

RQ1: *How do people who live in the immediate vicinity of potentially hazardous land uses and activities rate their neighborhoods?*

Forty-three percent of Elizabethport respondents rated their neighborhood as poor quality compared to 15 percent of Frog Hollow's, 8 percent of Peterstown's, and 3 to 4 percent of respondents to the AHS surveys of the United States, northern New Jersey, and the Philadelphia metropolitan area.

We used airplane noise to identify unusually insensitive people, train noise, utility rights-of-way, and furniture and metal factories to identify unusually sensitive respondents, and physical barriers and distance as hazard filters. We observed no more than 3 percent of respondents who could be labeled unusually insensitive and 4 percent as unusually sensitive.

RQ2: *What factors most influence neighborhood ratings, especially rating of a neighborhood as poor?*

Blight and behavioral risks clearly were the greatest stresses among respondents, especially in Elizabethport, the area with the worst neighborhood quality ratings in our surveys. Present neighborhood quality compared to previous neighborhood quality was also an extremely important filter. Good schools were the only notable attractions.

Airplane noise stresses east Elizabeth respondents. Many felt their present neighborhood was worse than their previous one as a result of airplane noise. Yet most of those stressed by airplane noise rated their neighborhood as fair or even good quality rather than poor.

The outsider perception model, which assumes that neighborhood residents focus on the kinds of hazards that outsiders see, smell, or hear, was the worst predictor of neighborhood quality. The aggregate hazard burden heuristic correctly classified almost as many respondents as the baseline discriminant model and more accurately predicted poor quality ratings. Overall, the east Elizabeth results were similar to the Marcus Hook area results (see chapter 4).

Neighborhoods Near Hazardous-Waste Sites

Edison, New Jersey, is where Thomas Edison invented the phonograph and other valuable products. During the 1970s, Edison was also where enormous quantities of hazardous waste from the manufacture of valuable products was discarded. The Kin Buc Landfill was opened in 1959 as a municipal sanitary landfill with the goal of reclaiming the meadows along the Raritan River (Greenberg and Anderson 1984). In the early 1970s, Kin Buc began to accept hazardous waste and experience the most unsightly and obvious ramifications of dumping (fig. 6.1).

Images of Hazardous-Waste Sites

From our faculty offices, located about four miles from the Kin Buc Landfill, we observed, on three occasions, plumes from a fire. On one occasion, when the plume was particularly large, a bulldozer driver was killed when a drum he was moving exploded. Kin Buc accepted waste from all over the East Coast of the United States. Waste-management practices, which one of us personally witnessed, included dumping garbage, burying drums in the garbage, and spilling liquid hazardous waste into pools dug into garbage.

By the time Kin Buc was closed, it was ninety feet high and covered more than two hundred acres, a massive eyesore from the New Jersey Turnpike, located about one-half mile away. After closure, it continued to make local news because of its potential impact on

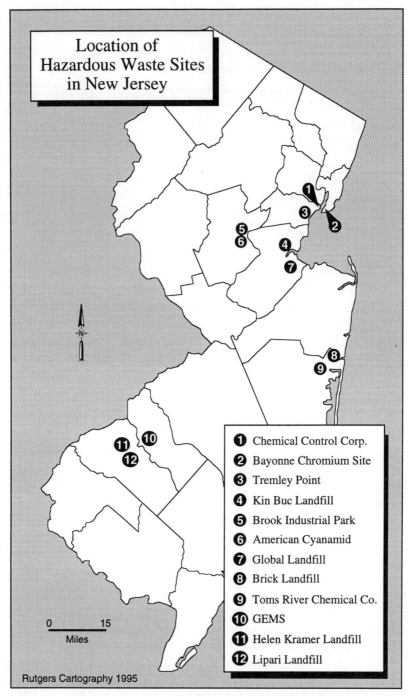

Figure 6.1. Location of Hazardous-Waste Sites in New Jersey

surrounding land uses. For example, a failed attempt was made to open Kin Buc II, locally known as "son of Kin Buc." The Mirror Lake Beach Club, about one-half mile from the landfill, remained open after much concern and discussion; Middlesex County College, about one mile away, expanded; and the Heller Industrial Park, a little more than one-half mile away, was constructed, as was a large garden apartment complex with a view of Kin Buc. Each of these land-use activities rekindled the image of blue liquid waste being poured onto fresh, dug-out garbage.

Kin Buc was our dominant image of a hazardous-waste site until Earth Day in 1980. The Chemical Control site (see discussion of east Elizabeth in chapter 5) exploded on that day. Chemical Control began accepting various types of waste in 1972. The wastes were supposedly incinerated. However, by the late 1970s, it was obvious that stacking rather than incinerating was occurring on the site located near the Frog Hollow neighborhood (see chapter 5).

In April 1979, the state of New Jersey began to remove explosives, compressed gases, radioactive materials, and other flammable materials from the Chemical Control site. Under state order, companies who had left the waste removed about eight thousand drums. Colleagues working for the state of New Jersey explained the nerve-wracking process of examining, testing, packing, and moving these ticking time bombs. When the site exploded in 1980, the contents of about thirty-five to fifty-five thousand drums stacked in sets of three to five were destroyed. The fire burned for about ten hours with numerous explosions (see chapter 5). The three-thousand-degree Fahrenheit fire accomplished the job that the incinerator did not. It was a terrifying experience.

Chemical Control left a health legacy. About half of the 250 firefighters dispatched to the site did not use respirators. Some of them developed respiratory problems. In addition, numerous unsubstantiated claims were made about the cause of the fire. For instance, one popular explanation was that the fire was deliberately set to hide bodies of murdered underworld members.

The combination of Kin Buc and Chemical Control were the cornerstones of our images of a hazardous-waste site. The Comprehensive Environmental Response and Compensation Liability Act (CERCLA), commonly known as Superfund, was built on the legacy.

CERCLA required the United States Environmental Protection Agency (EPA) to prepare a National Priority List (NPL) of four hundred sites for remediation. EPA created the Hazard Ranking System (HRS) to choose the sites. Sites were scored according to their potential to contaminate air, land, water, and people. The maximum (worst) score was 100.

In 1986, CERCLA was reauthorized and another $8.5 billion was added to Superfund. By 1993, the number of NPL sites exceeded twelve hundred, and the costs for remediating all NPL sites during the period 1990 to 2020 was conservatively estimated at $151 billion (Russell, Colglazier, and English 1991). The remediation of closed sites under the control of the EPA, United States Department of Defense, United States Department of Energy, other federal agencies, states, and other programs to control wastes at functioning hazardous-waste sites was estimated at $752 billion during the period 1990 to 2020 (Russell, Colglazier, and English 1991). A less conservative estimate is more than a trillion dollars.

Approximately two million Americans live within a mile of a Superfund site (Agency for Toxic Substances and Disease Registry 1992). Health effects studies have been inconclusive (National Research Council 1991). Economic and social impacts may be easier to measure (see, for example, Brown 1981; Dunne et al. 1990; Edelstein 1988; Fitchen 1989; Greenberg and Hughes 1992, 1993; McClelland, Schulze, Hurd 1990). We wanted to compare the perceptual impact of unremediated and remediated sites on neighborhood quality. How important is a hazardous-waste site compared to crime, blight, and other potential distressing neighborhood characteristics? Is there evidence that remediation improves neighborhood quality?

Choice of Neighborhoods

We chose ten areas near hazardous-waste sites in the following New Jersey municipalities: Bayonne, Bound Brook, Brick, Bridgewater, Dover Township, Gloucester, Linden, Mantua, Pitman, and Sayreville (see fig. 6.1). Each had a hazardous-waste site and at least thirty-five houses within one-half mile of the waste site. The ten hazardous-waste sites included three that were among the twelve worst on the Superfund NPL (New Jersey Department of Environmental

Protection 1989). Yet the three (GEMS, Helen Kramer, Lipari) had been substantially or fully remediated at a cost of more than $200 million at the time our surveys were conducted. They were closed, fenced, covered with a cap, treatment systems had been installed, and they looked liked grass-covered hills, not fire-breathing waste monsters. They were our "remediated" group. Residents who had lived adjacent to these sites for more than a decade were expected to have experienced a cycle beginning with fear of an out-of-control hazard and ending with less distress about a controlled nuisance. Furthermore, these neighborhoods did not contain other obvious locally unwanted land uses, such as a petroleum refinery or sewage plant, features that could confound the role of the hazardous-waste site. These made the three sites ideal for studying the effect of remediation on perception of neighborhood quality.

The Lipari landfill was the number 1 site on the EPA's National Priority List (NPL). Located in Mantua and bordering on Pitman, the sixteen-acre site, formerly a sand and gravel pit, was converted into a waste-disposal facility. Between 1958 and 1971, industrial and domestic wastes were disposed of at the site. Tens of thousands of drums were found on the site (*Home News* 1992). Leachate migrated from the site into an adjacent creek that empties into a nearby lake. Aquifers beneath the site were contaminated, including some potable groundwater wells serving about twenty thousand people (Dienemann, Ahlert, and Greenberg 1991; New Jersey Department of Environmental Protection 1989). A New Jersey Department of Health study of people living within one kilometer of the site was inconclusive. Some excess of adult leukemia and low-birth-weight babies were found. But normal or below-normal rates of other types of cancer were observed (New Jersey Department of Health 1989; *New York Times* 1989).

Homes were located within several hundred feet of the site, and new homes were being built about three-quarters of a mile from the site when we visited in mid-September and early October 1992. Except for warning signs, the area had the appearance of an affluent suburban neighborhood. Most of the fenced-off site was not visible because of heavy vegetation, including peach and other fruit trees.

A record of decision (ROD), which is the agreed upon methods chosen to remediate the site, was signed in June 1988. Initial remediation of Lipari consisted of a slurry wall and encapsulation by a synthetic membrane. This step reduced the unsightly appearance. A $16 million flushing system began operation in April 1992. In January 1993, three companies agreed to pay $52 million to partly pay for cleanup of contaminated creeks and marshes adjacent to the site (Gannon 1993; Hall 1994). Remediation should have greatly reduced stress among neighboring residents. However, we expected long-term residents to remember the on-site explosions and fires, fears of cancer, and pungent odors.

The Helen Kramer Landfill is located in Mantua Township less than five miles from the Lipari landfill. Another former sand pit, the sixty-six-acre site accepted liquid industrial waste, construction debris, septic tank pumpings, dewatered sewage sludge, hospital wastes, and an estimated two million cubic yards of municipal refuse during the 1960s. Leachate from the site contaminated both underground and surface water supplies (N.J. Department of Environmental Protection 1989). The Helen Kramer site was rated number 4 on the NPL list. When we visited the site, the immediately surrounding area included commercial food growing (pumpkins, corn, tomatoes), trailer parks, and scattered residential properties. We observed new developments under construction within one-half mile of the site.

The Helen Kramer Landfill was closed in 1981, and in 1985 the ROD included groundwater and leachate collection and treatment, a slurry wall, removal of materials from leachate ponds, and construction of a clay cap over the sixty-foot-deep site. At the time of our visit, the $90-million remediation was nearly complete (*Newark Star-Ledger* 1993) and was considered completed at the time this chapter was written in 1994. Like Lipari, we expected the Helen Kramer area to have a high quality rating among new residents. Distress would be associated with people who remember dumping at the site.

The Gloucester Environmental Management Services (GEMS) landfill covered a 60-acre site. Owned by Gloucester Township, New Jersey, the landfill accepted industrial and municipal waste for more than two decades. GEMS was ranked number 12 on the NPL. Ground and surface waters were contaminated.

Land use around this massive-appearing site was mixed. We observed a firing range, children riding up and down the sides of the landfill on their mountain bicycles, new middle-income suburban housing, and expensive-looking housing with many For Sale signs. Tractor noise and a sulfurlike sweet smell were apparent.

After lengthy negotiations, settlement was reached with the responsible parties for the GEMS site in 1989. The ROD required capping the site, constructing a treatment plant on site, bringing in a water line for homes whose wells were contaminated, and placing a fence around the site. The cost was approximately $40 million and growing when we visited.

Overall, we chose three sites in southern New Jersey that at one time epitomized so-called toxic time bombs that severely tainted neighborhoods. But all have been substantially remediated and none have another obvious locally unwanted land uses (LULU) nearby. Migration of distressed people from these neighborhoods during the 1980s and remediation of the sites should have substantially reduced stress, except, we expected, among long-term residents who wanted to leave the area but could not.

We summarize similarities and differences among the three sites that were expected to influence the results of our neighborhood surveys. Three elements were similar. The main hazard at each site was water pollution; the neighborhoods did not have another obvious LULU; and the municipalities were all middle-income, primarily occupied by white populations. But there were obvious differences among the sites in visibility and in site ownership and management. GEMS, the number 12 NPL site, appeared more threatening than Lipari and Helen Kramer (NPL numbers 1 and 4). GEMS rises above the landscape, literally looming over some adjacent housing, and was not well shielded by trees. We detected odors near the site. Lipari and Helen Kramer were both privately owned; GEMS was owned by the municipality, which was a principle responsible party. Furthermore, a controversy erupted at the GEMS site over use of state funds to pay for reduced property values (Singer 1993). In short, we expected recovery of the perception of neighborhood quality to be most hindered at the GEMS site.

We compared the three remediated study areas to seven areas we called "unremediated" sites. Some cleanup has occurred at some of these sites, but final remediation had not been accomplished at any of them. The seven areas adjacent to these unremediated sites are located in northern and central New Jersey, fifty to eighty miles from the three remediated sites that are located in southern New Jersey.

In addition to the difference in remediation, there were other important differences between the remediated and unremediated sites. The unremediated sites had much lower NPL ratings. Two were not on the NPL, and the other five had NPL ranks ranging from 59 to 275. These compared to 1, 4, and 12 for the three remediated sites. Despite the much higher NPL ratings of the remediated sites, we expected them to have higher neighborhood quality ratings for two reasons. First, much more site remediation had been done at the remediated sites, and there was extensive consultation between the federal and state agencies and the local populations. Neither statement can be made about the seven sites. In addition, many of the sites in the seven-site survey had multiple LULUs (e.g., sewage plants, oil and chemical tank farms, quarries, factories, major highways, adjacent airports, etc). We expected these massive technology sites to reduce neighborhood quality in the unremediated neighborhoods.

North of the Arthur Kill in the industrial districts of Bayonne and Jersey City were sites contaminated by industrial dumping of chromium. Two-family, middle-income housing and a baseball field had been built within one-quarter mile of one of these chromium sites during the last ten to fifteen years. We call this area the Bayonne Chromium site. Several residents explained that chromium had been scraped off the nearby baseball field. But they were certain that their back yards were "full of the stuff."

Multiple industrial sites were within one-quarter mile of the neighborhood. Back yards and decks directly faced a tank farm. Residents spoke about odors from a nearby sewage plant. Several residents pointed to the rail line running behind their houses and indicated that trains carrying chemicals had derailed spilling their contents. Despite these obvious hazards, we did not form an image of a poor quality neighborhood because the houses nearest to the chromium site were the newest housing, the residents we spoke with were articulate and well-dressed, and residents spoke fondly about their neighbors and their community. Their positive feelings, we expected, would soften the impact of the chromium site and the other massive technology sites.

The Brick Township Landfill was a forty-two-acre Superfund site used to dump sanitary and commercial wastes. The site contained hundreds of fifty-five-gallon drums, three ten-thousand-gallon storage tanks, and three open pits used for septic wastes during the early 1970s. The landfill ceased operating in 1979, a fence was placed around it, and the landfill was covered with shrubs and other green plants. It did not appear hazardous. Yet Brick had an HRS of 58.13 because of groundwater contamination and nearby housing.

Residential areas were within one-quarter mile of the site. A large townhouse development directly bordered the site to the south. The relatively new development appeared to be inhabited by middle-income families, many with young children. Trees completely hid the landfill from the view of these residents. A new (less than three years old) single-family housing development overlooked the site from the north. Neighborhood residents appeared to be middle to upper-middle income. Residents told us that they received city water. The back yards of some houses directly overlooked the landfill. More houses were being built with back-yard views of this Superfund site. A nearby billboard said houses were priced at $119,900 and up.

We expected the Brick area to have relatively high neighborhood quality ratings. The landfill was not expected to be a serious problem because so many of the residents had moved into the area after the landfill was closed, vegetation grew on the waste piles, and residents' did not depend on the water beneath their property. The Brick Township Landfill seemed to illustrate "out of sight, out of mind."

The Brook Industrial Park, a Superfund site contaminated with pesticide waste, is located on the north side of the Raritan River in Bound Brook. Houses were within one hundred feet of the site. The housing, signs, and census data suggested a lower-middle-income population with a growing Hispanic American component. This neighborhood was the most physically deteriorated of the ten we surveyed near hazardous-waste sites. Some of the attached housing and streets needed repair, and the public playground was badly deteriorated. A major train line cut the Brook neighborhood off from the remainder of Bound Brook. A parked diesel locomotive was making distressing loud noises at the time of our second visit. Despite an HRS score of 58.12, we expected the residents of this neighborhood to be more distressed by blight than by the hazardous-waste site at the end of the street.

In Bridgewater, adjacent to the Raritan River and the Elizabethtown Water Company intake for central New Jersey, was the 575-acre site of American Cyanamid, a chemical company that began manufacturing on the property during the First World War. The Cyanamid site contained buried wastes, dozens of lagoons, and had an HRS rating of 50.28 because of its threat to nearby water supplies. Residential areas nearest to the site were cut off from the site by a major road and numerous industrial activities, such as a sewage treatment plant, a recycling center, a railroad, and a sand and gravel operation. To us, Cyanamid's lagoons almost appeared benign compared to these other activities.

The closest houses were mostly single-family units clustered in locations about one-half mile from the site. Many of the houses off the main road were attractive, and some had back-yard swimming pools. People in the street did not appear to be distressed by Cyanamid. Their concerns were traffic congestion, noise, smells from the sewage plant, and dirt from the sand and gravel operation. We expected this area to have relatively low quality ratings because of the massive technology sites.

Global was a 57.5-acre inactive landfill located south of the Garden State Parkway, east of Route 9 and west of heavily used Cheesequake State Park in central New Jersey. Global had an HRS rating of 45.92 because it threatened nearby water supplies. The landfill closed in 1984, was covered with vegetation, and did not appear threatening.

Two apartment complexes were adjacent to the site. Residents' views of the landfill were partly blocked by garages and by the fact that the apartments sat at the top of a road and the landfill is at the bottom. Northeast of the site is an upper-middle-income neighborhood of large, single-family houses. Some of the houses had tennis courts and swimming pools. Although the site appeared harmless and was visible to only a few people, we expected long-term residents to be distressed by the recollection of garbage trucks driving through their neighborhood on the way to the landfill and by the absence of substantial remediation of the site.

One mile west of the Garden State Parkway and north of Route 37 was the Toms River Chemical Company, which was owned by Ciba-Geigy when we visited. The plant is surrounded by forests and state parks. Outsiders cannot see the active and lined landfill, unused lagoons, and inactive landfill, which led to an HRS of 50.33. Nearly all of the nearby housing was single-family and much of it is occupied by upper-middle-income people. Conversations with residents suggested that many new residents were unaware of the history of pollution, but older residents remembered local distress about well contamination. We expected this area to have high neighborhood quality ratings because of its attractive appearance.

In contrast, the Tremley Point neighborhood, located in Linden, is surrounded by massive technology sites. EXXON/Tosco's tank farm (see chapter 5) and manufacturing facilities owned by GAF, Cyanamid, and DuPont were clearly visible from the neighborhood. The New Jersey Turnpike, rail lines, small airplanes from Linden airport, and large ones from Newark airport surrounded the neighborhood with sound twenty four hours a day. Tremley Point Road is loaded with trucks on their way to the factories. The GAF property located just on the other side of the turnpike was the only location in New Jersey still being considered for a hazardous-waste incinerator at the time this chapter was written. The incinerator, which would be located at the end of Tremley Point Road, would incinerate toxins coming from all over New Jersey, but it was also needed, according to its sponsors, to incinerate the waste buried on the GAF site (Veronis 1993).

Despite the presence of these massive technology sites, the neighborhood contained mostly well-manicured, single-family houses, well-maintained playgrounds, and baseball fields. Several residents spoke fondly of the neighborhood, emphasizing that it was safe for children. We expected some stress because of the industry, airplanes, trains, trucks, and hazardous-waste site, but not many poor quality ratings.

Unlike the relative poverty of the east Elizabeth, Marcus Hook, and Camden study areas, our ten hazardous-waste site study neighborhoods were middle income. The 1989 per capita income of New Jersey was $18,714 (Department of Commerce 1992). Comparable figures for the study areas ranged from $21,100 near the Global site to $15,700 near the Brook one, and two of the ten had per capita incomes higher than the state's. Twenty-five percent of the state's population graduated college, compared to 19 percent in the ten study areas. Also, unlike the study areas in chapters 4, 5, and 7, these ten contained relatively few black or Hispanic Americans. In 1990, 4 percent of the population was Hispanic and 3 percent was black, about one-third of New Jersey's proportion.

Overall, the ten study areas had the desired contrasting characteristics: remediated and unremediated sites; sites with and without adjacent distressing land uses and blight; and urban, suburban, and rural environments. We did not expect these populations to be as seriously and consistently distressed by crime and blight as their counterparts in the other neighborhoods, and we expected to be able to observe the impact of site remediation on neighborhood quality.

Survey Questions, Methods, Problems, and Returns

The most important goal of the hazardous-waste site studies was to try to isolate the sites' impact on neighborhood quality. This goal had implications for the research design. Because we needed to center on hazardous-waste sites rather than functional approximations of neighborhoods, we had to pick residential areas that were not contiguous. That is, some hazardous-waste neighborhoods looked like donuts with a hole in the center, whereas the neighborhoods in chapters 4, 5, and 7 looked like danish. The areas surrounding the Brick, Cyanamid, GEMS, Helen Kramer, Lipari, and Toms River sites were not contiguous. A result of this physical separation was that the survey data at some sites represented the views of people who had not experienced the same perceptual environments. For instance, we think that the vast majority of residents of Linwood in the Marcus Hook area (chapter 4) saw, smelled, and heard the same neighborhood environment. The same could not be said of the residents of the Toms River area. In fact, one part of the Toms River neighborhood was separated from another by a large park and the chemical plant. Some residents of the area we called Toms River probably had never been in the other part of the area with the same label.

The need to explore a variety of types of neighborhoods adjacent to hazardous-waste sites led us to choose the Brook and Cyanamid sites, despite the fact that there were relatively few homes near the sites. Small sample sizes limit our ability to draw conclusions about respondents' ratings of these neighborhoods.

A third implication of focusing on hazardous-waste sites was that we asked more questions about the sites and did not ask any questions about amenities in the survey of the seven unremediated sites. Attractions were added to the survey of three remediated sites (GEMS, Helen Kramer, and Lipari). Because of these differences, attractions data presented in this chapter were only for the surveys of the GEMS, Helen Kramer, and Lipari areas.

A fourth difference between this research design and the one used in the other chapters was that the ten areas were so diverse that it was not feasible to identify a characteristic that could signal an unusually sensitive person. Instead, in this chapter we concentrated on the expected difference in perception between long- and short-term residents of remediated and unremediated areas to determine if long-term residents living near unremediated sites were the most sensitive and recent migrants to neighborhoods with remediated sites were the least sensitive.

The fifth difference between this chapter and the others is availability of twenty-eight structured, open-ended interviews done near the GEMS site and twenty-six near the Helen Kramer one. Done by single interviewer in December 1993 and January 1994, we sought to understand how residents integrate neighborhood quality and their image of a remediated hazardous-waste site with their images of "great" and "terrible" neighborhoods (see Appendix 2 for a copy of the survey instrument).

Eighteen potential problems and seven personal characteristics were included in both survey instruments. The survey for remediated sites included eight attractions, and the one for unremediated sites included none. We used hazardous-waste sites to identify unusually insensitive and sensitive people. All long-term residents of these areas should be aware of a nearby hazardous-waste site. We used the desire to leave as a result of the hazardous-waste site to identify the proportion of respondents who were extremely sensitive to the nearby hazardous-waste site.

We attempted to place an instrument in every occupied dwelling unit within one-quarter mile of each hazardous-waste site. We began at one-half mile at some sites because no one lived within one-quarter mile of the site. When the area adjacent to the waste site was cut off by a major highway or nonresidential land use, we stopped distributing the instrument.

Generic problems associated with distributing the survey instrument were described in detail in chapter 2. These problems were less prevalent in these ten study areas than in east Elizabeth, the Marcus Hook area, and east Camden. Only 6 percent of residents of the study areas indicated that they had difficulty with English. This compared, for example, to 39 percent in east Elizabeth. Vacant housing units, which exceeded 20 percent in parts of Chester, were only 4 percent near these hazardous-waste sites.

The first survey was distributed to 950 homes near the Bayonne, Brick, Brook, Cyanamid, Global, Toms River, and Tremley Point sites beginning on June 30, 1992. A total of 306 useful responses (32 percent) were received by the end of July 1992. The number of surveys received and distributed were as follows: Bayonne (42/100), Brook (13/38), Brick (51/150), Cyanamid (11/42), Global (72/295), Toms River (55/155), and Tremley Point (62/170).

We distributed 900 surveys in late September and early October of 1992 near the GEMS, Helen Kramer, and Lipari sites. A total of 377 usable surveys were returned by the end of 1992. The 42 percent response rate was the highest in our study. The response rate was 40 percent at GEMS (132/332), 34 percent for the Helen Kramer area (80/233), and 49 percent at Lipari (165/335).

In the previous chapters, a low response rate was associated with rental and vacant housing and people who identified themselves as Hispanic in the United States census. For these ten hazardous-waste site areas, we found a Spearman rank correlation of $-.48$ ($P < .05$) between response rate and percentage of residents who were Hispanic and $-.41$ ($P < .05$) with percentage of rental units. This means that potential respondents living in rental units and self-identified as Hispanic were less likely to respond. Correlations with measures of income, education, and age were not statistically significant at $P < .05$. The strongest rank correlation was $.76$ ($P < .02$) between HRS score and response rate for the eight sites on the NPL (Brick, Brook, Cyanamid, GEMS, Global, Helen Kramer, Lipari, Toms River). For instance, Lipari and GEMS, probably the two most controversial sites, had the highest response rates. This observation suggests that controversy associated with high-priority sites engendered substantial interest in communicating feelings about neighborhood quality.

As expected, the 683 respondents were not representative of all 48,700 residents who lived in the census tracts near the hazardous-waste sites. Ninety-three percent of respondents graduated high school, compared to 78 percent of area residents ($P < .01$); 58 percent were female, compared to 51 percent of residents ($P < .01$); and 81 percent were homeowners, compared to 69 percent of area residents ($P < .01$). Seven percent of respondents, compared to 9 percent of residents, were more than seventy years old (P < .05). Fifteen percent of respondents and 24 percent of residents were eighteen to thirty years old (P < .01). Finally, we note that 60 percent of area residents lived in the same house and 83 percent in the same county for at least five years, compared to 58 percent of respondents who lived in the neighborhood for at least five years. Overall, our respondents were more likely to be female, educated at least through high school, homeowners, and short-term residents of the neighborhood than the population of the ten areas as a whole.

Neighborhood Quality

The areas adjacent to the hazardous-waste sites had the highest neighborhood quality ratings in our field studies. Twenty-six percent of respondents rated their neighborhood as excellent (table 6.1). Another 51 percent rated their neighborhood as good. Twenty percent rated it as fair, and only 3 percent rated their neighborhood as poor quality. Respondents were almost as likely to rate their neighborhood as excellent or good quality as Americans as a whole and residents of the surrounding New Jersey and Philadelphia regions.

Respondents who lived near the Lipari and Toms River hazardous-waste sites had a higher or a similar proportion of excellent ratings than the United States and the two surrounding regions. In contrast, respondents from the Bayonne, Brook, Cyanamid, Global and Tremley Point sites were much less likely to rate their neighborhoods as excellent and more likely to rate them as fair or poor quality.

Problems, Attractions, and Comparisons with Previous Neighborhood

Only 29 percent of respondents reported at least one characteristic that was so distressing that they wanted to leave. A hazardous-waste site was identified by 23 percent of respondents as a serious problem. This result was not a surprising because every survey was placed in a home near a hazardous-waste site. Odors or smoke, and businesses and other nonresidential land uses were serious problems for over 10 percent of respondents (table 6.2).

Ten of the eighteen potential problems distressed fewer than 5 percent of respondents. None of the behavioral or blight hazards were

Table 6.1. Neighborhood Quality Near Ten Hazardous-Waste Sites with Selected Comparisons

Year	Area	Percentage Rating of Neighborhood Quality and 95% Confidence Limits			
		Excellent	Good	Fair	Poor
1992	All ten sites	25.5	51.0	20.2	3.4
	(n = 683)	(22.2, 28.8)	(47.3, 54.8)	(17.2, 23.2)	(2.0, 4.8)
	Bayonne	9.5	57.1	33.3	0.0
	(n = 42)	(0.6, 18.4)	(42.1, 72.1)	(19.1, 47.6)	(0, 0)
	Brick	25.5	51.0	21.6	1.8
	(n = 51)	(13.5, 37.5)	(37.3, 64.7)	(10.3, 32.9)	(−1.8, 5.5)
	Brook	7.7	53.8	15.4	23.1
	(n = 13)	(−6.8, 22.2)	(26.7, 80.9)	(−4.2, 35.0)	(0.2, 46.0)
	Cyanamid	0.0	18.2	81.2	0.0
	(n = 11)	(0, 0)	(−4.6, 41.0)	(58.1, 104.3)	(0, 0)
	GEMS	14.4	62.1	18.2	5.3
	(n = 132)	(8.4, 20.4)	(53.8, 70.4)	(11.6, 24.8)	(1.5, 9.1)
	Global	5.6	48.6	36.1	9.7
	(n = 72)	(0.3, 10.9)	(37.1, 60.1)	(25.0, 47.2)	(2.9, 16.5)
	Helen Kramer	26.3	53.8	17.5	2.5
	(n = 80)	(16.7, 35.9)	(42.9, 64.7)	(9.2, 25.8)	(0, 5.9)
	Lipari	53.0	43.4	3.6	0.0
	(n = 165)	(45.4, 60.6)	(35.9, 50.9)	(0.8, 6.4)	(0, 0)
	Toms River	34.5	45.5	18.2	1.8
	(n = 55)	(21.9, 47.1)	(32.3, 58.7)	(8.0, 28.4)	(−1.7, 5.3)
	Tremley Point	8.1	51.6	37.1	3.2
	(n = 62)	(1.3, 14.9)	(39.2, 64.0)	(25.1, 49.1)	(−1.2, 7.6)
1993– 1994	Other ten study neighborhoods	4.1	34.7	42.2	19.0
	(n = 735)	(2.7, 5.5)	(31.3, 38.1)	(38.6, 45.8)	(16.2, 21.8)
1991	United States	33.6	52.6	11.2	2.6
1991	Northern New Jersey[a]	32.9	54.7	9.7	2.7
1989	Philadelphia[b]	34.8	49.7	11.7	3.8

Source: Ratings of neighborhoods near ten hazardous-waste sites based on 683 valid respondents from all ten neighborhoods in New Jersey.
[a]Northern New Jersey includes Bergen, Essex, Hudson, Hunterdon, Middlesex, Monmouth, Morris, Ocean, Passaic, Somerset, Sussex, and Union Counties, New Jersey.
[b]Philadelphia includes Bucks, Chester, Delaware, Montgomery, and Philadelphia Counties, Pennsylvania, and Burlington, Camden, and Gloucester Counties, New Jersey.

major stresses to more than 6 percent of respondents. For example, abandoned or boarded-up buildings, inadequate street lighting, and crime caused less than 3 percent of respondents to want to leave, a sharp contrast with the results reported in chapters 4 and 5.

Although problems were less prevalent near hazardous-waste sites

Table 6.2. Prevalence of Neighborhood Characteristics Near Ten Hazardous-Waste Sites, 1992

Characteristic	Percentage of Respondents
Problems:[a]	29.4
Sites with hazardous waste	23.4
Odors or smoke	12.3
Businesses, electrical power, sewage treatment plants, other nonresidential	10.0
Polluted water	9.1
Motor vehicle noise and heavy traffic	8.2
Traffic congestion	6.6
Unfriendly neighbors	6.4
Litter or trash in streets, elsewhere	5.4
Noise from airplanes or trains	4.8
Dogs, cats, uncontrolled animals	4.4
Streets, roads, and sidewalks in disrepair	3.7
Occupied buildings in poor or dangerous condition	3.7
Crime	2.8
Inadequate street lighting	2.3
Recreational facilities that attract rowdy people	2.0
Right-of-way for a utility	1.9
Abandoned or boarded-up buildings	1.8
Flooding	1.5
Attractions:[b]	
Looks/design of neighborhood	81.2
House was key	69.5
Good schools	69.2
Convenient to job	61.0
Convenient to friends/relatives	61.0
Convenient to leisure activities	55.4
Other public services	47.2
Convenient to public transport	20.1
Neighborhood comparison:	
Present neighborhood is better	48.7
Present neighborhood is same	38.6
Present neighborhood is worse	12.7

Source: Problems and neighborhood comparisons are based on 683 responses from all ten neighborhoods in New Jersey; attractions are based on 377 responses from the GEMS, Helen Kramer, and Lipari sites.
[a]Percentage who found condition so disturbing that they wanted to leave.
[b]Percentage who gave these as reasons they live in the neighborhood.

than in the other study areas, table 6.3 shows an obvious difference between respondents from neighborhoods with remediated and unremediated sites. Seventeen of the eighteen potential problems were more distressing in the seven unremediated site areas than in the three remediated ones. Notably, the largest differences were for

Table 6.3. Problems Causing Residents to Want to Leave Neighborhoods Near Ten Hazardous-Waste Sites, 1992

	Percentage of Respondents	
	(Three Sites)	(Seven Sites)
Characteristic	Remediated	Unremediated
Sites with hazardous waste	33	18
Odors or smoke	22	5
Businesses, electrical power, sewage treatment plants, other nonresidential	16	5
Polluted water	13	6
Motor vehicle noise and heavy traffic	15	4
Traffic congestion	11	3
Unfriendly neighbors	10	4
Litter or trash in streets, empty lots	9	3
Noise from airplanes or trains	10	1
Dogs, cats, uncontrolled animals	8	2
Streets, roads, and sidewalks in disrepair	5	3
Occupied buildings in poor or dangerous condition	7	1
Crime	4	2
Inadequate street lighting	3	2
Recreational facilities that attract rowdy people	4	1
Right-of-way for a utility	3	2
Abandoned or boarded-up buildings	2	2
Flooding	3	<1

Source: Based on 683 responses from all ten neighborhoods in New Jersey. Unremediated sites are Bayonne, Brick, Brook, Cyanamid, Global, Toms River, and Tremley Point; remediated sites are GEMS, Helen Kramer, and Lipari.
Note: Percentages are those respondents who found condition so disturbing that they wanted to leave.

hazardous-waste sites and odors or smoke. The latter may also be partly associated with waste sites.

Table 6.2 shows that looks/design of the neighborhood, good housing, good schools, and convenience to work and friends/relatives were considered attractions by over 60 percent of respondents who lived near the GEMS, Helen Kramer, and Lipari sites. Forty-nine percent of all respondents rated their neighborhood as better than their previous one compared to 39, 44, and 54 percent of Americans, residents of northern New Jersey, and the Philadelphia region who rated their neighborhood as an improvement, respectively. Only 13 percent of residents of neighborhoods with hazardous-waste sites rated their neighborhood as worse.

Table 6.4 shows a strong association between number of problems

Table 6.4. Neighborhood Characteristics/Variables Associated with Poor Neighborhood Quality Rating Near Ten Hazardous-Waste Sites, 1992

Characteristic/Variable	Percentage	95% Confidence Limits
All respondents	3.4	2.0, 4.8
Problems:[a]		
Number of problems:		
0	0.0	0, 0
1–3	6.0	2.2, 9.8
4+	27.5	15.3, 39.8
Specific problems:		
Odors or Smoke	11.9	5.0, 18.8
Sites with hazardous waste	10.6	5.8, 15.4
Businesses, sewage treatment		
plants, other nonresidential	7.4	1.2, 13.6
Attractions:[b]		
Number of attractions:		
0	2.0	−1.7, 5.7
1–4	3.0	0.4, 5.6
5+	0.0	0, 0
Specific attractions:		
Looks/design of neighborhood	1.6	0.2, 3.0
Other public services	1.7	−0.2, 3.6
Good schools	1.9	0.2, 3.6
Convenience to public transportation	1.9	−0.7, 4.5
Convenience to leisure activities	2.4	0.3, 4.5
Convenience to friends/relatives	2.6	0.5, 4.7
Convenience to job	3.0	0.8, 5.2
House was key	3.1	1.0, 5.2

Source: Problems based on 683 responses from all ten New Jersey sites; attractions based on 377 responses from the GEMS, Helen Kramer, and Lipari sites.
[a]Percentage who rated their neighborhood as poor quality of those who found condition so disturbing that they wanted to leave. Only problems noted by at least 10 percent of respondents are listed. Fifteen of the 18 potential problems are not included.
[b]Percentage who rated their neighborhood as poor quality of those who found condition an attraction.

and poor quality. The proportion of poor quality ratings increased as the number of perceived problems increased. Those who identified no problems did not rate the neighborhood as poor quality. One to three problems were associated with 6 percent of respondents rating their neighborhood as poor, and four or more problems with 28 percent rating their neighborhood as poor quality.

What specific problems were most likely to be associated with poor neighborhood quality? Almost 12 percent of respondents who wanted to leave as a result of odors or smoke also rated their neighborhood as poor quality. The comparable percentages for hazardous-waste sites and businesses and other nonresidential land uses were 11 and 7 percent, respectively.

Amenities should reduce the likelihood of a neighborhood being labeled poor quality. Table 6.4 shows that the expected inverse relationship between attractions held for five or more attractions, but not for less.

With respect to preventing a low quality rating, table 6.4 suggests that looks/design of the neighborhood, other public services, good schools, and convenience to public transportation were the most protective. Conversely, 3 percent of those who were attracted by housing still rated their neighborhood as poor quality. Recapitulating, as in the other chapters, housing is not protective of neighborhood quality and good schools are a buffer.

Personal Filters

Table 6.5 lists seven respondent characteristics. In order of their likelihood to rate their neighborhood as poor quality, the four characteristics most strongly associated with a poor neighborhood quality rating were as follows: Brook neighborhood respondent (23.1 percent), present neighborhood is worse (19.8 percent), Global neighborhood respondent (9.7 percent), and renter (8.5 percent).

Remediation of Sites and Neighborhood Quality

Table 6.5 does not suggest that length of residence is a markedly important filter. Long-term residents were only slightly more likely to rate their neighborhoods' as poor quality (3.7 percent). The 95 percent confidence limits suggest that the differences could easily be explained by chance.

These results were misleading because length of residence was not controlled for type of site. Our hypothesis was that residents who lived near an unremediated site for more than a decade would be the most distressed and respondents who lived near a remediated hazardous-waste site for a short period of time would be the least distressed.

Table 6.6 presents the results controlled for site remediation. Eighty-four percent of those who had lived near GEMS, Helen Kramer, and Lipari—the three highly controversial remediated sites —for more than a decade acknowledged the presence of a hazardous-

Table 6.5. Respondent Characteristics/Responses Associated with Poor Neighborhood Quality Rating Near Ten Hazardous-Waste Sites, 1992

	Respondents Who Rated Neighborhood as Poor	
Characteristic/Response	Percentage	95% Confidence Limits
All respondents	3.4	2.0, 4.8
Neighborhood comparison:		
Present neighborhood is better	0.0	0, 0
Present neighborhood is the same or same neighborhood	2.3	0.5, 4.1
Present neighborhood is worse	19.8	11.4, 28.2
Age:		
18–30	4.0	0.1, 7.9
31–50	3.3	1.5, 5.1
51+	3.5	1.0, 6.0
Sex:		
Male	3.1	1.1, 5.1
Female	3.6	1.8, 5.5
Tenure:		
Owner	2.2	1.0, 3.4
Renter	8.5	3.7, 13.3
Length of residence, years:		
0–2	3.4	0.1, 6.7
>2–10	3.0	1.1, 4.9
>10	3.7	1.4, 6.0
Education:		
Grades 1–11	8.0	0.5, 15.5
High school graduate	5.0	2.1, 7.9
Some college or college	2.0	0.6, 3.4
Neighborhood of Residence:		
Bayonne	0.0	0, 0
Brook	23.1	0.2, 46.0
Global	9.7	2.9, 16.5
GEMS	5.3	1.5, 9.1
Tremley Point	3.2	−1.2, 7.6
Helen Kramer	2.5	−0.1, 5.9
Brick	2.0	−1.8, 5.8
Toms River	1.8	−1.7, 5.3
Cyanamid	0.0	0, 0
Lipari	0.0	0, 0

Source: Based on 683 responses from all ten neighborhoods in New Jersey.

Table 6.6. Responses of Residents Living Near Ten Hazardous-Waste Sites, 1992

Characteristic	Type of Site	Percentage and 95% Confidence Limits Based on Length of Residence		
		<2 years	*2–10 years*	*11+ years*
Site does exist	Unremediated[a]	37.7	66.5	83.8
		(25.7, 49.7)	(58.2, 74.8)	(77.2, 90.4)
	Remediated[b]	44.4	55.3	65.0
		(31.0, 57.8)	(48.0, 62.7)	(57.3, 72.7)
Site causes respondent to want to leave	Unremediated	20.6	28.5	36.7
		(10.6, 30.6)	(20.5, 36.5)	(28.1, 45.3)
	Remediated	5.7	14.2	27.0
		(−0.5, 11.9)	(9.0, 19.4)	(19.9, 34.2)
Percentage of respondents distressed by hazardous-waste site who rated neighborhood poor or fair quality	Unremediated	4.8	19.5	27.0
		(−0.5, 10.1)	(12.5, 26.5)	(19.1, 34.9)
	Remediated	3.8	6.2	20.8
		(−1.3, 9.0)	(2.6, 9.8)	(14.3, 27.3)

Source: Based on 683 responses from all ten neighborhoods in New Jersey.
[a]Unremediated sites are the Bayonne, Brick, Brook, Cyanamid, Global, Toms River, and Tremley Point sites.
[b]Remediated sites are the GEMS, Helen Kramer, and Lipari sites.

waste site in their neighborhood, compared to 38 percent who had lived in these same areas for less than two years (P < .01). The comparable percentages for the seven unremediated sites were 65 and 44 percent (P < .01). In other words, about three-fourths of respondents who lived near waste sites for more than a decade acknowledged the site's existence, compared to about 40 percent of those who lived near them for less than two years.

There was a greater difference in recognition that a waste site existed between long-term and short-term residents of neighborhoods with remediated sites than unremediated ones: 46 percent for remediated sites (84–38 percent) compared to 21 percent (65–44 percent) for unremediated ones. These data suggest that cleanup programs have substantially reduced perceived site-related hazards in the remediated neighborhoods. Even though unremediated sites are covered over by weeds and other green plants and therefore appear less dangerous than they did a decade ago, the seven unremediated sites conceivably pose a continuing health and environmental threat and are a symbolic irritating reminder to residents that the neighborhood did not have sufficient political power to demand a cleanup.

The greater stress caused by unremediated hazardous-waste sites is apparent in the third part of table 6.6. It reports the percentage of respondents who wanted to leave as a result of the hazardous-waste site and also rated their neighborhood as poor or fair quality. The difference between the unremediated and remediated sites was particularly notable among residents of two to ten years. Almost 20 percent who had moved into neighborhoods with unremediated sites were stressed by their waste site and rated their neighborhood as poor or fair quality, compared to only 6 percent of their counterparts living near remediated waste sites (P < .01).

Several responses suggested that this difference was related to frustrated people who had purchased property with the goal of selling it and moving into better housing. Because the nearby site stigmatized the neighborhood, they could not get the price to buy a better piece of property. For instance, an angry respondent who moved into a house near an unremediated site two to five years ago wrote that he "was advised that the landfill was a ski mountain being built by government officials." A second wrote that he was "extremely disturbed by the site. [The] landfill was not known to us. We moved from Philadelphia to escape a bad neighborhood, only to step into this mess."

Looking only at those who rated their neighborhood as poor quality, we found that not a single respondent out of fifty-three who had lived in a remediated neighborhood for less than two years rated their neighborhood as poor quality, compared to 1.7 percent who had lived near one of the former ticking time bombs from two to ten years, and 4.1 percent who had lived near one of them for more than a decade.

Although remediation doubtless played a role in removing the taint of living in a toxic neighborhood from the GEMS, Helen Kramer, and Lipari areas, the availability of inexpensive housing also seems to have played a central role in attracting newcomers. Seventy-seven percent (41 of 53) of new residents (<2 years) indicated that housing was an important consideration in attracting them to GEMS, Helen Kramer, and Lipari areas, compared to 61 percent (90 of 148) long-term residents (>10 years) (P < .05). About 50 of the 377 respondents appended statements to their questionnaires to explain why they moved to the area. The availability of inexpensive housing was mentioned more often than all the other factors combined: 12 who moved to the GEMS area, 9 near the Helen Kramer site, and 10 to the vicinity of Lipari. A recent migrant to the GEMS area wrote: "I was only able to buy a house and property because its adjacent to the landfill." A second wrote: "GEMS allowed us to buy more for [our] money."

It would be a mistake to assume that those who took advantage of the vacancies caused by the flight of people who feared the waste sites were oblivious to the waste sites. A thirty-one to fifty-year-old female college graduate wrote: "[We] had an EPA friend relate test results to us. This neighborhood is better than the last neighborhood." A second recent migrant agreed: "GEMS was cleaned up. More important, everyone knows there is not much crime or any problems in this area."

Three residents of the GEMS and Helen Kramer areas for more than twenty years felt assured that their health was not threatened. One wrote: "People in white suits [at Gems] were kind of scary. Traffic is now the big issue, not GEMS." A second concluded: "Helen Kramer's not a problem now. Burning and odors stopped, it is caped and fine now. What we need is better policing to control the drugs on the other side of the highway." A third wrote that she "liked the area. Its quiet, schools are good. I went to a meeting, and they said it is safe. Water tests show its okay."

Our finding that neighborhoods of remediated sites are no longer viewed as tainted by middle-class Americans was supported by housing-sales data. For example, in 1980 the median sales price of a home in Mantua Township, which contains Lipari and Helen Kramer, was 99 percent of the county value (Greenberg and Hughes 1992). In 1985, after Lipari and Helen Kramer were declared Superfund sites, the median sales price slipped to 96 percent of the county's. But by 1988 it was back up to 99 percent. Furthermore, these two sites have not disrupted sales. For instance, the number of homes sold in Mantua decreased from 85 in 1980 to 77 in 1985, but jumped up to 111 in 1988.

The township tax assessor confirmed our data and added that he knew of only one housing development that was abandoned because of the hazardous-waste sites. Furthermore, he added that Mantua had 36 percent of the new county (Gloucester) housing construction in 1992. In other words, this township with the number 1 and number 4 rated NPL sites in the United State is clearly seen as a good place to live by middle-class Americans.

Discriminant Analysis of Neighborhood Quality

To investigate potential associations among the problems, attractions, and personal filters, five stepwise discriminant analyses were done for the three remediated and five were done for the seven unremediated sites. We first present the baseline runs, then the results of the two sets of four heuristic runs.

Baseline Run for Unremediated Sites

The baseline run for the unremediated sites contained eighteen problems, no attractions, as well as age, gender sex, tenure, length of residence, education, seven neighborhoods of residence, and comparison of present and previous neighborhood. Twenty-three of the thirty-one potentially discriminating variables were statistically significant discriminators at $P < .05$ (table 6.7). Only one or two would have been expected to be statistically significant by chance. Measured by their F-values, inadequate street lighting ($F = 48.4$), occupied buildings in poor condition ($F = 41.9$), present neighborhood is worse ($F = 36.5$), and streets in need of repair ($F = 29.2$) were the most powerful discriminators.

We would not be surprised if the reader stopped at this point and assumed that we had accidentally copied the results from the east Elizabeth and Marcus Hook baseline runs. Blight variables were also the most powerful discriminators in those study areas. The apparent difference between this analysis of the seven unremediated site areas and the case studies of east Elizabeth and the Marcus Hook area is the absence of crime, unfriendly neighbors, uncontrolled animals—that is, the behavioral hazards—from this discriminant analysis.

Two functions help interpret the interrelationships among the discriminating variables in the baseline run. The first, like its counterparts in east Elizabeth and Marcus Hook, focused on poor neighborhood quality ratings. The six strongest correlates of the first function were as follows: inadequate street lighting ($r = .556$), occupied buildings in poor or dangerous condition ($r = .463$), streets in need of repair ($r = .377$), abandoned and boarded-up buildings ($r = .360$), litter or trash in the street ($r = .281$), and Brook neighborhood respondent ($r = .250$).

Table 6.7. Discriminant Analysis: Seven Neighborhoods Near Unremediated Hazardous-Waste Sites, Baseline Run

		Correlation of Variable with Function	
Variable	F-value	Poor Quality Blighted Function 1	Worse Neighborhood Function 2
Inadequate street lighting	48.4	.556	
Occupied buildings in poor or dangerous condition	41.9	.463	
Streets, roads, sidewalks in disrepair	29.2	.377	
Abandoned and boarded-up buildings	20.3	.360	
Litter or trash in the street, roads	20.1	.281	
Brook neighborhood respondent	5.4	.250	
Present neighborhood is worse	36.5		.564
Odors or smoke	20.1		.550
Businesses, gasoline station, other nonresidential	13.1		.471
Polluted water	14.6		.458
Hazardous-waste sites	14.6		.398
Cyanamid neighborhood respondent	7.5		.356
Renter	10.5		.279
Toms River Neighborhood respondent	3.7		−.260
Motor Vehicle Noise and Heavy Traffic	15.6		.252
Canonical correlation with neighborhood quality dependent variable (P-value)		.724 (.001)	.478 (.01)
Average standardized Z score with poor quality respondents		4.02	1.72

Source: Based on 306 responses from the Bayonne, Brick, Brook, Cyanamid, Global, Toms River, and Tremley Point sites.

Note: Variables with a correlation of >0.25 with one of the two functions are shown. All correlations shown were statistically significant discriminators at P < .05.

This first function shows that an unremediated hazardous-waste site may not be the most distressing characteristic in a neighborhood. Train noise and occupied buildings in poor or dangerous condition were more likely to motivate respondents to want to move from the Brook neighborhood (46 percent and 38 percent vs. 23 percent for the site), businesses and other nonresidential activities were more of a stress near the Cyanamid site (55 percent vs. 46 percent), odors or smoke distressed more people at Tremley Point (37 percent vs. 33 percent), and traffic congestion was an equally distressing problem in the Global area (29 percent).

Residents of the Brook area illustrate the perceptions of people who live in a neighborhood with a waste site and with behavioral and blight problems. Two males, aged fifty-one to seventy, residents of the neighborhood for more than a decade, described their assessments of the site and the neighborhood's major problems. One wrote: "Long ago it was a wool factory, then a bulb factory. The factory itself doesn't bother us, but the trucks ruin the street. Older people got to rent. When people move in, they live 3–4 families in a one family house, cars go with it, then fights." The second commented: "The plant, no, it doesn't affect us, not that I know of. This was a nice neighborhood, now its a transient neighborhood. Lots of unemployed and [they] don't give a damn about the neighborhood. Just a place to live for the time being. Dirty sidewalks, nothing maintained, people walk with booze in their hands, kids getting hurt."

The second function identified nine characteristics associated with respondents who perceived that their present neighborhood was worse than their previous one. It focused on people who perceived their present neighborhood as worse (r = .564), were troubled by odors or smoke (r = .550), businesses, gasoline stations, and other nonresidential land uses (r = .471), polluted water (r = .458), hazardous-waste sites (r = .398), and motor vehicle noise and heavy traffic (r = .252). These respondents tended to live in the Cyanamid neighborhood (r = .356), not in Toms River (r = −.260), and live in rental units (r = .279).

A female respondent who had lived in the Cyanamid area for two to five years but said she was moving in a week described her dissatisfaction with local industry, including Cyanamid's chemical works: "Cyanamid used to dump, and I used to drink that water. That and the other stuff around here make this area a living hell."

A Bayonne resident, a thirty-one to fifty-year-old female high school teacher with two master's degrees, summarized her ambivalence about living in a neighborhood that she considered worse than her previous one because of industrial activity: "My neighborhood is aesthetically and visually utopian for ugly Bayonne, except for chemicals. Trees, kids, gorgeous houses and yards, little traffic, wealthy people, great friends, but full of weird odors."

In contrast to these residents of the Cyanamid area and the Bayonne Chromium site, nineteen of fifty-five (35 percent) of Toms River respondents rated their neighborhood as excellent. Only one rated it as poor. Fifty-six percent knew the hazardous-waste site

Table 6.8. Discriminant Analysis: Three Neighborhoods Near Remediated Hazardous-Waste Sites, Baseline Run

		Correlation of Variable with Function	
		Poor vs.	*Poor vs.*
		Excellent/Good	*Fair*
		Quality	*Quality*
Variable	*F-value*	*Function 1*	*Function 2*
Hazardous waste sites	57.7	.549	
Businesses, electrical power, sewage treatment plants, other nonresidential	51.9	.521	
Motor vehicle noise and heavy traffic	48.1	.474	
Odors or smoke	58.9	.466	
Present neighborhood is worse	42.8	.463	
Streets, roads, sidewalks in disrepair	36.1	.411	
Traffic congestion	44.8	.403	
Polluted water	36.3	.395	
Lipari neighborhood respondent	15.6	−.295	
Looks/design of neighborhood	15.9	−.290	
Inadequate street lighting	19.7	.282	
Noise from airplanes and trains	32.8	.267	.354
Unfriendly neighbors	31.0		.479
Right-of-way for utility	13.6		.263
Canonical correlation with neighborhood quality dependent variable (P-value)		.739 (.001)	.500 (.01)
Average standardized Z score with poor quality respondents		5.00	3.59

Source: Based on 377 responses from the New Jersey GEMS, Helen Kramer, and Lipari sites.
Note: Variables with a correlation of >0.25 with one of the two functions are shown. All correlations shown were statistically significant discriminators at P < .05.

existed, yet nine (16 percent) wanted to leave as a result of it. The tree-lined streets, new housing, and beautiful neighborhood school more than compensated for some concern about the site.

A notable difference between the two functions is the concentration of blight-related variables in the poor quality neighborhood function and characteristics associated with land uses, such as hazardous-waste sites, odors or smoke, businesses, traffic, and polluted water with the worse neighborhood quality function.

Baseline Run for Remediated Sites

The baseline run for the three remediated sites contained eighteen problems, eight attractions, as well as age, gender, tenure, length of residence, education, three neighborhoods of residence, and comparison of present and previous neighborhood. Twenty-seven of the thirty-five potentially discriminating variables were statistically significant discriminators at P < .05 (table 6.8). Only one to two would have been expected to be statistically significant by chance.

The first function in this discriminant analysis is the only one in this book that did not begin with blight and crime variables. The strongest correlates of the first function were as follows: hazardous-waste site (r = .549), businesses and other nonresidential activities (r = .521), motor vehicle noise and heavy traffic (r = .474), and odors or smoke (r = .466). These five are massive technology sites, local activity spaces, or results of activities associated with these land uses.

Present neighborhood is worse (r = .463) was part of this poor neighborhood quality function. Residents who identified strongly with this poor quality neighborhood function also were stressed by streets and roads in need of repair (r = .411), traffic congestion (r = .403), polluted water (r = .395), inadequate street lighting (r = .282), and noise from airplanes and trains (r = .267). Finally, these respondents were not happy with the appearance of the neighborhood (r = −.290), and they were not residents of the Lipari neighborhood (r = −.295).

One distressed respondent who purchased a home near the GEMS site wrote about the landfill as part of her disappointing new neighborhood: "We moved from Philadelphia, loved the fresh air and single houses. The landfill, noisy neighbor with motorcycles and souped up cars destroyed our tranquil neighborhood." A second wrote: "The dump sucks. I've tried to sell and move up. But this was supposed to be a move-up."

These angry respondents were rare. Only 9 of 377 who responded to the GEMS, Helen Kramer, and Lipari surveys rated their neighborhood as poor quality. The flip side is represented by the 288 who rated their neighborhood as excellent or good. Three summarize the more typical sentiments we encountered. A female aged thirty-one to fifty with a college degree wrote: "The site (Helen Kramer) was bad, but they cleaned it up. People keep up their places and neighbors watch for each other." A second added: "I can't see GEMS. The water is safe. Schools are good, houses are kept up. We like the people." Another resident of the GEMS area compared it to Camden,

Table 6.9. Summary of Discriminant Analysis Runs, Ten Hazardous-Waste Sites, 1992

Sites Runs	Canonical Correlation Function		Percentage Correctly Classified	
	1	2	Total	Poor
Unremediated:				
Baseline (table 6.7)	.724	.478	76	79
Heuristic:				
Outsider perception	.298	—	54	64
Specific hazard type	.671	.433	73	71
Specific hazard type checkoff	.628	.293	71	79
Aggregate hazard burden	.636	.296	71	79
Remediated:				
Baseline (table 6.8)	.739	.500	89	89
Heuristic:				
Outsider perception	.486	—	79	89
Specific hazard type	.702	.169	87	78
Specific hazard type checkoff	.661	.125	79	67
Aggregate hazard burden	.678	.163	85	89

Source: Before runs based on 306 responses from 7 New Jersey sites, after runs based on 377 responses from 3 New Jersey sites.

where he had previously lived (see chapter 7 about Camden): "GEMS is not problem. Rather have GEMS than Camden."

The second function identified three characteristics associated with respondents who rate their neighborhood as poor quality rather than fair quality. It identified people who were stressed by unfriendly neighbors (r = .479), were troubled by noise from airplanes and trains (r = .354), and right-of-way for utility (r = .263).

Heuristic Runs

The four heuristics attempt to model people's thinking about their neighborhoods. The outsider perception heuristic assumes that insiders, like outsiders, focus on massive landscape features, in this chapter hazardous-waste sites. Table 6.9 compares the canonical correlations and accuracy of the classification produced by the baseline and four heuristics. The baseline analysis had slightly higher canonical correlations than any of the heuristics, and was as effective or more effective at classifying all respondents than the heuristics.

Again, the outsider perception heuristic was the worst model for both remediated and unremediated sites. In other words, knowing that someone is distressed by a hazardous-waste site is insufficient

Table 6.10. Neighborhood Characteristics and Neighborhood Quality Near Ten Hazardous-Waste Sites, 1992

Neighborhood Quality	Total Number Of Hazards (maximum is 10)	Specific Hazard Type (maximum is 4)	Hazardous Waste Site (1 = yes)
Excellent/good	0.5 (0.4, 0.6)	0.3 (0.3, 0.4)[a]	.14 (.11, .17)
Fair	2.6 (2.2, 3.1)	1.6 (1.4, 1.9)	.49 (.41, .58)
Poor	5.8 (4.3, 7.4)	2.7 (2.3, 3.1)	.74 (.55, .93)

Source: Based on 683 responses from all ten neighborhoods in New Jersey.
[a]Respondent gets a score of 1 for noting great distress with one indicator of a behavioral risk, blight, local activity space, and massive technology sites. For example, a respondent who expresses a desire to leave as a result of crime (behavioral risk), and airplane noise (massive technology site) would receive a score of 2.

to accurately predict how they will classify their neighborhood.

The two specific and aggregate hazard models were better than the outsider one at classifying respondents. The aggregate hazard burden model was the best of the four heuristics. It assumes that people do not care about categories of problems. Rather the greater the number of problems of any kind, the more likely they are to rate their neighborhood as poor quality. It accurately classified the same proportion of poor quality ratings as the baseline run.

Table 6.10 provides additional support for the aggregate heuristic model. A hazardous-waste site was identified as a major stress by 74 percent of respondents who rated their neighborhood as poor quality. This compared to 49 and 14 percent who rated their neighborhood as fair and excellent/good, respectively. The overlap of the 95 percent confidence limits show that the hazardous-waste site was not able to clearly distinguish between fair and poor quality rating.

The specific hazard type heuristic was better able to distinguish between fair and poor ratings, that is, none of the 95 percent confidence limits overlap. The average respondent who rated his or her neighborhood as poor quality identified 2.7 of the 4 hazard types (behavioral, blight, local activity space, massive technology site). The aggregate hazard variable, by far, was the best at distinguishing among the three quality groups of poor, fair, excellent/good. An average of only .5 problems were identified as distressing by respondents who rated their neighborhood as excellent or good, compared to 2.6 who rated their neighborhood as fair and 5.8 who rated their neighborhood as poor quality. In other words, respondents who lived near these ten hazardous-waste sites and rated their neighborhood as poor quality typically identified 4 to 7 major stresses in their neighborhoods, not just the hazardous-waste site.

Image Analysis of Remediated GEMS and Helen Kramer Sites

The fifty-four qualitative interviews at GEMS and Helen Kramer support the findings that behavioral and blight-related hazards are perceived to be a much greater threat by people who live near a remediated hazardous-waste site than the site itself. We asked respondents to imagine that they were walking, biking, or riding through a neighborhood that they dislike—that is, one they hate being in and would try to avoid. We then asked them to make a list of the feelings about this terrible neighborhood. We also asked them to make a list of their feelings about a great neighborhood, one they would go out of their way to spend time in.

Table 6.11 shows that the fifty-four people responded with 120 feelings about a great and 106 feelings about a terrible neighborhood. Unsafe-safe and ugly-beautiful dimensions dominated. Feelings of insecurity were responsible for 66 percent (70 of the 106) word associations with a terrible neighborhood; feelings of security accounted for 51 percent (61 of the 120) with a great neighborhood. The ugly-beautiful dichotomy accounted for 26 percent of the terrible (28 of 106) and 30 percent (36 of 120) of the great neighborhood feelings. Neighborliness was responsible for most of the remaining feelings about great and terrible neighborhoods.

The goal of this qualitative analysis was to determine the characteristics associated with the feelings of ugly and insecurity. How many feelings were associated with the hazardous-waste sites, antisocial behaviors, and blight? Respondents provided an average of about four word associations. Only seven of the two hundred word associations relate to pollution. Only two mentioned a nearby waste site. Both mentioned "Helen Kramer before remediation." One, a homeowner aged fifty-one to seventy, charged that "the dump is the biggest problem. Officials don't listen, payment doesn't come." This angry resident was one of the homeowners who had been promised money to compensate for alleged property devaluation. Although he was furious about the economic costs he associated with GEMS, he added many other distressing characteristics, including the follow-

Table 6.11. Images of Respondents Living in Two Neighborhoods with Remediated Hazardous-Waste Sites, 1993/94

Feelings and Images	Number of Responses
Terrible Neighborhood	
Unsafe: afraid, anger, can't leave my house, concerned, conflict, dislike, don't want to be there, fear, insecure, nervous, paranoid, pissed off, scared, tense, terrified, uncomfortable, uneasy, unsafe, want to run, worried	70
Unfriendly neighbors: nasty, terrible, unkind	6
Ugly: crowded, dark, dirty, disgusting, loud, noisy, repulsive, scummy, terrible unhealthy	28
All others:	2
Total	106
Great Neighborhood	
Safe: comfortable, cozy, contented, enjoy, fun, happy, peace-of-mind, positive, relaxed, safe, satisfied, secure, trusting, very good	61
Friendly neighbors: cheerful, concerned, cooperative, friendly, harmonious, helpful, neighborly	22
Beautiful: Beautiful, better, bright, decent, few people, good appearance, good, hills, mountains, nice, no commotion, open space, peaceful, pretty, quiet, trees	36
All others:	1
Total	120
Characteristics of a Terrible Neighborhood:	
Blight	69
Buildings: Abandoned houses, blighted buildings, boarded-up houses, crowded houses, defaced houses, rundown housing	(20)
Streets: broken, broken streets, dirty, grimy, no light, not enough light, potholes, unclean, unkempt	(19)
Trash: beer cans, cigarette butts, garbage, junk, litter, rusty barrels, trash	(20)
Other blight: abandoned cars, cars stripped, graffiti	(10)
Violence	
Crack, crime, dealers, dope, drugs, fighting, guns, innocent hurt, killing, mugging, robbery, robbing	47
Vagrants	
Alcoholics, bums, drinking, drunks, foul-language, gangs, homeless, loitering, sleeping in street, unemployed hanging around	33
Government	
Bad government, cops seem irresponsible, corrupt business, corrupt government, high taxes, insufficient signs, lack of facilities, lack of facilities for kids, lack of recreation facilities, not enough police, too many cops	19
Motor-vehicle operations	
Cars on front lawn, car noise, cars racing around, horns honking, traffic	10
Pollution	
Bad manufacturing nearby, dirty air, Helen Kramer before remediation, living near a refinery, loud noise from factory, unhealthy environment	7
Other appearance	
Cement, no privacy, no trees too many people	11
Other	4
Total	200

Source: Based on open-ended interviews with twenty-eight residents near the New Jersey GEMS site and twenty-six interviews near the New Jersey Helen Kramer site.

ing ending statement: "We've been robbed. Police don't seem to care." The second respondent, a former city planner, said that "Helen Kramer is a major negative—puts children at higher risk." He then added that GEMS is a problem, but not the worst problem in the area.

These two respondents were a clear minority. We had to prompt the vast majority of respondents to get them to talk about the waste site. They had other concerns. Table 6.11 shows blight and crime dominated their images of a terrible neighborhood. Sixty-nine of the two hundred word associations were about blight and forty-seven were about violence. The images described are the problems of residents of east Elizabeth, the Marcus Hook area, Camden, and residents of the Brook area. Some of these concerns crept into the imagery of our waste-site neighborhood respondents because of their previous neighborhoods. One commented: "I see it (Helen Kramer) through the trees, but we aren't affected. Crime, crooked politicians, lack of facilities for kids—like where I lived before—are our problems."

A second said: "There's no odor anymore at the site. I came from Philadelphia where there were guns and killing. This is a nice place, great people who take care of the property. I'm contented." A third remarked: "We came from s.w. Philadelphia. It's really much better here. I forget it's (Helen Kramer) there. Schools are excellent." And a fourth added the same idea: "Don't hear much about it (Helen Kramer). It's not really on my mind. I came from Camden where there was crime, dirt, and stripping of cars."

While commenting on American society as a whole, an elderly male respondent summarized his feelings about nearby GEMS: "GEMS is the least of our problems."

Summary of Findings

RQ1: *How do people who live in the immediate vicinity of potentially hazardous land uses and activities rate their neighborhoods?*

Only 3 percent of respondents who lived near the ten hazardous-waste sites rated their neighborhoods as poor quality. This was about the same as their counterparts in the United States as a whole, northern New Jersey, and the Philadelphia metropolitan area.

RQ2: *What factors most influence neighborhood ratings, especially rating of a neighborhood as poor?*

Crime was not a major issue in these neighborhoods, yet it was acknowledged by respondents as part of the image of a terrible neighborhood. Many respondents had moved from nearby cities were crime was prevalent. Blight was noted in several areas, and when present was considered a bigger problem than a hazardous-waste site.

Hazardous-waste site was the most frequently cited problem because all the areas we chose had a hazardous-waste site. Unremediated sites were a bigger concern than remediated ones. Sewage treatment plants, major roads, tank farms, and other massive technology sites were problems in some neighborhoods. They combined with a hazardous-waste site to lower neighborhood quality to fair and much less frequently to poor.

Length of residence was a surrogate for exposure to the history of the waste site and helped explain responses to remediated and unremediated hazardous-waste sites. Seventy-five percent of those who had lived near a hazardous-waste site for more than a decade acknowledged the existence of the site, compared to 40 percent who lived near one for less than two years. Residents who lived near remediated sites for less than two years were the least stressed and least likely to rate their neighborhoods as fair or poor quality (4 percent), and those who lived near unremediated ones for more than a decade were the most likely to be distressed and rate their neighborhood as poor or fair quality (27 percent).

The outsider perception model, which assumes that neighborhood residents focus on the kinds of hazards that outsiders see, was a poor predictor of neighborhood quality. The aggregate hazard burden model, which assumes that the greater the number of hazards, irrespective of type, the greater the likelihood of a poor quality rating, was the best of the heuristics.

7

Painful, Violent Landscapes

Camden was a city of patriots. A major cog in the World War II machine, tens of thousands of men labored in the Camden shipyards to build ships. Camden also made Campbell Soup and Esterbrook pens, household items in many American homes. In 1950, Camden's population was 125,000, with more than 30,000 people employed in manufacturing.

Images of Camden

Camden's role quickly changed after the war ended. The shipyards all but closed, and many of the shipyard workers developed asbestosis, mesothelioma, and lung cancer. The city lost more than two-thirds of its manufacturing jobs. In addition, it lost 60 percent of its retailing employment and a third of its wholesaling jobs. The increase of a few hundred service jobs did not compensate for these loses.

The patriotic "Rosie the riveter" jobs that were the essence of our image of Camden have been replaced by mostly low-paying service and laborer jobs. Few Camden residents work in managerial and executive positions. In 1970, 23 percent of Americans classified their jobs as professional and managerial, and in 1990, more than 30 percent said they worked in professional and managerial occupations. In Camden, the proportions were 12 and 14 percent, respectively.

Camden's population fell from 125,000 in 1950 to 103,000 in 1970 and to 87,000 in 1990. By 1990, the population was 57 percent black and most of the rest of the residents identified themselves as Hispanic. Although the population of the United States became older, Camden's population became younger. In 1990, 37 percent of the population was less than eighteen years old and the proportion was increasing.

Poverty in Camden is brutal. Camden is New Jersey's sixth largest city and its poorest. Thirty-seven percent of Camden's residents have incomes less than the federal government poverty level. Among cities with 50,000 people or more, Camden rated fifth in this painful indicator. Greenberg, Schneider, and Martell (1994) analyzed the economic stress of all 436 Northeast and Midwest U.S. cities with populations of 25,000 to 500,000. Using twenty-one demographic and economic variables to measure economic stress, they ranked the 436 cities from most (436) to least (1) stressed. Camden ranked 430. In short, whether compared to cities in the United States, Northeast, or Midwest, or to New Jersey, Camden is a city with few economic resources and tremendous economic burdens.

Violence in New Jersey is centered in places like Camden. Researchers have found that murder and other forms of violence flourish in unstable personal, neighborhood, and regional environments (Dodge, Bates, and Petit 1990; Gelles 1973; Hinkle and Loring 1977; Leighton 1959; Zabrin et al. 1986). Numerous destabilizing factors impacted life in cities like Camden during the 1980s and 1990s: increased availability of firearms and illegal drugs; more poverty and segregation; limited educational and employment opportunities; withdrawal of police, fire, and health services; increased mass media emphasis on violence; lack of family planning and other prevention services; siting of LULUs, such as trash to steam incinerators; and rapid formation and spread of TOADS, such as abandoned houses.

All of these destabilizing activities increased the probability of violent behavior and deadly outcomes in a city as debilitated as Camden. As part of a health study of violence, we calculated age-adjusted death rates for Camden and the rest of New Jersey (minus Camden, Newark, and Trenton) for the period 1985–90 (Greenberg and Schneider 1994; Schneider and Greenberg 1994). Five specific categories of violent death were chosen as representative of urban violence based on the *International Classification of Diseases* (ICD-8 and ICD-9): falls, fires, homicides, poisonings (including overdoses from illegal drugs), and suicides. Fatal falls and fires were expected to be high in areas with dilapidated and deteriorated housing, abandoned buildings, and lots strewn with garbage. Homicides were expected to express rage turned outward, and poisoning and suicide were expected to represent raged turned inward.

The United States government prepared a 1987 baseline and year 2000 goals for death rates for all Americans (Department of Health and Human Services 1991). We make fifteen comparisons between Camden, the rest of New Jersey, and the United States. The comparisons in table 7.1 are striking. Camden's resident death rates for all people from homicide, poisoning, falls, and fire are three to eight times the year 2000 objectives for the United States. Only the suicide target has already been met, with the notable exception of males aged twenty to thirty-four.

The data for young black men is the most striking. Camden's rates are two to three times the rates calculated for young black males in the rest of New Jersey. In contrast to Camden, the rest of New Jersey has already met the year 2000 goals for homicide and suicide and is close to the national targets for poisoning, falls, and fire deaths. This shows the seriousness of Camden's problems. The city not only has overwhelming economic and social stress but terrible violence as well.

Our new image of Camden is not based on the employment, population, or death rates, although all of them create a depressing visage. Camden's painful physical landscape is the core of our image. The problems of TOADS and LULUs described in chapter 1 are magnified in Camden. Much of Camden's industrial plant is abandoned, derelict, rusting, and collapsing. Scrap of all sorts is found where workers once built war ships. But the abandoned housing in Camden seems even worse than the rotting industrial plant and scrap heaps because of its prevalence. More than 20 percent of the city's housing is abandoned. Some blocks have mostly abandoned and deteriorating houses. These numerous industrial and residential TOADS give the impression that the entire city is a throwaway.

The blighted landscape in Camden worsened during the 1980s and 1990s. For example, the proportion of vacant housing units doubled between 1980 and 1990. A *Time* magazine article featured Camden as a place where "only people with no other choice" would live (Fedarko 1992:21). The article describes the problems of crime and

Table 7.1. Comparisons of Camden, Rest of New Jersey, and United States: Selected Causes of Violent Death

Cause of Death	Population	Death Rate per 100,000			
		Camden	Rest of New Jersey	United States	
		1985–1990	1985–1990	1987	2000
Homicide	All people	31.4	3.6	8.5	7.2
	Children <4	6.6	2.2	3.9	3.1
	Black men, 15–34	82.2	34.7	90.5	72.4
	Black women, 15–34	27.7	12.8	20.0	16.0
Poisoning	All people	12.2	3.6	3.8	3.0
Falls	All people	7.3	3.5	2.7	2.3
Fires	All people	9.9	1.4	1.5	1.2
	Children <4	16.4	2.0	4.4	3.3
	All 65+	20.5	3.8	4.4	3.3
	Black men	10.3	3.9	5.7	4.3
	Black women	6.8	2.8	3.4	2.6
Suicide	All people	9.0	9.0	11.7	10.5
	Youth 15–19	8.4	7.3	10.3	8.2
	Males 20–34	27.4	19.1	25.2	21.4
	White males 65+	35.8	28.3	46.1	39.2

Source: The source for the United States figures is *Healthy People 2000* 1990.
Note: The rest of New Jersey includes all of New Jersey, expect the cities of Camden, Newark, and Trenton.

abandoned properties, but it also emphasizes that Camden is now the place to site facilities that no one else wants, such as the Camden County incinerator, prisons, and a sewage treatment plant. It is difficult to avoid the conclusion that Camden, like south Chester, has become a place for land uses and people that mainstream Americans do not want located near them. Apropos this observation, a *New York Times* article (Gray 1992) complemented Rutgers University for providing training for Peace Corps volunteers in Camden. The article quoted a Rutgers professor as seeing Camden as "perfect training for the third world" (B5). One of the trainees observed that he "had no idea that things could be this bad in this country. I'm embarrassed and I'm ashamed."

Choice of Neighborhoods

We chose census tract 10 in Camden (fig. 7.1), which we will also call east Camden. Tract 10 is about three-fifths of a square mile in area and in the year 1990 had a population of fifty-five hundred. It

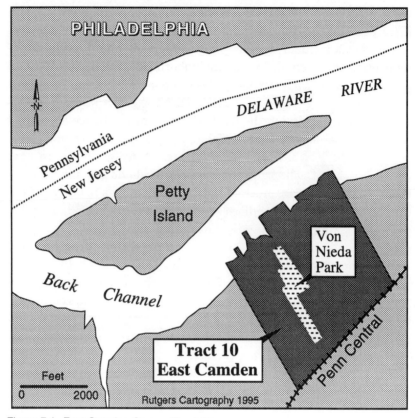

Figure 7.1. East Camden Census Tract 10

is bordered on the north by Pennsauken Township, on the west by the Delaware River.

Problems in east Camden are obvious. A railroad line forms its eastern edge. During our second visit, one train sat on the tracks, another slowly rumbled through, making our conversation difficult. Unlike many rail lines that run through neighborhoods in the urban Northeast, this right-of-way has no buffer of trees or fencing. Debris and assorted garbage were strewn along the right-of-way. Stray dogs crossed the tracks. Factories sit on the other side of the railroad line. A water treatment facility is found in the northwest corner. Its tanks and part of the water line are visible along the western edge of the tract. An old abandoned landfill lies about one-half mile south of the tract.

Dogs roam throughout east Camden. Residents told us that people leave their unwanted dogs in Camden. One dog, perhaps one of these jilted pets, bit the first author, leading to rabies shots. Probably because of this incident, roaming dogs supersede blight as his dominant image of tract 10. In most neighborhoods, the dogs, train and water treatment facilities would be the most distressing problems. But not in tract 10. Blight and crime are the major stresses. About 10 percent of housing in the tract is abandoned, a figure about half the proportion for the City of Camden. The appearance and cause of the blight is what is so frightening. Many buildings in east Camden are not collapsing because landlords do not take care of them. In other words, much of north Camden does not suffer from the classical tenement landlord syndrome (Sternlieb 1966). Instead, perfectly sound single-family houses on residential streets are stripped and burned out. Residents explained that "drug vandals" wait for someone to die or go on vacation. The vandals attack, stripping the aluminum siding and pulling out the copper plumbing and fixtures. They set fire to the house and take the vandalized metals to a recycling facility in an adjacent town. One resident pointed to a pleasant looking, single-family house about two hundred feet from her house and indicated that the elderly man who owned the house had died. Vandals were expected to attack the house within the next few weeks. Long-term residents always inform each other and the police if they are going to be out of town for more than a day. Unfortunately, this is not always effective in protecting their properties.

Evidence of efforts to prevent crime were apparent. The nearby school had rolls of curbed razor wire on the top of the fence. Residents had the usual Keep Out and Beware of Dog signs. One house featured the following creative message: "Due to the high crime rate, we will not answer the door unless we are expecting someone. Please call if you desire an appointment with us."

Residents described some of the successes and failures in their "war" against drug-related crime. For instance, one of the successes was the use of a police helicopter to track the dealers and the deals. In fact, the helicopter was overhead during our second visit. One resident wrote: "We have lots of drug traffic, but its lightened up since the helicopter has been patrolling the area." In another neighborhood, in another city, a noisy helicopter flying over the neighborhood would bring protests. In east Camden, like Belfast (Northern Ireland), many residents welcomed the sound.

Other efforts to control crime were less successful. Residents described the building of a police substation in the neighborhood in November 1992. Drug dealers waited until it was constructed, broke in, stole the air-conditioning unit, and burned it down the night before it was scheduled to open. Residents expected the police to rebuild.

The effects of blight and crime are evident in east Camden's mortality statistics. Tract 10 has a higher age-adjusted death rate from violent causes than the city as a whole. The death rate from fires and falls is three times the rate of the city, and the death rate from homicide and drugs is about three-fourths of the city's rate.

Yet tract 10 has attractions, a fact that makes it preferable to other areas of beleaguered Camden. Von Nieda Park is a thirty-acre linear green area. Much of the housing around the park was built during the 1970s, new housing by Camden standards. The neighborhood has good bus service and many churches. The comprehensive master plan for Camden (Wallace et al. 1977) said that "census tract 10 is one of the two neighborhoods in the city that is closer to being a stage 1 community in terms of homogeneity of population, of high level of homeownership, and of social cohesiveness."

In other words, east Camden is one of the few places in this city where we expected a sense of neighborhood. This sense was conveyed by the people who spoke with us. For example, an eighteen to thirty-year-old woman remarked: "At the present time our neighborhood suffers from several bad conditions (crime, drugs, distasteful neighbors). However, I believe if we worked together, as a concerned community, the neighborhood could improve."

East Camden's population is among the poorest of any community described in this book. The 1989 per capita income of New Jersey's population was $18,714 (Department of Commerce 1992). The comparable figures for tract 10 was $8,079. Twenty-five percent of the state's population graduated college, compared to only 5 percent in the study area. Tract 10 contains a wide variety of ethnic/racial groups. In 1990, 31 percent of the tract's population was black and 43 percent was Hispanic. Overall, even though east Camden has a few industrial and commercial sites, it was the area we expected to be most besieged by the pain of crime and blight.

Survey Questions, Methods, Problems, and Returns

Ten attractions, six personal characteristics, and nineteen hazards were included in our survey instrument. Seventeen of the nineteen clearly were present. We did not observe a metal or furniture plant, or a chemical plant, refinery or tank farm. The main utility right-of-way for the water plant is visible yet seemed pleasantly green. The closed landfill, which is located about one-half mile south of tract 10, was also not expected to be much of a problem because so many other problems were located within the tract itself. We used these four land uses to identify unusually sensitive people. In other words, these should be identified as problems by few people.

We used crime and abandoned housing to identify the proportion of respondents who were insensitive to an obvious stress. That is, no one should indicate that crime or abandoned housing were not present.

We attempted to place an instrument in every occupied dwelling unit within one-quarter mile of the water line, the railroad right-of-way, and on the streets adjacent to two corners identified as locations where drugs were sold, and those bordering Von Nieda Park.

We undertook the east Camden survey with the expectation that we would obtain a low response rate and biased responses for two reasons. Thirty-seven percent of the population lived in rental units. Many of these units were owned by a single company, which did not provide a place where an instrument could be safely left. We spoke with a representative of the company who explained that the company constructed front-door mail slots to reduce stealing. She could not think of an easy way to deliver the instrument to apartment dwellers. Neither could local postal officials, who warned us not to place the instrument in the mail slot. We left surveys on the front step of these apartments, under a door mat when one was present. Yet we were not sanguine about a high return. Second, 19 percent of the study area's population indicated in the 1990 U.S. Census that they "did not speak English very well."

We distributed one thousand surveys on December 15, 1993. A total of 158 useful responses (15.8 percent) were received by March 14, 1993. East Camden had the lowest response rate of any of our study areas. Respondents were not representative of all fifty-five hundred residents of east Camden. Seventy-seven percent of respondents graduated high school, compared to 47 percent of area residents (P < .01); 72 percent were female, compared to 51 percent of residents (P < .01); and 73 percent were homeowners, compared to 60 percent of area residents (P < .01). Six percent of respondents and 8 percent of residents were more than seventy years old. Twenty-two percent of respondents and 33 percent of residents were eighteen to thirty years old (P<.01). Finally, we note that 49 percent of area residents had lived in the same house and 86 percent in the same county for at least five years compared to 67 percent of respondents who had lived in the neighborhood for at least five years. Overall, our respondents were more likely to be female, educated at least through high school, middle-aged, and homeowners than the population of the area as a whole.

Neighborhood Quality

Twenty-five percent of east Camden respondents rated their neighborhood as poor quality (table 7.2). Another 42 percent rated their neighborhood as fair, 31 percent as good, and only 1 percent (two people) rated it as excellent. Only Elizabethport (chapter 5) and the Main and River areas of Chester (chapter 4) had such a large proportion of poor and fair neighborhood quality ratings.

More than 70 percent of east Camden respondents reported at least one characteristic that was so distressing that they wanted to leave (table 7.3). Crime was identified by 46 percent of respondents. Many wrote notes describing their fears. For instance, a male aged thirty-one to fifty crossed out our rating of 4 (poor) and wrote in 5 and the word "disgraceful." He focused on the crime problem in a written note: "No one is safe outdoors. Crime is rampant. Drugs are on every corner and also in schools zones. Robbers are everywhere. There is no safe place in this city fit to live in." Blight caused 44 percent of respondents to want to leave the neighborhood. One respondent wrote: "This neighborhood is not that bad, but there is an abandoned burned up house right next door to me that bothers me to no end!!"

Overall, the proportion of respondents in east Camden who were distressed by crime was the highest we observed in our neighborhood studies, and the proportion stressed by abandoned housing was the second highest (after the Chester Main area). Litter or trash,

Table 7.2. Neighborhood Quality in East Camden Compared with Other Study
Neighborhoods

Year	Neighborhood	Percentage Neighborhood Quality Ratings and 95% Confidence Limits			
		Excellent	Good	Fair	Poor
1993	East Camden	1.3	31.0	42.4	25.3
	(n = 158)	(–.5, 3.1)	(23.8, 38.2)	(34.7, 50.1)	(18.5, 32.1)
1992–94	Other nineteen study neighborhoods				
	(n = 1,262)	16.0	44.0	30.3	9.7
		(14.0, 18.0)	(41.3, 46.7)	(27.8, 32.8)	(8.1, 11.3)

Source: East Camden ratings are based on 158 respondents.

inadequate street lighting, dogs and other uncontrolled animals, and streets and roads in need of repair were also noted as major stresses by more than 25 percent of respondents.

A utility right-of-way, metal or furniture plant, chemical plant/refinery/tank farm, and landfill/hazardous-waste site were major problems for less than 6 percent of respondents. The minimal attention to these four land uses is notable because these were the four selected to signal the presence of unusually sensitive respondents. The fact that the water plant and line were a problem for only 6 percent of respondents confirms the greater concern with crime and blight and the fact that the plant is located along the edge of the tract. In fact, only one respondent mentioned it specifically in a written note. He complained about "periodic odors."

We expected to find crime and blight identified by all respondents. We did not. Forty-four percent did not perceive that crime existed in their neighborhood and 27 percent did not acknowledge abandoned housing. In fact, 18 percent (29) of respondents perceived that neither crime or abandoned houses existed in their neighborhood. We studied the geographical distribution of these seemingly 29 highly insensitive people. We did not find a geographical cluster. We did find a plausible explanation. Twenty of the 29 respondents rated their present neighborhood as better than their previous one and were residents of tract 10 for two to ten years. Only 10.8 of these responses were expected by chance (P < .01). Furthermore, 55 percent (11 of 20) of these risk-insensitive respondents were attracted by convenience to work, compared to 38 percent for the other

Table 7.3. Prevalence of Neighborhood Characteristics, East Camden, 1993

Characteristic	Percentage of Respondents
Problems:[a]	70.2
High crime rate	46.2
Abandoned houses	44.3
Litter or trash in the street, elsewhere	31.6
Inadequate street lighting	27.8
Dogs, cats, uncontrolled animals	26.6
Streets, roads, sidewalks in disrepair	25.9
Motor vehicle noise and heavy traffic	21.5
Occupied buildings in poor or dangerous condition	20.3
Unfriendly neighbors	19.6
Abandoned factories and businesses	14.6
Odors or smoke	11.4
Train or airplane noise	10.1
Recreational facilities that attract rowdy people	8.2
Junkyard, gasoline station, other nonresidential	7.6
Sewage or water treatment plant	6.3
Chemical plant, oil refinery, tank farm	5.7
Metal or furniture plant	5.1
Landfills or hazardous-waste sites	5.1
Right-of-way for utility	4.4
Attractions:[b]	
House was inexpensive/inherited	66.5
Convenient to public transport	50.0
Convenient to friends/relatives	44.9
Convenient to hospital	40.5
Convenient to job	40.5
Convenient to religious activity	34.0
Convenient to shopping	27.2
Other public services	26.6
Good schools	25.9
Convenient to leisure activities	19.6
Neighborhood comparison:	
Present neighborhood is better	35.3
Present neighborhood is same	39.7
Present neighborhood is worse	25.0

Source: Based on 158 responses.
[a]Percentage who found condition so disturbing that they wanted to leave.
[b]Percentage who gave these as reasons they live in the neighborhood.

respondents (P = .16). In comparison, these 20 respondents were less drawn to the other nine attractions than their 138 counterparts. It is plausible that east Camden is considered such a convenient place by some people that they do not acknowledge the shortcomings of their environment.

Table 7.3 shows that inexpensive housing and convenience to public transportation were attractions for at least half of respondents. In strong contrast, convenience to leisure activities, good schools, and other public services were attractions to less than 27 percent of respondents. These were the lowest proportions of any neighborhood in this research. Obviously, Von Nieda Park was not the attraction we had expected. Residents described two problems with it. One said: "Von Nieda is pretty, but it was a tributary of the Delaware that was filled. It floods every time we have a heavy rain. It floods River Road, Pierce, Harrison." A second resident complained about the "noise from loud car radios of people in there [Von Nieda Park] who then drive through the neighborhood."

Good schools were attractive to only 26 percent of respondents. One wrote: "The condition of the public schools is poor. I prefer to take my son to private school in another town." Other public services, such as police and fire were an attraction to only 27 percent of respondents. In fact, more than a dozen people complained about insufficient police protection. A typical sentiment we heard in the streets and read in the comments was written by a fifty-one to seventy-year-old male: "Drugs on all streets. No police. Gun-shots every night. No police. They ride by." But comments were not confined to police services. For example, an eighteen to thirty-year-old female wrote: "We need more activity centers, safer streets—get rid of pot holes, more cops, shopping centers, get rid of drug dealers, stricter laws on drug pushers."

A female aged thirty-one to fifty who had lived in the neighborhood for more than a decade complained about the lack of support from the city. "If I had the money, I would move in a minute. At one point we had 15 burglaries in a 12 day period of time. You have to watch all night long. It's horrible at times. No one listens to us. No one helps us. My neighbors are good people who want to change things. We can't do it alone."

Thirty-five percent of east Camden respondents rated their neighborhood better than their previous one, compared to 39, 44, and 54 percent of Americans, residents of northern New Jersey, and the Philadelphia region, respectively.

Table 7.4 shows a strong association between number of problems and poor quality. Forty-six respondents were not distressed by any problems. Only one of these (2.2 percent) rated the neighborhood as poor quality. The proportion of poor quality ratings rose rapidly as the number of perceived problems increased. Twenty-two percent of those who perceived one to four problems rated their neighborhood as poor quality, 48 percent of those who listed five to nine problems rated their neighborhood unfavorably, and 75 percent of respondents with ten or more serious problems rated their neighborhood as poor.

What specific problems were most likely to be associated with poor neighborhood quality? Blight and behavioral problems were dominant. For instance, 70 percent of those who identified abandoned factories and businesses and 63 percent who felt occupied buildings in poor or dangerous condition were major problems also rated their neighborhood as poor quality. Unfriendly neighbors (52 percent) was the most strongly associated behavioral characteristic associated with poor quality ratings. Uncontrolled animals (50 percent) and crime (48 percent) were also strongly associated behavioral problems in east Camden.

Attractions should reduce the likelihood of a neighborhood being labeled poor quality. Table 7.4 suggests that good schools were the most protective amenity. Only 12 percent of those who rated their school as an attraction also rated their neighborhood as poor quality. Unfortunately, only one-fourth of respondents feel that the schools are good. Two-thirds thought housing was inexpensive. Yet 29 percent of those who were attracted by inexpensive housing still rated their neighborhood as poor quality. In other words, like other neighborhoods in this study, inexpensive housing is not protective of neighborhood quality. One female respondent aged seventy-plus who rated the neighborhood as poor quality stated what we heard from some residents on the street of Camden and other cities: "All the houses were excellent when built and purchased in 1961. Most of those homeowners have fled to suburbs—the sorry few, like me 'hungin.' We have bars on our windows and a dog. Fear of consequences prevent my fuller cooperation with you."

Personal Filters

Table 7.5 lists six respondent characteristic variables. The perception that the present neighborhood was better than the previous one was the only characteristic that was protective. Nine percent of respondents who rated their present neighborhood as better also rated it as poor. In sharp contrast, 41 percent of respondents who rated it as worse concluded that their neighborhood was poor quality.

Table 7.4. Neighborhood Characteristics/Variables Associated with Poor Neighborhood Quality Rating, East Camden, 1993

Characteristic/Variable	Percentage	95% Confidence Limits
All respondents	25.3	18.5, 32.1
Problems:[a]		
Number of problems:		
0	2.2	−2.0, 6.4
1–4	21.9	12.4, 31.4
5–9	47.8	27.4, 68.2
10+	75.0	53.8, 96.2
Specific problems:		
Abandoned factories and businesses	69.6	50.8, 88.4
Odors or smoke	66.7	44.9, 88.5
Occupied buildings in poor or dangerous conditions	62.5	45.7, 79.3
Motor vehicle noise and heavy traffic	52.9	36.1, 69.7
Unfriendly neighbors	51.6	34.0, 69.2
Dogs, cats, and other uncontrolled animals	50.0	34.9, 65.1
Litter or trash in streets, on empty lots, or properties	48.0	34.2, 61.9
High crime rate	47.9	36.4, 59.4
Abandoned houses	47.1	35.4, 58.8
Streets, roads, sidewalks in disrepair or open ditches	46.3	31.0, 61.6
Inadequate street lighting	38.6	24.2, 53.0
Train or airplane noise	37.5	13.8, 61.2
Attractions:[b]		
Number of attractions:		
5–10	16.1	7.0, 25.3
1–4	31.8	21.9, 41.7
0	27.3	1.0, 53.6
Specific attractions:		
Good schools	12.2	2.2, 22.2
Convenient to shopping	16.3	5.3, 27.3
Convenient to religious activities	16.4	6.6, 26.2
Other public services	19.0	7.1, 30.9
Convenient to leisure activities	19.4	5.5, 33.3
Convenient to friends/relatives	19.7	10.5, 29.0
Convenient to public transportation	21.5	12.4, 30.6
Convenient to job	21.9	11.8, 32.0
Convenient to hospital	23.4	13.0, 33.8
House was inexpensive or inherited	28.6	20.0, 37.2

Source: Based on 158 responses.

[a]Percentage who rated their neighborhood as poor quality of those who found condition so disturbing that they wanted to leave. Those who cited inexpensive housing still rated their neighborhood as poor quality. Only problems noted by at least 10 percent of respondents are listed.

[b]Percentage who rated their neighborhood as poor quality of those who found condition an attraction.

Table 7.5. Respondent Characteristics Associated with Poor Neighborhood Quality Rating, East Camden, 1993

	Respondents Who Rated Neighborhood as Poor	
Characteristic	Percentage	95% Confidence Limits
Comparison of present and previous neighborhood:		
Present neighborhood is better	9.1	1.5, 16.7
Present neighborhood is the same or same neighborhood	29.0	17.7, 40.3
Present neighborhood is worse	41.0	25.6, 56.4
Age:		
18–30	32.4	16.7, 48.1
31–50	25.3	15.5, 35.1
51+	20.4	9.1, 31.7
Sex:		
Male	26.7	13.8, 39.6
Female	24.8	16.8, 32.8
Tenure:		
Owner	23.3	15.6, 31.0
Renter	28.2	14.1, 42.3
Length of residence (years):		
0–2	23.8	5.6, 42.1
>2–10	13.0	5.0, 21.0
>10	37.7	26.3, 49.1
Education:		
Grades 1–11	22.2	8.6, 35.8
High school graduate	28.6	16.0, 41.3
Some college or college	23.5	13.7, 33.3

Source: Based on 158 responses.

Discriminant Analysis of Neighborhood Quality

Tables 7.6 to 7.8 present the discriminant analysis runs. We describe the baseline run and summarize the results of the four heuristic runs.

Baseline Run

The baseline run contained nineteen problems, ten attractions, as well as age, gender, tenure, length of residence, education, and comparison of present and previous neighborhood. Twenty of the thirty-five potentially discriminating variables were statistically significant discriminators at P < .05. Only one to two would have been expected to be statistically significant by chance.

The first function in the baseline run (table 7.6) contrasts respondents who rated their neighborhood as poor quality with those who rated tract 10 as excellent/good. It identifies respondents who perceived their present neighborhood as worse than their previous one (r = .581), were troubled by abandoned houses (r = .559), inadequate street lighting (r = .453), crime (r = .377), and streets and roads in disrepair (r = .290). We labeled this the "worse versus better neighborhood" function. In other words, respondents who perceived their neighborhood was excellent or good believed it was a better neighborhood than their previous one and were not troubled by abandoned houses, inadequate street lighting, crime, and streets in need of repair.

Two pairs of respondents illustrate that people can see the same environment differently because of their previous neighborhoods. The first was from a female aged eighteen to thirty who rated the neighborhood as poor and her present neighborhood as worse: "When I came to this neighborhood it wasn't that bad. But it gets worse every single day. I cannot have my children play outside any more." The second response is from a female aged thirty-one to fifty who wanted to leave as result of crime yet rated her present neighborhood as good and better than her previous neighborhood: "The neighborhood would be a lot cleaner if everyone got together and kept their own property clean."

These women lived on the same block, as did the following two respondents. One, who rated his neighborhood as poor and previous neighborhood as better, wrote: "Burn it down and start over." The second rated this same neighborhood as good and better than her previous one: "I (have) lived in Camden for 20 years, and for me this is the best place I found."

The second function in the baseline run has four strong correlates: occupied buildings in poor or dangerous condition (r = .558), odors or smoke (r = .534), abandoned factories and businesses (r = .469), and crime (r = .465). In addition to these four, table 7.6 shows that this poor quality neighborhood function includes other behavioral problems (unfriendly neighbors, uncontrolled animals, recreational facilities that attract rowdy people), blight (abandoned houses, litter

Table 7.6. Discriminant Analysis: East Camden, Baseline Run

		Correlation of Variable with Function	
Variable	F-value	Worse vs. Better Neighborhood Function 1	General Poor Quality Function 2
Present neighborhood is worse	21.9	.581	
Abandoned houses	35.0	.559	.255
Inadequate street lighting	9.9	.453	
High crime rate	32.2	.377	.465
Streets, roads, sidewalks in disrepair	12.4	.290	
Occupied buildings in poor or dangerous condition	23.9		.558
Odors or smoke	11.5		.534
Abandoned factories and businesses	17.5		.469
Junkyard, gasoline station, other nonresidential	7.5		.384
Unfriendly neighbors	11.0		.374
Motor vehicle noise and heavy traffic	11.0		.373
Water or sewage plant	3.8		.368
Uncontrolled animals	13.3		.339
Landfills, hazardous-waste sites	3.4		.322
Litter or trash in the street	16.5		.314
Recreational facilities that attract rowdy people	5.9		.304
Chemical plant, oil refinery, tank farm	5.4		.303
Convenient to religious activities	1.6		−.273
Metal or furniture plant	4.0		.266
Canonical correlation with neighborhood		.747	.347
quality dependent variable (P-value)		(.001)	(.04)
Average standardized Z score with poor quality respondents		1.06	1.23

Source: Based on 158 responses.
Note: Variables with a correlation of >0.25 with one of the two functions are shown. All correlations shown were statistically significant discriminators at P < .05.

or trash), local activity spaces (junkyard, gasoline station, and other nonresidential activities), motor vehicle noise and heavy traffic, and massive technology sites (landfill/hazardous-waste site, water or sewage plant, metal or furniture plant). We labeled this function "general poor quality."

A male resident aged seventy-plus testified to the multiplicity of behavioral problems in east Camden: "I've been mugged in front of my house. I can't take walks to the church. Drugs! Very seldom see police. The mail has been stolen, snow shovels, ladder, lawn mower all stolen." A female aged thirty-one to fifty wrote: "Kids are nasty. Boys and men urinate anywhere. Animals are always loose and running in the street. And drugs and crime."

Many east Camden residents, although they admitted that serious problems existed, had a variety of reasons to remain in the area. A female homeowner aged fifty-one to seventy wrote: "I've been here all my life. No one is going to run me out." A male college graduate aged thirty-one to fifty, who noted that this neighborhood was worse than his previous one, wrote: "I believe this is where God wants me to be to help make a positive difference. The devil can't have it as long God's people occupy the area."

An eighteen to thirty-year-old female who rated this neighborhood as better than her previous one recognized problems but wanted to the community to respond: "Within one month there has been seven robberies in nearby houses. It effects our family when we want to go out all at the same time. We are scared to leave our house alone. I would like to see our neighbors get together and create a town watch system."

Heuristic Runs

Table 7.7 compares the canonical correlations and accuracy of the classification produced by the baseline and four heuristics. Judged by the percent of respondent ratings that were accurately classified, the aggregate hazard burden and specific hazard type models were not better predictors than the much simpler outsider perception model, which contained only the crime and abandoned housing variables. This was contrary to our other neighborhood sites, where the outsider model was the poorest predictor.

Table 7.8 provides additional support for the importance of crime and abandoned housing. Only 14 and 8 percent of respondents who rated their neighborhood as excellent or good wanted to leave as a result of crime and abandoned housing, respectfully. The comparative percentages for those who rated their neighborhoods as fair were 46 and 49 percent, respectively. These percentages jumped to 88 and 83 percent for those respondents who rated their neighborhoods as poor quality. In short, crime and abandoned housing are able to sharply discriminate among respondents who rated their neighborhoods as excellent/good, fair, and poor. Furthermore, the 95 percent confidence limits do not overlap. In the east Elizabeth, Marcus Hook,

Table 7.7. Summary of Discriminant Analysis Runs, East Camden, 1993

Run	Canonical Correlation Function		Percentage Correctly Classified	
	1	2	Total	Poor
Baseline (table 7.6)	.747	.347	76	82
Heuristic:				
Outsider perception	.668	.078	63	73
Specific hazard type	.708	.192	63	62
Specific hazard type checkoff	.707	.209	67	74
Aggregate hazard burden	.664	.165	64	62

Source: Based on 158 responses.

and hazardous-waste areas, the 95 percent confidence limits of the outsider perception problems (e.g., hazardous-waste site, incinerator, petroleum refinery, airplane noise, petroleum refinery, and gas tanks) overlapped. That is, we could not be 95 percent certain that the differences in proportions attributed to specific hazards did not occur by chance.

Even though crime and abandoned housing were able to accurately classify respondent ratings in east Camden, the aggregate hazard data show that multiple problems are strongly associated with poor quality neighborhoods. An average of .7 problems were identified as distressing by respondents who rated their neighborhood as excellent or good, compared to 3.3 who rated their neighborhood as fair and 7 who rated their neighborhood as poor quality. In other words, those who rated their neighborhood as poor quality typically identified five to nine major stresses in their neighborhoods.

Summary of Findings

RQ1: *How do people who live in the immediate vicinity of potentially hazardous land uses and activities rate their neighborhoods?*

Twenty-five percent of east Camden respondents rated their neighborhoods as poor quality compared to 3 percent of their counterparts in the United States as a whole, northern New Jersey, and the Philadelphia metropolitan area.

RQ2: *What factors most influence neighborhood ratings, especially rating of a neighborhood as poor?*

Blight and behavioral risks clearly were the greatest stresses

Table 7.8. Neighborhood Characteristics and Neighborhood Quality, East Camden, 1993

Neighborhood Quality	Total Number of Hazards (maximum is 19)	Specific Hazard Type (Maximum is 4)	Crime (1 = yes)	Abandoned Houses (1 = yes)
Excellent/good	0.7 (0.3, 1.2)	0.5 (0.2, 0.8)[a]	.14 (.04, .24)	.08 (.00, .16)
Fair	3.3 (2.5, 4.2)	1.7 (1.4, 2.0)	.46 (.34, .59)	.49 (.37, .62)
Poor	7.0 (5.5, 8.5)	2.8 (2.5, 3.1)	.88 (.77, .98)	.83 (.70, .95)

Source: Based on 158 responses.
Note: Average and 95 percent confidence limits figures in parentheses.
[a]Respondent gets a score of 1 for noting great distress with one indicator of a behavioral risk, blight, local activity space, and massive technology sites. For example, a respondent who expresses a desire to leave as a result of crime (behavioral risk), and airplane noise (massive technology site) would receive a score of 2.

among respondents in east Camden. Yet almost 20 percent of respondents did not acknowledge the presence of crime or abandoned housing in their neighborhood. This finding may be caused by respondents who rate their neighborhoods as an improvement over their prior living circumstances. They may like the convenience of east Camden to their jobs, have family in the neighborhood, or may appreciate the neighborhood's amenities. Alternatively, it may be caused by the respondent choosing a very narrow definition of their neighborhood.

Present neighborhood quality compared to previous neighborhood quality was an extremely important filter. Good schools were the only notable attractions.

The outsider perception model was a better or as good a predictor of neighborhood quality than the more complex heuristics models. The outsider model, which used only crime and blight as variables, was almost as strong as the baseline model, which included all thirty-five variables. We think that this result is due to the dominance of crime and blight in respondents' perceptual fields.

8

Findings, Limitations, and Research Needs

T his chapter restates the research questions and hypotheses, summarizes the tests of these hypotheses reported in chapters 4 to 7, discusses the limitations of the present study, and describes follow-up research.

Summary of Findings

RQ1: *How do people who live in the immediate vicinity of potentially hazardous land uses and activities rate their neighborhoods?*

We chose twenty neighborhoods in New Jersey and Pennsylvania that had abandoned houses, crime, hazardous-waste sites, incinerators, nearby airports, and various other environmental hazards. These can devastate a neighborhood by undermining its economic and social fabric, polluting the environment, and contributing to illness and injury.

Ten of the neighborhoods were chosen primarily because they were near abandoned hazardous-waste disposal sites, seven were known to suffer from blight and crime, nine were adjacent to oil refineries and tank farms, six were close to a major garbage incinerator, and three were adjacent to an international airport. Many had multiple potential hazardous land uses and activities.

H1.1: *Residents of environmentally devastated neighborhoods rate their neighborhoods as lower quality than Americans as a whole rate their neighborhoods.*

This hypothesis was supported by the data, but not in every neighborhood. Only 57 percent of our respondents rated their neighborhood as excellent or good quality. In comparison, 87 percent of Americans rated their neighborhood as either excellent or good. The comparable proportions from the American Housing Surveys for Northern New Jersey and the Philadelphia metropolitan area were 88 and 85 percent, respectively. In other words, 13 percent of Americans rated their neighborhoods as fair or poor, compared to 43 percent of our respondents.

Considerable variation was observed among the twenty neighborhoods. The Main and River areas of Chester, Elizabethport in east Elizabeth, and east Camden had the lowest neighborhood quality ratings. Less than 2 percent of respondents in these four areas rated their neighborhood as excellent quality, and more than 25 percent rated it as poor. In strong contrast, 53 and 35 percent of respondents who live in the areas around the Lipari and Toms River hazardous-waste sites rated their neighborhoods as excellent, respectively. These percentages exceed or equal Americans' ratings of their own neighborhoods.

H1.2: *People who live in stressed neighborhoods have an accurate perception of what potential hazards are actually present and not present in the neighborhood. In other words, there are relatively few respondents who are unusually sensitive or unusually insensitive to potential hazards.*

This hypothesis was supported by the data. We deliberately selected potential hazards, such as a metal or furniture factory, that should not bother respondents because they were not present. Less than 5 percent of respondents in each area could be labeled unusually sensitive—that is, they wanted to leave as a result of problems that did not exist. In addition, utility rights-of-way with towers and hanging lines were considered problems by very few respondents, despite the well-publicized potential threat from electromagnetic fields.

We chose one or more prominent land uses or activities that existed in order to estimate unusually insensitive populations. Every respondent should have acknowledged the existence of airplane noise in east Elizabeth, the refineries and trash incinerator in the Marcus Hook area, the hazardous-waste site in the ten neighborhoods surrounding them, and crime and blight in east Camden. As expected, acknowledgment of these potential hazards was attenuated by distance and physical barriers. In general, respondents who lived a mile or two away, whose view was blocked by a road, rail road line, large buildings, factories, parks, forests, and rivers often did not consider the facility to be a problem in their neighborhood. With a few notable exceptions, those who resided within one-half mile of an incinerator, refinery or tank farm, the runway of an international airport, and corners where drugs were sold acknowledged the existence of the problem and usually were extremely distressed by it.

There were three interesting exceptions. Thirty percent of respondents from the Chester River area did not acknowledge the nearby massive trash-to-steam incinerator, about 20 percent of east Camden respondents did not indicate the presence of crime and abandoned housing in their neighborhood, and about half of the respondents who lived near a hazardous-waste site did not acknowledge it. We developed plausible explanations. The cluster of Chester River residents who did not acknowledge the existence of the incinerator, we think, do not consider the incinerator to be in their neighborhood. They have a much narrower definition of their neighborhood than most of their neighbors. East Camden respondents, we speculate, overlook the problems because they consider their neighborhood to be better than their previous neighborhood and convenient to their jobs. The vast majority of respondents who did not acknowledge the existence of a hazardous-waste site tended to be recent migrants to the neighborhood. Some of the new residents may not know that a site exists, and others may not consider a fully or partly remediated facility to be hazardous.

In summary, we found relatively few unusually insensitive or sensitive respondents. However, there were more unusually insensitive people in these neighborhoods than there were people who could be labeled sensitive to neighborhood hazards.

RQ2: *What factors most influence neighborhood ratings, especially ratings of a neighborhood as poor quality?*

We compiled a list of more than twenty potential problems, ten possible attractions, and six characteristics of respondents that were expected to influence their neighborhood quality ratings.

H2.1: *Massive technology sites are not as important as crime and blight, especially if the technology sites are being controlled, but are more important than local activity spaces and amenities.*

Massive technology sites in our study areas include land uses that can create odors, smoke, noise, and other forms of pollution around a fixed site, such as a factory, hazardous-waste site, incinerator, land-fill, natural gas tank, and petroleum refinery or tank farm. Other massive technology sites impact an area along a line, such as the flight path of an airport, and road beds of trains and major high-ways.

Even though massive technology sites are the most prominent landscape features, we expected that a poor quality rating would oc-cur only if the local public felt personally threatened by a site. An uncontrolled hazardous-waste site that experienced explosions, fires, and constant odors would be perceived as directly threatening and would cause a poor neighborhood quality rating. A controlled site that looks like a hilly golf course or a parking lot with a fence around it is more likely to be perceived as an aesthetic smudge. We are not saying that residents enjoy living next to a closed waste dump or an old oil refinery and tank farm, nor do we conclude that there is no health risk, but our hypothesis was that a neighborhood with a controlled massive technology site is likely to be rated fair, good, or even excellent if other, more directly threatening problems are not present.

Our hypothesis was supported by the data. Airplane noise, haz-ardous-waste sites, incinerators, gas tanks, refineries and tanks farms, and the odors and smoke associated with them were the prob-lems nominated most often as the reasons respondents wanted to leave east Elizabeth, Marcus Hook, and areas adjacent to hazardous-waste sites. Yet prominence as a problem that causes respondents to want to leave the neighborhood usually did not translate into a poor quality neighborhood rating. Twenty-one percent of respondents who wanted to leave as a result of the most prominent massive tech-nology site in east Elizabeth, Marcus Hook, and the hazardous-waste site areas also rated their neighborhood as poor quality. Yet 79 per-cent did not; more often they rated their neighborhood as fair or good.

For example, airplane noise and odors or smoke were the two most distressing characteristics in east Elizabeth. Yet airplane noise had only the ninth highest statistical explanatory power and odors and smoke the fourteenth in the baseline discriminant analysis of 293 surveys. Airplane noise and odors or smoke, in fact, did not identify with the poor quality neighborhood function that resulted from the stepwise discriminant analysis. Instead they both identified with the function that described people who considered their present neighborhood worse than their previous one.

The same patterns were observed in Marcus Hook and near the hazardous-waste sites. Odors or smoke, petroleum refinery or tank farm, and chemical plant ranked one to three as problems in Marcus Hook. Yet in the discriminant analysis, none were among the ten strongest discriminating (e.g., predictor) variables. Like east Elizabeth, all three prominent massive technology sites correlated with the better or worse neighborhood quality discriminant function rather than with a poor neighborhood quality one.

Respondents living near a hazardous-waste site identified the site and odors or smoke as the two most distressing problems. But these had only the tenth and seventh highest statistical strength in the baseline discriminant analysis of the unremediated waste sites, respectively. Once again, both variables identified with the worse neighborhood quality function, not with the poor quality one.

In summary, east Elizabeth, Marcus Hook, and neighborhoods surrounding hazardous-waste sites were selected to determine the relative importance of massive technology sites as a cause of a poor quality neighborhood. We found a consistent pattern. The prominent massive technology sites were the major reason given by respondents for wanting to leave the neighborhood. Yet these same respondents often rated their neighborhoods as good or fair, as well as poor. They associated massive technology sites with a neighborhood worse than their previous one rather than as a poor quality neighborhood. In short, our respondents have sent an intriguing mixed message: massive technology sites can make a neighborhood worse but not necessarily make it the worst.

H.2.2. Crime, other behavioral risks, and blight are the characteristics most likely to result in a poor quality rating.

Our hypothesis was based on the assumption that violent and other aggressive antisocial behaviors and neighborhood deterioration were frightening threats that would lead to a poor quality neighborhood rating. The data supported this hypothesis. Forty-eight percent of respondents in all twenty neighborhoods who wanted to leave as a result of crime also rated their neighborhood as poor quality, and 50 percent who wanted to leave as a result of abandoned housing rated their neighborhood as poor quality.

This result was further confirmed by the discriminant analyses. In east Elizabeth, the five strongest discriminators in order of their statistical strength were crime, inadequate street lighting, occupied buildings in poor or dangerous condition, litter or trash, and streets roads and sidewalks in disrepair. In the Marcus Hook area, the three strongest and nine of the ten best predictors were indicators of behavioral and blight-related hazards. East Camden was chosen because of its reputation for blight and crime. Abandoned housing and crime were the two strongest discriminators. Six of the eight other strongest discriminating variables were behaviors and blight.

The neighborhoods surrounding the ten hazardous-waste sites were not expected to have many behavioral and blight problems. They did not. Only 6 percent of respondents said they wanted to leave as a result of unfriendly neighbors, 5 percent because of litter or trash, 4 percent because of dogs and uncontrolled animals, 3 percent due to crime, and 2 percent said they wanted to leave because of inadequate street lighting. Yet the problems of a poor quality neighborhood near a hazardous-waste site are remarkably like a poor quality neighborhood found in east Elizabeth, Marcus Hook, and east Camden. Five of the six strongest discriminating variables were measures of blight: inadequate street lighting; occupied buildings in poor or dangerous condition; streets, roads, sidewalks in disrepair; abandoned and boarded up buildings; and litter or trash in the street. An exception was crime, which was not among the most powerful discriminating variables.

In summary, crime and various forms of blight are powerful predictors of a poor quality neighborhood. As a summary of this destructive combination, we found that only 3 percent of respondents in our twenty neighborhoods who were not troubled by crime or abandoned and dangerous buildings rated their neighborhood as poor quality. Fifty-four percent who wanted to leave as a result of two or more of these problems rated their neighborhood as poor quality.

H2.3: *Local activity spaces are an important stress to people who live immediately adjacent to them but are the least important of the four types of potential hazards.*

This result was only partly supported by the surveys. The local bar, shopping mall, county and local road, park and playground, fire and police station, and ambulance dispatch center are attractions to the community as a whole but may be nuisances to some people who live near them. Our indicators of local activity spaces were limited to traffic noise and congestion, facilities that attract rowdy people, and junkyards, gasoline stations and other nonresidential land uses. In other words, there were only three local activity space categories. The second limitation is that in the case of east Elizabeth, we did not have a separate variable for the New Jersey Turnpike and state roads on the one hand and local and county ones on the other. Based on written and verbal comments from respondents, we treated traffic noise and congestion in east Elizabeth as a local activity space.

With these caveats in mind, the data suggest that local activity spaces are moderate problems for the neighborhoods and are moderately associated with a poor quality neighborhood. They are less important than crime or blight. Motor vehicle and traffic congestion was the most distressing local activity in every area. Thirty-six percent of respondents who wanted to leave as a result of automobile traffic rated their neighborhood as poor quality.

The discriminant analyses supported these observations. For example, in east Elizabeth motor vehicle noise and heavy traffic was the fourth ranked problem causing people to want to leave, recreational facilities that attract rowdy people was the seventh ranked, and junkyards, gasoline stations, and other nonresidential land uses was the eleventh.

Similar results were obtained in the Marcus Hook area. Motor vehicle noise and heavy traffic, junkyards, gasoline stations and other nonresidential land uses, and recreational facilities that attract rowdy people ranked fourth, twelfth, and fifteenth as problems causing people to want to leave their neighborhood. They ranked fifth, seventh, and thirteenth, respectively, in the baseline discriminant analysis. Once again, crime and blight were stronger discriminators of poor quality neighborhoods and massive technology sites were weaker predictors of poor quality.

The same findings were made in areas hosting the hazardous-waste sites and east Camden. Motor vehicle noise and traffic congestion were among the ten most important problems and discriminating variables and the other two indicators of local activity spaces were ranked between twelfth and fourteenth as problems and discriminators of poor neighborhood quality.

In summary, local activity spaces are less likely than crime and blight but more likely than massive technology sites to be associated with a poor quality neighborhood.

H2.4: *Personal experiences, especially previous neighborhood experiences and length of residence in the neighborhood, are important filters.*

This hypothesis was only partly supported by the research. Quality of present compared to previous neighborhood was one of the three most important predictors of neighborhood quality ratings. Only deteriorated or abandoned buildings and crime were stronger. Almost 30 percent of all respondents who perceived that their present neighborhood was worse than their previous one rated their present neighborhood as poor quality, compared to less than 3 percent of respondents who rated their present neighborhood better than their previous one. This neighborhood comparison variable ranked third, fourth, ninth, and twelfth in the baseline discriminant analyses in hazardous-waste site, east Camden, Marcus Hook, and east Elizabeth study areas, respectively.

The combination of worse neighborhood and desire to leave as a result of crime and abandoned/deteriorated buildings was a powerful heuristic found in the data. Fifty-eight percent of respondents who noted these three on their survey instrument rated their neighborhood as poor quality; 41 percent rated it as fair. Only one respondent who was stressed by dilapidated buildings, crime, and perceived her new neighborhood as worse than her old neighborhood rated her neighborhood as good or excellent.

With two exceptions, no other personal filter was consistently important. Residents of their present neighborhood for more than a decade had the highest proportion of poor quality ratings in three of the four study areas. The most marked difference was near unremediated hazardous-waste sites, where long-term residents experienced the sights, sounds, and smells of these hazards, and declining property values. This legacy, we think, caused a relatively large proportion of these respondents to rate their neighborhood lower quality than more recent migrants into these hazardous-waste site neighborhoods.

With the exception of Marcus Hook, a larger proportion of renters than homeowners rated their neighborhoods as poor quality. The renter-owner dichotomy was a significant variable (P < .05) near the waste sites. In addition to the neighborhood comparison (better-worse than previous neighborhood) variable, it was the only personal filter variable that was a statistically significant discriminating variable. It was the twelfth strongest variable in the stepwise discriminant analysis of the unremediated hazardous-waste sites.

In summary, our hypothesis about the importance of personal filters was not supported by the data, with the exception of the neighborhood comparison variable.

H2.5: *Amenities are not important filters in environmentally devastated neighborhoods, except for the presence of friends and relatives.*

More than one-half of respondents indicated that they were attracted by convenience to work, friends and relatives, and inexpensive housing. Frequent mention of an attraction was not a buffer against a poor quality rating. Inexpensive housing, including inherited housing, is the best illustration. Ranked among the most prevalent attractions in every neighborhood, it ranked last in ability to buffer against a poor quality rating. For example, 17 percent of east Elizabeth respondents rated their neighborhood as poor quality. If inexpensive housing was a buffer, then less than 17 percent of those who were attracted by inexpensive housing should have rated their neighborhood as poor quality instead of the 20 percent who did. In addition, some of the strongest written notes were from respondents who lived in inexpensive housing but were terrified about their neighborhood. Convenience to public transportation was a second attraction that clearly did not buffer against a poor quality neighborhood.

Good schools and presence of leisure activities were the only attractions that reduced the likelihood of low quality ratings. For example, only 8 percent of east Elizabeth respondents who were attracted by good schools and 11 percent who gave convenience to leisure activities as attractions rated their neighborhood as poor quality. This compared to 17 percent of east Elizabeth respondents as a whole.

The baseline discriminant analysis runs confirmed the limited explanatory power of attractions. Good schools were the fifteenth most important discriminator in the east Elizabeth analysis; good schools

and convenience to leisure activities were both statistically significant discriminators only in the Marcus Hook analysis; and convenience to religious activities was a significant discriminator in the east
Camden analysis. In fact, two to three significant attractions would
have been expected to be significant discriminating variables in the
five baseline runs at $P < .05$ (5 runs $\times$ 8 to 10 attractions in each
run $\times .05 = 2$ to 3).

In summary, the empirical analyses support our hypothesis that
a few attractions and amenities are not enough to substantially
buffer against a poor quality neighborhood. Our expectations that
convenience to friends and relatives might be a buffer against a poor
quality rating was not supported by the data. A perception of good
schools and convenience to leisure activities did reduce the likelihood of a poor quality neighborhood designation.

H.2.6. *Residents use mental shortcuts—that is, heuristics—to help
them integrate their perceptions into an overall neighborhood evaluation.*

We developed four simple heuristics: (1) outsider perception, (2)
specific hazard type, (3) specific hazard type checkoff, and (4) aggregate hazard burden. We also had a baseline run that served as a
point of comparison.

The outsider heuristic assumes that residents focus on the prominent hazards that outsiders see as they travel through the neighborhood or learn about in the mass media. The outsider perception
heuristic is a naïve model because it makes simplistic assumptions
about residents' image-building processes. It was expected to have
the least ability to predict neighborhood quality ratings.

The specific hazard type hypothesis was created to test the concept that people think about problems in categories of massive technology sites, behavioral hazards, blight, and local activity spaces.
These aggregates were computed by adding each respondents' scores
by category.

The specific hazard type checkoff heuristic also focuses on the four
hazard categories. Any extremely distressed designation for any
problem within a category results in a maximum score for that entire category and triggers a poor quality rating for that neighborhood. This model assumes that respondents who perceived one
behavioral and one blight problem would be more likely to rate their
neighborhood poor quality than those who perceived four types of a

single category, such as blight. The aggregate number of hazards heuristic assumes that the total number of burdens is more important than any specific one or specific type. The greater the number of hazards that cause the respondent to want to leave, irrespective of their type, the greater the likelihood that the neighborhood will be scored poor quality.

We expected the specific and aggregate heuristics to be better at predicting poor quality ratings than they would at predicting excellent/good and fair ones. Poor ratings require a model that can capture the interaction of multiple distressing neighborhood characteristics while taking into account demographic filters. Excellent and good ratings were expected to be associated with few neighborhood problems.

Table 8.1 compares the accuracy of the baseline and four heuristics. The results were in the expected direction, although not as strong as we had projected. The outsider perception heuristic was the least accurate model for predicting all neighborhood quality responses and poor quality ones. The baseline model, which includes all the problems, attractions, and filters, was better than the outsider one at predicting the total set of responses. But, as expected, the aggregate burden and specific heuristics were even better at accurately classifying poor quality responses than the baseline. In other words, with the exception of the outsider heuristic, all the heuristics were as effective or more effective at capturing the interactions underlying a poor quality rating as the baseline. This is an important finding because the heuristics sacrifice considerable precision compared to the baseline model. In addition to the formal heuristics we proposed and tested, the research found concern about crime, abandoned buildings and rating the present neighborhood as worse to be a powerful heuristic to explain poor quality neighborhood ratings.

Limitations

Chapter 2 described the major limitations of this research. Five of these limitations are revisited here focusing on how the limitations impact the utility of the results.

We followed the American Housing Survey (AHS) practice of having respondents define their neighborhood. Did this obfuscate the

Table 8.1. Accuracy of Heuristic and Baseline Discriminant Models at Predicting Respondent Neighborhood Ratings

Model	Percentage Correctly Classified and 95% Confidence Limits			
	All Neighborhood Ratings		Poor Quality Neighborhood Ratings	
Baseline	77.4	(75.2, 79.5)	74.1	(67.4, 80.9)
Heuristic:				
Outsider perception	61.7	(59.2, 64.2)	67.9	(60.7, 75.1)
Specific hazard type	71.2	(68.8, 73.6)	73.4	(66.6, 80.2)
Specific hazard type checkoff	68.1	(65.7, 70.5)	74.7	(68.0, 81.4)
Aggregate hazard burden	73.6	(71.3, 76.9)	74.7	(68.0, 81.4)

Source: All neighborhood ratings are based on 1,418 responses; poor quality neighborhood ratings are based on 162 responses.
Note: 95 percent confidence limits figures in parentheses.

results? A small geographical cluster of respondents in Chester and dispersed populations of respondents in east Camden and around some of the hazardous-waste sites were insensitive to obvious problems in their neighborhood. In the Chester case, we are convinced that the respondents had a narrower definition of their neighborhood than the vast majority of their counterparts. Otherwise, allowing respondents to define their own neighborhood does not seem to have prevented us from finding neighborhood patterns that make sense.

A second concern was the location of the study areas. We avoided the problem of having urban, suburban, or rural biases by deliberately picking some neighborhoods that would be considered to be inner city, small city, suburban, and rural. How much did selecting areas in New Jersey and the Philadelphia area limit the generalizability of the results? We suspected that New Jersey's and Philadelphia's regional problems and attractions could be different from the United States' as a whole. But they were not. AHS summary tables show that concern about crime and blight, two key problems, were almost identical. Compared to all Americans, residents of the two regions are slightly more likely to be stressed by noise, traffic, and poor city services, but are less likely to be stressed by people. Attractions were similar, although New Jersey and Philadelphia area respondents had more satisfaction associated with good schools, the presence of friends and relatives, and mass transportation.

The only notable difference between the two regions and the nation was the neighborhood comparison variable. Thirty-nine percent of Americans considered their present neighborhood better than their previous one compared to 49 percent in the two regions (P < .01). Seventeen percent of American respondents considered it worse, compared to 19 percent of regional ones. In other words, respondents from the New Jersey and Philadelphia areas were more likely to have a stronger negative or stronger positive assessment than their national counterparts. This implies that the neighborhood comparison variable might be more important in the New Jersey and Philadelphia areas than elsewhere in the United States.

Our twenty neighborhoods are in two states that are among the most innovative at developing environmental health policies. Using published interstate comparisons, Greenberg, Popper, and West (1991) ranked New Jersey third and Pennsylvania fifteenth in the strength of state programs to protect public health and the environment. Aggressive state programs engender more mass media and public attention to the neighborhood problems studied in this research.

This observation, combined with the greater propensity of regional residents to rate their present neighborhoods as better or worse than national counterparts, leads to the conclusion that regional respondents might be more sensitive to the full set of environmental hazards we analyzed than their national counterparts. This conclusion is speculative. Nevertheless, prudence suggests that caution should be used in generalizing the results of this study to the United States as a whole until studies are done in other regional settings.

The survey instrument was a third limitation. Our closed-ended and fully labeled instrument is similar but not identical to the American Housing Survey instrument. How much would differences between our more detailed form and the AHS's less specific instrument hinder our ability to infer conclusions from the twenty case studies? Our survey lists many more potential hazards than the AHS's. Furthermore, the AHS requests attractions and neighborhood comparison data only from recent migrants. We requested this information from all respondents. This means that we could not compare the extent of some problems and attractions in our neighborhoods to national and regional data. The main limitation is the inability to pursue in the national data the unexpected finding that massive technology sites were consistently associated with the perception that their present neighborhood was poorer quality than their previous one.

The testing of the heuristics was a fourth concern. Given the dearth of literature about poor quality neighborhoods, we felt it appropriate to present only conservative forms of the heuristic tests. Would these models in their simple form perform adequately, that is, provide insights about poor quality ratings? For example, we counted only stress that was sufficient to cause a respondent to want to leave (1) or not leave (0). The data we collected contains the distinction between acknowledging that the problem does not exist (0), exists (1), exists and bothers the respondent (2), and bothers respondents so much that they want to leave (3). That is, we collapsed a response of four categories into two.

We also tested but do not report here the idea that the 0,1,2,3 scale is more discriminating than the 0,1 scale. For example, assume that Ms. Smith scored three local activity space problems 0, 3, and 3, respectively. Her score in the discriminant analysis presented in this book for local activity spaces was 2 (3 activities x 1 point for each problem that causes a respondent to want to leave). When the same data were scored 0,1,2,3, then her score was 6 (3 + 3). We also tested another version, which multiplied all the scores between 1 and 3. Ms. Smith's score is 9 (3 x 3) for this version. The results of the additive and multiplicative versions of the heuristic create greater statistical variance in the independent variable set, which might mimic people's responses to different groups of hazards. Several of these exploratory tests increased the ability of the heuristics to predict responses. However, others did not. Without adequate theory to support a more complex version of the heuristics and rather than presenting the results of a mathematical fishing expedition for the best empirical fit to the data, we fell back to the more conservative version presented here. This means that we doubtless understated the ability of these heuristics to accurately recreate respondents' ratings.

Before we began this research, we knew that surveys in these environmentally devastated neighborhoods would not yield response rates of 60 percent or more. How much bias would be introduced by a limited response rate? Would these biases seriously distort the results? Almost fifty-three hundred surveys were distributed and more than fourteen hundred were returned. The overall response rate was 27 percent, but varied from less than 20 percent in east Camden, the Main area of Chester, and Elizabethport and Frog Hollow in east Elizabeth to more than 40 percent near the Lipari, Bayonne, and GEMS hazardous-waste sites. High school graduates, females, and homeowners were disproportionately represented in the respondent group. There was no consistent bias in the responses by age. It was not possible to make a precise comparison of the length of residence variable because the question we asked was not the same as the question asked by the United States census.

Did these biases impact the results? Because our major concern was poor quality neighborhoods, we reexamined the poor quality ratings for statistically significant differences in education completed, gender, age, tenure, and length of residence. With one exception, these demographic characteristics did not significantly alter the propensity to rate a neighborhood as poor quality.

We demonstrate this observation by summarizing the results by demographic category for the east Elizabeth, Marcus Hook, hazardous-waste sites, and north Camden study regions. Persons without a high school diploma were more likely to rate their neighborhood as poor quality in two regions, but less likely in two others. None of these differences in educational achievement were associated with a statistically significant difference in poor quality ratings at P < .05. Females were more likely to rate their neighborhood as poor quality in two regions, but less likely in the other two. None of the female-male differences were statistically significant at P < .05. The eighteen to thirty-year-old population was the most dissatisfied in three of the four regions, but the differences were not statistically significant.

We do not know how our respondents compare to the population in their respective census tracts in length of residence because the questions were posed differently. Assuming that the respondents were not representative of the census tract populations in age distribution, the data show that respondents who lived in their neighborhood for more than a decade were the most likely to rate their neighborhood as poor quality in three of the four areas. Yet only in east Camden was this difference statistically significant (P < .05). We did not recalculate the proportion who rate east Camden poor quality because we do not know if long-term residents are over or underrepresented in the respondent group.

The owner/renter dichotomy did make a difference. Renters were more distressed in three of the four areas but the difference was statistically significant only in the hazardous-waste site areas. The fact that renters are underrepresented in the responses implies that the overall proportion of respondents who rated their neighborhood as poor quality in these ten neighborhoods is too low. We weighted the actual proportion of renters and owners in the census tracts reported in the 1990 census by the respondent neighborhood quality ratings. The weighted percentage who rated their neighborhood as poor quality was 4.2. The unweighted percentage reported in chapter 6 was 3.4 percent.

In summary, the responses were biased toward more educated, females, owner-occupied, and middle-aged populations. Yet only in the single case of the hazardous-waste site neighborhoods and the owner-renter dichotomy did the bias obviously impact the estimate of poor quality neighborhoods. In short, poor quality ratings were not substantially distorted in any of the four regions because of these biases.

It would be begging the question to assume that the 73 percent who did not respond to our survey are mirror images of the 27 percent who did. It could be that respondents are disproportionately positive-minded about their neighborhoods—that is, they are able to rationalize problems and feel an inner need to paint a rosier picture than their real life assessment to support their self-esteem. Those who did not respond might be more suspicious of outsiders like us and unwilling to tell us how bad it is to live in their neighborhood. Unfortunately, there is no way of confirming or rejecting these speculations without surveying nonrespondents. The low response rate is a second reason why we suggest caution about generalizing the results of these surveys.

Even though the regional results are not significantly distorted by the sampling response bias, the bias does mean that the aggregate neighborhood quality rating calculated for all fourteen hundred respondents—14 percent excellent, 43 percent good, 31 percent fair, and 12 percent poor—is misleading. Specifically, the twenty neighborhoods taken as a whole show unambiguous relationships between response rate and social characteristics. The strongest was a

Spearman rank correlation of .71 (P < .01) with percentage of the population in the census tract that graduated high school. Other significant relationships were in order of their correlation as follows: .60 (P < .01) with per capita income; −.59 (P < .01) with percentage of population residing in rental units; −.59 (P < .01) with percentage Hispanic; −.58 (p.<01) with percentage black population; and −.47 (P < .01) with percentage who said that they did not speak English well.

These strong associations with social indicators are unlikely to surprise readers. Indeed, the difficulty of getting a good and unbiased response in low socioeconomic status neighborhoods is one reason why so much of the risk literature ignores people who reside in these marginalized neighborhoods.

The overall impact of the 15 to 25 percent response rates in low socioeconomic status neighborhoods and 35 to 50 percent response rates in middle-income ones is to bias the aggregate neighborhood quality estimate toward middle-income neighborhoods with excellent and good ratings. In fact, the Spearman rank correlation between response rate in the twenty neighborhoods and percentage excellent neighborhood quality was .84 (P < .01), −.71 (P < .01) with poor neighborhood quality ratings. The obvious bias toward excellent ratings means that the aggregate ratings for the full set of fourteen hundred responses is not representative and should not be cited as indicative of neighborhood quality in environmentally stressed neighborhoods in the United States.

Research Needs

The findings and limitations of this research raise questions that can only be answered with additional research. Here we state five questions and suggest studies to find answers to the questions.

1. *How do residents of environmentally devastated neighborhoods in the Midwest, South, and West and in other urban-industrial nations rate their environmentally stressed neighborhoods?*

Neighborhood quality research is needed in other regions of the United States where there are concentrations of behavioral, blight, and land-use hazards. Many western European nations have implemented policies that prevent the brutal impoverishment of cities that has occurred in the United States. In addition, crime rates, especially violent crime rates, are lower in western Europe. Poland, Russia, and other former members of the eastern bloc also have had lower rates of crime than the United States but gross pollution in some areas. A different set of associations among neighborhood quality, problems, attractions, and filters should be expected in these nations.

2. *What are the relationships between neighborhood quality and quality of life?*

Quality of life has become a consideration of the American public health community and federal and state agencies, such as the Centers for Disease Control and the Agency for Toxic Substances and Disease Registry (Von Allem et al. 1992). Do people who rate their personal quality of life high also rate their neighborhoods as excellent? Is the converse true? That is, do people who have a poor quality of life also rate their neighborhood as fair or poor quality? Are more aggressive people more likely to rate their neighborhood as excellent/good or fair/poor? To answer these questions in future studies we added questions to our survey instrument. Two questions taken from the set used by the Centers for Disease Control behavioral risk factor surveys ask respondents to rate their own health and any recent activity limitations. We added ten activities to measure what respondents have done about neighborhood quality and their own quality of life. Five ask if the respondent had their blood pressure, cholesterol, teeth, and eyes checked, or visited a doctor during the last two years. Respondents are also asked if they have attended a public meeting during the last two years, voted in a local election, called the police, contacted an elected official about a problem, or volunteered for a civic or church duty. These questions should ascertain relationships about what people living in environmentally devastated neighborhoods do to improve their own and neighborhood environments and how these activities are imbedded in their neighborhood and personal quality ratings. In addition, we can utilize measurements of the quality of the air, water, and land, and monitor mortal and morbid states, such as infant mortality, low-birth-weight babies, cirrhosis, tuberculosis, homicide, suicide, deaths by fire and illegal drugs, and AIDS in these environmentally devastated neighborhoods to better understand that relationship.

3. *What heuristics most effectively explain neighborhood quality ratings?*

Our four existing heuristics assume a very simple linear hierarchy of respondent concerns and preferences. Focus groups and use of an open-ended survey, such as the one we used in chapter 6, are the best ways of trying to better understand insiders realities in a way that will allow us to create better heuristic models.

4. *What differences exist among subpopulations?*

Our studies did not gather data about differences between racial and ethnic groups, and our decision to use an English-language survey doubtless led to a low response rate in some areas. The increasing number of Americans born in Asia and Latin America who reside in devastated neighborhoods suggests that this issue needs to be confronted. We plan to conduct several survey experiments with and without the racial/ethnic question and to prepare the survey instrument in Spanish. We also plan to survey neighborhoods, such as south Chester, that are almost exclusively African American and neighborhoods that have almost exclusively Vietnamese, Chinese American, and other sizable minority populations. We believe such strategies are needed to understand actual differences in neighborhood perception.

The most problematic population to sample in environmentally devastated neighborhoods are residents of multi-unit dwellings. Increasingly, apartments in these neighborhoods are being redesigned like fortresses with no access to individual apartments. A telephone survey staffed by multilingual surveyors who can offer a payment for participation might be the only way of obtaining information from residents of these multi-unit dwellings. Of course, as noted in chapter 2, as many as 20 percent of the residents of some of these neighborhoods do not have phones. To address this problem, we are designing a project that will allow us to hire persons from some of these neighborhoods to conduct door-to-door surveys in their own neighborhoods.

The results of this work contradict studies that suggest major differences by gender and educational achievement in risk perception. One plausible explanation is that the literature accurately reflects differences in excellent and good neighborhoods but not in poor and environmentally devastated ones. In order to learn more about male-female differences, we are designing a survey that will be limited to men and women of approximately the same age who live in the same dwelling unit.

5. *How do neighborhood quality, problems, and amenities change in neighborhoods that once were economic jewels but have become environmentally devastated?*

The importance of the neighborhood comparison variable suggests a series of studies in neighborhoods undergoing change. Neighborhoods that once vibrated with economic vitality because of an iron and steel plant, coal mines, a military base, and asbestos factories but now are abandoned and rusting would be excellent places to learn about the dynamics of neighborhood quality.

These studies should include a few environmentally devastated neighborhoods in each region of the United States. Studies repeated every three to five years in places like south Chester, Marcus Hook, and east Elizabeth have the advantage of relating specific land uses and behaviors to changes in neighborhood quality. These studies would be the neighborhood quality and quality of life equivalents of the Framingham, Massachusetts studies that have made major contributions to understanding the health of a population.

Poor Quality, Multiple-Hazard Neighborhoods

The initial goals of this research were to learn how residents of neighborhoods burdened with blight, crime, and industrial and other noxious land uses rate their neighborhoods, and to understand the environmental and personal factors that influence these ratings. As a consequence of pursuing these objectives, we observed two strong and consistent relationships in neighborhoods with multiple hazards. Respondents associated poor quality neighborhoods with blight and crime, and a neighborhood worse than their previous one with massive technology sites.

If our respondents' observations are accurate, neighborhood quality in these stressful multiple-hazard places is not going to be substantially improved without dealing with behavioral, blight, and technological hazards. These observations lead us to question existing narrowly focused state- and national-based policies as they apply to multiple-hazard neighborhoods. Is it prudent to spend tens of millions of dollars building noise barriers along roads, remediating waste sites to *de Minimis* risk, or reducing odors from sewage treatment plants while doing nothing about blight and crime in these neighborhoods? Likewise, is it logical to increase police surveillance, fix streets and street lights, and rehabilitate housing while continuing to allow odors from a sewage treatment plant or petrochemical complex to make the neighborhood unpleasant to anyone with sufficient resources to live, work, and recreate elsewhere?

We need a national policy and complementary state ones that address the special reality of these multiple-hazard, for the most part densely packed city neighborhoods. Our purpose is not to formulate and argue for a single "best" policy approach. The idea of a policy device that optimizes public health, economic efficiency, equity, and political concerns is naïve. Nor do we fixate on a radical new idea or borrow one of the many discarded by the Nixon, Reagan, and Bush administrations. They have little to no chance of gaining political support. Instead, we describe a policy and two different and complementary ways of implementing it that could help to improve neighborhood quality to *de Minimis* levels (chapters 1 and 3) and doubtless reduce individual risk. Specifically, we want to develop a "target-of-opportunity" policy for multiple-hazard neighborhoods, a strategy we consider plausible in the 1990s context.

Before focusing on targets of opportunity, we review other approaches we considered. We favor comprehensive master planning, especially if the neighborhood plays an important role in the process. Yet in a political economy in which elected officials compete for the "reducing government," "reducing government interference," and "reducing taxes" labels, we do not envision many opportunities to implement comprehensive master plans.

A second option not addressed in detail is to remove residents from the most beleaguered neighborhoods. That is, forget about the neighborhoods. Instead, help the residents by relocating them in more salubrious environments. This policy option would undoubtedly engender fierce opposition from residents of the proposed host neighborhoods. Furthermore, residents of devastated neighborhoods might resist location. In neighborhoods where the risk is demonstrably hazardous to a limited number of people and the cost of reducing it is unrealistically high, an evacuation and relocation policy would be prudent. Relocation, however, is unrealistic for the many thousands who live in multiple-hazard neighborhoods.

Our research supports a third option, which is reallocating funds from existing narrowly focused national or state programs to broader local environmental concerns in multiple-hazard neighborhoods. But proposals to reallocate funds from building a sewage plant, remediating a hazardous-waste site, or building a noise barrier to building a police substation or rehabilitating structures in the same neighborhood are highly unlikely to succeed in the United States political context. In fact, three of our readers with more than sixty years of experience in policy formation argued that we should avoid proposing a reallocation scheme because it would anger many potential readers and divert attention from our scientific findings and more plausible policy options below.

We bow to their advice, focusing on a target-of-opportunity program. Eligibility for the program requires that a local government prove that a major investment by sources external to the neighborhood is going to occur and that added funds would enable them to address one or more important neighborhood problem. To simplify the terminology, we refer to the externally supported project that is going to be built as "external." A mandated hazardous-waste site or municipal landfill cleanup, the construction of a noise barrier, the expansion of a hospital, renovation of a baseball stadium, building of a center for the arts, renovation of a train station, or construction of a prison complex or hospital could be external sparks.

The project that our policy would facilitate is called "internal," that is, the project initiated by the local government. The internal project could be fixing the streets, rehabilitating housing, adding more police patrols, building a fire station. Funds for internal projects, along with resources for the external one, could help raise the neighborhood quality rating from poor or fair quality to good. In other words, while stipulating to the great complexity of coordinating multiple redevelopment projects, our premise is that more benefit will be derived from a combination of external and internal projects than from a single, narrowly focused, external one.

Two Approaches for Obtaining Internal Funds

This section describes two ways of implementing the policy. Both are extensions of existing approaches with long track records.

Inside Initiative for Internal Projects

This approach requires federal, state, or local government or private organizations to set aside a small amount of funding for planning and marketing purposes so that municipalities representing multiple-hazard neighborhoods can try to obtain existing large funding sources. For example, when a mandated cleanup of a hazardous-waste site is announced for the south side of Jones City, Jones' local government, in cooperation with the neighborhood, requests funds to develop a plan to address blight and behavioral problems that also severely stress the neighborhood. The municipality/neighborhood uses the planning money to develop their internal plans and market them to business interests, nonprofit organizations, and government agencies that have funds to remediate blight and reduce crime.

A key sales pitch is that the externally mandated federal government project will increase the desirability of the neighborhood as a place of residence and work, but only if blight and crime are also addressed. In short, the inside initiative approach places the burden for planning and marketing the internal project idea on local government. Local governments must compete for very limited, already existing government and private resources.

Hundreds of projects in big and small cities and towns have followed the path of getting small planning grants and trying to access large funds. For example, the Environmental Enterprise Center (1994) compiled a list and abstracted hundreds of primarily locally initiated redevelopment projects that they consider environmentally sensitive. Some of these are in cities. The difference between our policy and most of these is two preconditions, which are that planning funds for internal projects would be set aside only for places that qualify as multiple-hazard neighborhoods and can prove an external project is going to be built.

Outside Initiative for Internal Projects

Federal or state government, or private organizations, aggressively initiate the process of neighborhood remediation by providing a sizable fund for internal projects in poor quality, multiple-hazard neighborhoods where an external project is already scheduled. For instance, a state prison is to be built in Smithtown. The proposed site is derelict and used by drug dealers. The planned jail complex will eliminate some blight and dramatically reduce the propensity for drug sales and arson in the neighborhood. Smithtown applies for multiple-hazard neighborhood funds to cleanup and rehabilitate other blighted properties in the same neighborhood.

A bill introduced in the United States Senate on August 10, 1992 (102d Cong., 2d sess.) illustrates the outside initiative. S.3164 called for $100 million in fiscal 1993 and $100 million in fiscal 1994 to demonstrate the feasibility of linking hazardous-waste site cleanup with neighborhood redevelopment. Up to fifty sites were to be provided funds in each fiscal year. State as well as local governments were required to play a role. No more than $4 million was to be made available to a site, no more than three projects could go to a state, and 25 percent was to be provided in nonfederal contributions. The bill did not become law.

The EPA has created a scaled-down version of S.3164, the so-called brownfield development program. A pilot program, it allocates planning grants of $200,000 to redevelop abandoned and contaminated industrial sites. By our definition, the brownfield program is an internal initiative—that is, the external project is waste remediation, and the grants are only for planning. Depending on the results of pilot studies (awarded to Bridgeport, Connecticut; Cleveland, Ohio; and Richmond, Virginia, at the time this chapter was written), a much larger national program to cleanup sites and simultaneously stimulate economic redevelopment in multiple-hazard neighborhoods might be possible (Salvesen 1994). In other words, if successful, the brownfield program might lead to a large outside fund for internal projects.

States have their own versions of outside initiatives. For example, New Jersey designated twenty "urban enterprise zones." Among the benefits for a business to located in these zones are a cut in the sales tax to 3 percent and a one-time corporate tax credit of fifteen hundred dollars to businesses for hiring full-time employees who were unemployed or receiving public assistance. These twenty zones, which include Elizabeth and Camden, also have priority when it comes to other state assistance programs (Carter, Jaffe, and Dilworth 1995).

In summary, there are a variety of externally initiated programs that could help multiple-hazard neighborhoods. They range in scale from allowing business advertising on abandoned lots predicated on the business cleaning up that lot to the creation of multiple-neighborhood zones that receive a variety of economic benefits. The difference between our target-of-opportunity policy and these is that eligibility for our program depends upon proving that an external project is about to occur and demonstrating that crime, blight, and pollution-related hazards all exist in the neighborhood.

Evaluation of the Target-of-Opportunity Policy

We examine the policy for the issues of health and safety, economic efficiency, equity and consent, and political acceptability. These evaluation criteria were developed by Michael Greenberg over the course of two decades and applied to projects including the siting of nuclear power stations, landfills, incinerators, and dams.

Health and Safety

Would this policy compromise health and safety? First we must determine if focusing on blight, crime, and massive technology sites is consistent with the best science known about public health problems. Nationally, deaths attributed to smoking, alcohol, fires, falls, and handguns can be compared with fatality estimates from cancer and a few selected other diseases based on risk assessments done by the EPA and ATSDR. Even after acknowledging that risk assessments typically produce high estimates of mortality and morbidity (Harris and Burmaster 1992a, 1992b; Robertson 1994; Silbergeld 1993a, 1993b; Talcott 1992), comparisons show that deaths related directly to behaviors and blight far exceed fatalities from technological hazards (Slovic, Fischhoff, and Lichtenstein 1980; Environmental Protection Agency 1987).

Yet national comparisons may be problematic guides for neighborhoods in places with densely packed technological hazards, such as east Elizabeth and Chester. In some of these multiple-hazard neighborhoods, crime and blight could be amplified and pollution understated. The cumulative public health impact to workers and residents from pollution could be substantial, even if the public is more afraid of the immediate threat of the mugger and arsonist.

To be certain that we protect future generations and population outside the neighborhood from contamination caused by massive technology sites, we need to consult experts. Indeed, one important potential outcome of our research would be to provoke scientists into determining methods to estimate the aggregate public and environmental risk in multiple-hazard neighborhoods. Such an endeavor would show the elevated risks in multiple-hazard neighborhoods. That is, if risk analysis is applied across all environmental risks rather than separately to individual ones, it would demonstrate the

212 Multiple-Hazard Neighborhoods

need to address these neighborhoods under a "worst things first" policy (Finkel and Golding 1994).

We obtained public health expertise by surveying the local health officers (LHO) of each municipal government in ten of our neighborhoods with multiple densely packed hazards. LHOs are the professionals best suited to integrate the relative importance of threats to the neighborhoods ranging from environmental contamination to violence. Specifically, we called health officers from Bayonne, Bound Brook, Bridgewater, Camden, Chester (three neighborhoods), and Elizabeth (three neighborhoods) and asked them to identify the five most important public health problems in the study neighborhoods. Their responses were consistent. In order of mention they listed: (1) drug abuse and alcohol; (2) violence and crime; (3) HIV infection and spread of AIDS; (4) reaching the high-risk elderly, pregnant mothers, and children; and (5) crowded, dilapidated, and abandoned housing, which contribute to injuries, fires, rodent infestations, garbage dumping, drug problems, homelessness, and numerous other neighborhood problems.

The LHOs regarded industries and other commercial land uses as much less important, although not unimportant. For example, the LHO of a city with a Superfund site was afraid that failure to control the local site would eventually pollute the local groundwater supply. He was also concerned about spills and accidents along roads, railroads, and inside factories. The health officer of a city with a nearby airport and oil refinery reported that airport noise was a chronic problem, which had been partly remediated by soundproofing all schools in the direct path of the airplanes. However, he described the impact of the airport noise, refinery, and other nearby land uses as "minuscule" compared to the problems of violence, other behavioral problems, and blight. Another LHO said local residents complained about the waste facility, especially dust and traffic. She felt that violence, substance abuse, and AIDS were the critical problems, and lead poisoning from old houses and rats were the most important environmental health problems. Overall, the health officers clearly support the argument that blight and crime are central to public health problems in these neighborhoods.

A survey of health officers in all cities with a population of 25,000 to 500,000 in the Midwest and Northeast United States (Greenberg, Schneider, Martell 1994) further supports our LHO interview results.

That study ranked the cities from least economically stressed (rank 1) to most economically stressed (rank 436). Cities representing eight of the ten multiple-hazard neighborhoods were included in the quartile of most stressed cities (328 to 436): Chester (349), Bayonne (384), Elizabeth (422) and Camden (430). The LHOs of these 109 most economically stressed cities ranked twenty-one public health concerns. In order of their importance, the five most important were: (1) reducing alcohol and drug abuse, (2) preventing and controlling the HIV infection and AIDS, (3) improving maternal and infant health, (4) preventing and controlling sexually transmitted diseases, and (5) reducing violent and abusive behavior. Four of the five from this 436-city study (numbers 1, 2, 3, and 5) match the set of five from the ten neighborhoods with densely packed hazards.

Overall, the local and multistate surveys of LHOs support the contention that blight and crime are deeply embedded in the public health problems that plague neighborhoods with multiple, densely packed behavioral, blight, and technological hazards. It follows, then, that obtaining funds to combat blight and crime while technological hazards are being remediated provides an opportunity to jump start a meaningful improvement in neighborhood quality and public health.

It can be argued that whatever funds are provided to an internal project, such as rehabilitating housing in a poor quality, multiple-hazard neighborhood, subtracts funds from an external one that would improve neighborhood quality in places with only a single hazard, such as a hazardous-waste site or noise pollution from automobiles. We could not devise a plausible way that either approach could compromise the health and safety of the residents of multiple-hazard neighborhoods.

Investment Efficiency

Will the proposed policy increase the benefits relative to the costs of the project? The idea of increasing the benefit-to-cost ratio in environmental programs by engaging in complementary activities rather than narrowly focused ones is appealing because environmental protection programs are no longer sacred cows. They are more carefully scrutinized for benefits and costs, partly because costs have dramatically increased. For example, environmental investments associated with EPA programs were estimated at $27 billion in 1986 dollars (Carlin 1990), or .9 percent of the gross national product (GNP). In 1994, they were estimated at $127 billion, or 2.4 percent of GNP. They are forecasted to rise to $160 billion, or 2.8 percent of GNP, by the year 2000.

A second reason for questioning environmental programs is their relative lack of economic efficiency. Reacting to tighter budgets and the need for better investments, Minard (1991) called for "replac[ing] crisis management, inertia and conventional wisdom with informed judgement." The Carnegie Commission (1993) called for reforming risk regulation in the United States to achieve greater environmental protection for less cost. Van Houtven and Cropper (1994) found that the EPA implicitly attaches values ranging from $10 to $45 million to avert one cancer. It is a figure two to ten times what people claim they are willing to pay to prevent their own death.

Increasing attacks on programs such as Superfund focus on their lack of cost effectiveness. A University of Tennessee study (Russell, Colglazier, and English 1991) estimated that if current policies are continued, Americans will spend about $750 billion between 1990 and 2020 to clean up hazardous-waste sites. Total costs could increase to $1.7 trillion if considerable off-site contamination is found and if policy requires cleanups to destroy more of the waste. Costs would be closer to $400 billion if wastes could be contained and managed on site.

Because the Tennessee group's scenarios were developed to have roughly the same human health effect, the extra $350 ($750 minus $400) to $1300 ($1700 minus $400) billion represents an enormous opportunity cost. Although the Tennessee researchers' estimates may be high because of the way costs were discounted, opportunity costs were underscored by ten case studies that found that residents did not necessarily expect contaminated sites to be returned to a pristine state.

Critics argue that Superfund cleanup dollars should be reallocated to other public health and environmental programs. Charging that it is built on "overzealous abatement of hypothetical risks," for example, Orme (1992:2) labeled Superfund "an expensive dump site beautification exercise that has minuscule, if any, impact on improving health." Orme concluded his attack by calling for "redirect[ion] of the wasted dollars toward activities that are more likely to enhance public health" (1992:4).

Newspapers, once ardent proponents of environmental programs, now routinely question them. Writing in the *Washington Post,* Jessica Mathews (1991), vice-president of World Resources Institute, labeled the waste-management program a "boondoggle" and noted that "just a fifth [of the money] that is wasted could enable Head Start to enroll half instead of a quarter of eligible children." Passell (1991:1) argued that "most health dangers could be eliminated for a fraction of the billions now estimated." Notably, Dan Dudek, an economist with the Environmental Defense Fund, is cited in the article as favoring a policy that would gave back a portion of the money to towns willing to settle for residual contamination instead trying to return the site to its precontamination level. The newspaper article suggests that the money could be used for buying better fire-fighting equipment or by testing every home for radon and lead contamination.

Will our multiple-hazard neighborhood policy increase the economic efficiency of heavily criticized programs such as Superfund? Marginal utility theory suggests that it will. Briefly, the value of the first few dollars invested in solving a problem are normally more important than the value of the same number of dollars invested later in the program. For example, a $5 million investment in odor abatement at a sewage plant might reduce complaints from four days a week to four times a year. Another $5 to $15 million might be required to completely eliminate the odor problem. Investing part of that second $5 to $15 million to rehabilitate and convert an abandoned factory across the road from the sewage plant into warehousing and small spaces for entrepreneurs should have a far greater impact on the area, we expect, than achieving no odor days while neglecting redevelopment.

Rehabilitating an abandoned factory without dealing with sewage plant odors is also imprudent. Neighborhoods must have a sufficient number of civic-minded residents who will work for better schools, more fire, police, and sanitation services, and in other ways advocate for the neighborhood. The results of this research suggest that a critical mass of these dedicated people is going to be difficult to assemble in a poor quality neighborhood suffering from odors or chemical contamination.

To examine this multiple-project versus single-project idea for our study neighborhoods, we spoke with the city planners or town administrators of Bound Brook, Camden, Chester, and Elizabeth, four municipalities with many poor quality, multiple-hazard responses. We posed a hypothetical investment of funds to be allocated in whatever proportion the local official deemed most efficient to neighborhood remediation. How would they use these funds?

There was remarkable agreement among what stressed our respondents and what their local officials chose as priorities. East Elizabeth respondents were distressed by inadequate street lighting, streets and roads in disrepair, blight, and crime. Their planner identified a greater police presence and physical rehabilitation of buildings, streets, and roads as his priorities. He added that his third priority was to establish better communications with neighborhood residents, which we think was a fortuitous suggestion.

Bound Brook residents were distressed by blight and noise. The borough administrator was concerned about the deteriorated infrastructure of the area. He would use the money to fix the broken and misshapen roads, streets, and sidewalks. His second priority was to fix the sewer system, which he knew to be badly deteriorated. Finally, he would use some funds for housing inspections, which would pressure landlords to keep up their property and not permit overuse of apartments.

Chester's residents pointed to crime, abandoned buildings, rowdy people, litter or trash, and uncontrolled animals. A planning official immediately pointed to addressing severe physical blight, including rehabilitating housing, fixing curbs, sidewalks and streets. Second, he would add lighting to protect residents against crime. In addition, the planning official recommended planting trees and shrubs to improve the neighborhood's appearance, and last he would address the legacy of industrial pollution of the neighborhood.

East Camden respondents focused on abandoned houses, inadequate street lighting, crime, and streets, roads, and sidewalks in disrepair. Their planner identified the need for a police presence, housing rehabilitation, and physical improvements to lighting, streets, and roads. She noted that these were essential to support the strong neighborhood organizations in east Camden. She also mentioned several other projects that were identified by a few residents in their written comments. One was to redesign some of the streets near the park and add trees to improve the neighborhood's appearance. She also wanted to redevelop the nearby landfill as open

Table 9.1. Factors Associated with Reduced Appreciation of Property Values in 150 New Jersey Municipalities, 1987–1991

Factor	Ten Municipalities With Multiple Hazards (n = 10)		Other Municipalities (n = 140)
	Mean	Median	Mean
Area is unattractive culturally or physically	6.0	6.5	3.6
Economic recession	5.4	5.5	5.4
Industrial decline	4.9	5.0	3.6
High taxes	4.7	5.5	4.6
Commercial decline	4.6	4.0	3.7
Inferior services (schools, police, fire)	4.4	4.5	2.2
State environmental regulations	4.0	4.0	5.1
Area fully developed	3.9	3.0	3.1
No major highway linkage	3.1	1.5	2.4
State planning policies	2.9	2.5	4.1
Hazardous-waste sites	2.4	1.5	2.3
Local planning policies	2.1	1.5	4.3
Area too remote	1.6	1.0	2.6
Agricultural decline	1.4	1.0	2.6

Source: Greenberg and Hughes 1993.

space. Only this last idea was not mentioned by our respondents.

A study in New Jersey lends further credence to our survey of respondents' collective judgment (Greenberg and Hughes 1993). A survey containing six questions was mailed to the tax assessors of each of New Jersey's 567 minor civil divisions (e.g., boroughs, towns, cities). A total of 150 responded. Question six asked assessors to rate the relative importance of fourteen constraints on the appreciation of property values in the municipality during the years 1987 to 1991. On a scale of 1 to 9, in which 1 was not important and 9 was extremely important, table 9.1 compares two groups of municipalities. Ten municipalities, including four of the ones included in our twenty neighborhoods, have serious crime, blight, and massive technology site problems (Greenberg et al. 1992). The other 140, to the best of our knowledge, do not have all these problems.

Almost all the tax assessors agreed that economic recession and high taxes were important constraints to property value appreciation. However, the assessors of ten municipalities containing multiple-hazard neighborhoods focused on relative unattractiveness (culturally and physically), inferior services, and industrial and commercial decline as much more serious constraints. In other words, the combination of crime, blight, and decline of economic base leading to deteriorated buildings, loss of jobs, and reduction of public services has made these ten places unattractive to people and businesses with other choices.

Another economic efficiency question is what are the advantages and disadvantages of initiating the target-of-opportunity policy with a large external fund from outside sources? Outside initiative would doubtless be applauded by those who care about the potential benefits of substantially raising neighborhood quality in extremely stressed neighborhoods through coordinated investments. Although we have no proof, we believe that the benefit-to-cost ratios of programs targeted at poor quality, multiple-hazard neighborhoods could produce much higher aggregate economic benefits than programs aimed at a single problem. For example, the relatively low benefit-to-cost ratios of many EPA programs would be improved because insider programs could save lives from drugs, fires, and homicides and make the neighborhood more attractive for outside investment.

Others might view the outside initiative as fiscally irresponsible because it requires setting aside new funds to support the policy. Furthermore, it is risky because some parts of a multiple-hazard neighborhood plan could fail. For example, suppose a multiple-hazard plan required reducing odors for a sewage plant (external project), rehabilitating and leasing an abandoned factory (internal project), and reclaiming the streets from criminals (internal project). Rehabilitation of the factory could coincide with a recession. The rehabilitated property might not attract tenants and become politically embarrassing. Potential investors might be so put off by the neighborhood reputation as a center of criminal activity that they will not underwrite endeavors in the neighborhood even if crime is controlled. Reducing odors from the sewage plant, the external project, is probably the only safe investment.

Crime prevention is particularly worrisome. Our surveys and the literature show that safe streets are a prerequisite for successful redevelopment. Yet we have doubts that safe streets can be guaranteed. Some cities have recently noted a decline in violent and nonviolent crime (Krauss 1995). Among other explanations for this phenomenon: there are fewer teenagers to commit crimes, many criminals have been imprisoned, and police presence in neighborhoods has been increased. But criminal activity occurs in cycles and no one knows for sure what causes crime rates to decrease.

Clearly, we feel a moral imperative to reduce crime in devastated neighborhoods, especially as our studies show that residents are more concerned about crime than they are about massive technology sites. Yet neither the ethical imperative nor residents' perceptions automatically justify making crime reduction the highest priority unless there is some assurance that funding will have a lasting effect.

Equity and Consent

How will the proposed policy effect distributional inequities and consent? Scholars assert the principle that the distribution of burdens and benefits should be roughly equal (Rawls 1971; Beatley 1994). In other words, economically and politically disadvantaged populations, including future generations, should not be unfairly burdened with land uses and activities that no one else wants in their neighborhood.

The dense packing of technological hazards and relatively poor people into some of the neighborhoods we studied demonstrate that scholars' words and deeply rooted ways of locating people and activities do not match. Collin (1992) asserts that distributional inequities "snowball" in politically powerless environments. East Elizabeth, south Chester, and east Camden neighborhoods epitomize the kinds of highly vulnerable places and people that have led to the charge of "environmental racism," "environmental inequity," and the PIBBY—Place in Blacks' Back Yards—acronym. Our call for a multiple-hazard neighborhood policy is an opportunity to redress this distributional effect, to send a responsive message to a frustrated population. In addition, our call for internal projects to accompany and complement externally initiated outsider ones is, we think, of way of gaining the consent, and, we hope, enthusiastic support, of residents.

Two traps could sabotage this effort to address inequitable burdens. One is to dilute the potential funds and message by making too many neighborhoods eligible. We call this the "accessibility" trap. Multiple-hazard neighborhoods should not include middle-class places, such as the areas surrounding the Global Landfill in

Sayreville, the Cyanamid site in Bridgewater, and the Bayonne Chromium site. These neighborhoods do have multiple hazards, but the neighborhoods are not rated as poor quality and relatively few of the people are poor. Inclusion of middle-class neighborhoods would doubtless make the multiple-hazard neighborhood policy more politically acceptable. However, we believe that the money should be focused on multiple-hazard neighborhoods that have a poor or fair quality rating as well as behavioral, blight, and land-use hazards.

Our policy requires the development of eligibility criteria based on vulnerability. Cutter (1993) defined place vulnerability as combining hazards with political and social contexts to create a measure of place and population vulnerability. Hazard vulnerability could be judged from perception studies, such as the ones presented in this book; from age, income, and housing data gathered from United States census; from land-use data gathered from master plans; from published FBI uniform crime data; and from environmental monitoring data, right-to-know data, and other indicators of environmental pollutants. Only neighborhoods that demonstrate high vulnerability across all three dimensions (behavior, blight, pollution) should be given access to the funds.

Our restriction of the policy to poor quality, multiple-hazard neighborhoods follows the precedent that led to the Orphan Drug Act of 1983. Briefly, some serious but relatively rare diseases have not been addressed by pharmaceutical companies because the cost of developing the product could not be recouped by sales. In order to address the socially desirable goal of developing drugs for rare diseases, pharmaceutical companies were granted market and tax credit incentives. It is not a stretch to label our poor quality, multiple-hazard neighborhoods as political and economic orphans of the United States.

Wide variations exist in the ability and willingness of states and local governments to support public health, environmental protection, and planning programs in their neighborhoods (Greenberg, Popper, and West 1991). This reality is also part of the accessibility trap. We predict that medium and large cities in proactive states, such as California, Massachusetts, Minnesota, New Jersey, New York, and Wisconsin will obtain a disproportionate share of the funding, if not nearly all of it. Small cities in poor states that normally do not support environmental and public health programs are unlikely to be able to obtain either resources to develop plans or required funds to match federal government revenues. For example, the Evergreen Enterprise Center's list of community environmental successes includes twenty-four projects in the United States listed as "urban." Seventeen of the twenty-four are in seven of the fifteen states classified as the most affluent and innovative (Greenberg, Popper, and West 1991). None are in the fifteen states that are least affluent and least innovative, even though these have neglected cities.

We do not expect every poorly rated, multiple-hazard neighborhood to want to apply for funds, nor is it reasonable to expect every neighborhood to have exactly the same opportunity to obtain funds. Limits must be set on the number of projects that can be approved for a single state and for the largest municipalities. To encourage a variety of applications, it may also be necessary to provide simpler decision criteria and extra planning funds for neighborhoods located in small cities and/or in poor states.

The second and perhaps the most dangerous ethical trap is abuse of the target-of-opportunity policy by a local or state government. The most likely maneuver is to try to use funds to attract private investors who will seek to drive out current residents and gentrify the neighborhood for a higher-income population.

Another potentially unethical option is to use funds to reindustrialize the neighborhood without consent of the residents and without proper risk analyses. Funds would be employed to clean up pollution, rehabilitate houses and other buildings, add a ramp to the nearby highway, and rehabilitate the old railroad spur with the idea of attracting new industrial clients. Local residents would be trained to do as much of the work as possible. The idea of shoehorning incinerators, sewage plants, factories, maximum security prisons, junkyards, and all other land uses and activities that cannot be politically fit elsewhere into existing poor quality, multiple-hazard neighborhoods is not without merit. It can be argued that concentrating LULUs in these areas saves pristine ones.

The potential trap is sprung by reducing the levels of cleanup required on abandoned or underused industrial properties in multiple-hazard neighborhoods to less than that demanded of industrial properties in other neighborhoods (Schneider 1993). It is possible that trying to resuscitate poor quality neighborhoods through reindustrialization could fail because of the unpredictability of production-based economies in the 1990s. Before allowing a policy created to correct inequities to be used for reindustrialization, we must confront the strong probability that land uses perceived as dangerous and/or unsightly for many decades will continue to be perceived as undesirable by outside investors who have the resources to really upgrade devastated neighborhoods. We suspect that these land uses, even if much cleaner than their earlier counterparts, will scare away outsiders and could begin anew a process that ends with blight, crime, and other elements of a low quality neighborhood a generation later. Such an outcome would amount to what Calabresi and Bobbit (1978) call "tragic choices."

It is essential that the neighborhood within one-half mile of the projects be strongly represented in developing the plans and be able to modify plans that in the eyes of the neighborhood are not in their best interest. Some residents of neighborhoods might support the reindustrialization of their neighborhoods if pollution, crime, and blight were reduced, and if money saved by requiring a lower level of decontamination is reallocated to bring jobs into and rebuild the neighborhood. Others would be outraged, especially if they believe that reindustrialization might fail.

Political Support

Can the policy secure political support? Our policy requires a broader definition of environmental hazard, an ability to get national and state government to focus on the neighborhood scale and work with local governments and neighborhoods, and the flexibility to move funds among different levels of government in new ways. In this section, we propose and respond to questions that we think will be the main political stumbling blocks. Before presenting the questions, we note that a considerable literature addresses these questions. We cannot possibly do justice to it. We use the literature to present our sense of the prospects for overcoming serious political obstacles.

Insider Input. How much credence will be given to insiders' collective judgments about neighborhood quality and environmental hazards by outside experts and officials who control funds? If government scientists and regulators believe that residents and municipal officials are ignorant of what really impacts neighborhoods, they will not support a policy that encourages municipal governments and neighborhood advocates to play a central role in decision making. Or if experts and bureaucrats want a convenient excuse to ignore or disregard a neighborhoods' self-stated needs, they can turn to experts to suggest public ignorance as a rationalization for agencies maintaining full control.

The different views of hazards and risks held by experts and the public has been addressed by many scholars (Hapgood 1979; Krimsky and Plough 1988; Michalos 1974; Nelkin 1981; Shrader-Frechette 1985, 1991a, 1991b; Zielhuis and Wibowo 1989). Kasper (1980:77) summarized the typical expert view of the public prior to the decade of the 1990s: "The experts' approach to their differences with the rest of the public has been to somehow persuade the public to alter its perception. . . . I know of no serious effort directed toward shifting expert's views so that they will coincide with those of the rest of the public." A typical comment associated with this view appeared in *Science* as a letter to the editor: "Surely the responsibility lies with the educable but ignorant adults to enlighten themselves" (Robinson 1987:19).

Criticizing public ignorance of science, overzealous mass media for hyping some problems and understating others, and political officials for creating phantom risks and creating policies that ignore the best science will not disappear. For example, commenting on the Medical Waste Tracking Act of 1988 in the *New England Journal of Medicine,* Rutala and Weber (1991:581) state: "Because of the intense and often misleading media coverage of this issue and a lack of understanding of disease transmission, the states and the federal government created strict regulations, which aggravated the problem. . . . The result is an extraordinary increase in cost with no environmental or public health benefit. The medical-waste policies that have evolved from perceived risks over the past few years should be supplanted by rules based on scientific considerations."

Despite this legacy, we expect scientists and especially officials will become increasingly responsible to the public because it is becoming politically hazardous to do otherwise. In some cases, statutes require consultation with the public, which, of course, does not guarantee anything more than perfunctory compliance. The bigger risk to the expert/bureaucrat is being so out of touch with the public that their recommendations are ignored.

Sentinels of the need to listen to the public were apparent by the mid-1980s. For example, former EPA assistant administrator Milton

Russell (1987:20) wrote that "when it comes to protecting health and environment, it is public, not expert, opinion that counts." Evidence of this change is sprouting, at least on paper. In February 1994, the EPA Office of Policy Analysis distributed a memo that directed the Pollution Prevention and Toxics Branch to empower communities to help redevelop industrial areas. In sharp contrast to failed U.S. Department of Energy attempts to educate the citizens of Nevada about the safety of the planned Yucca Flats high-level radioactive waste storage facility (Flynn, Slovic, and Mertz 1993), a National Research Council Committee (1994) recommended to the DOE that stakeholder involvement must be planned as carefully as risk assessment and risk management.

A 1994 issue of the newsletter to members of the Society of Risk Analysis, reported an interview with Mark Schaefer, described as the "point person for risk assessment issues in the Clinton administration" (Society for Risk Analysis 1994:1). Schaefer was quoted as follows: "Another high priority is ensuring that there is a two-way communication between the public and federal officials. We don't view risk assessment as experts telling the public what they should be concerned about. Communication should flow in both directions." This statement is testimony to the fact that senior political officials have grasped the message that one of the reasons that officials have lost credibility is their failure to listen.

State and federal officials and their experts ignore the public and local experts at their own political peril (Shrader-Frechette 1985, 1991a, 1991b). They play a high-stakes game using science that is not presently able to estimate cumulative risk, and regulations are not geared to address multiple-hazard neighborhoods. We do not expect the fight for control between scientific experts, regulators, elected officials, and the public to fade away. We do expect it to be supplanted by an effort to find solutions based on the best science that incorporates the wisdom of the residents in places like multiple-hazard, poor quality neighborhoods.

To be very clear, we are not calling for neighborhood residents and local health officers and planners to vote on how resources are to be used. Residents who "get what they want" because of misinformation or anger at outside experts and regulators will probably not be better off in the long run. Nor will multiple-hazard neighborhoods get much better when national and state government officials force narrowly conceived programs down the throats of insiders because of a congressional mandate that makes perfect sense for the nation as a whole but not for multiple-hazard places. In short, it is hard work to reconcile democratic values with the methods of science and mandate of regulators. The United States has created knowledge and rule-based elites that too often think they have the "answer." Our data suggest that local agency experts in public health and planning are in strong agreement with neighborhood residents about problems and solutions in poor quality, multiple-hazard neighborhoods. Their knowledge must be at the core of multiple-hazard neighborhood redevelopment projects. The experts and regulators in Washington, D.C., and state capitals rightfully should be at the periphery and involved primarily through external projects and technical backup.

Social Science Input. How much credence will be given to social science–based findings about neighborhood quality and environmental hazards by traditional environmental health scientists? As our research progressed, it became clear that unless social science is given an important role to play in poor quality neighborhoods, the sociological, economic, political, psychological, and other foundations of these complicated places will not be sufficiently understood to intelligently inform redevelopment. We obviously need to know the value of property; the age, race/ethnicity, and educational characteristics of the population; the characteristics of community groups; street-, park-, and school-use patterns; residents' perceptions of the local government, businesses, and community leaders; and a variety of other facts about neighborhoods at least as much as we need to know facts about pollution, architecture and planning.

But basic facts are insufficient to inform policy in complex multiple-hazard neighborhoods. Risk perception is influenced by the extent that the public feels that they can control the hazard, its scale and memorability, the degree of trust that the public feels about those imposing the risk, and other factors described in detail elsewhere (Slovic 1993; Sandman et al. 1993). We need more information about these "outrage" factors by race, ethnicity, economic class, age, and other demographic characteristics for environmentally devastated neighborhoods.

The absence of support for social science research is a serious concern. Social sciences have been made subordinate to natural sciences in risk analysis. As a prelude to the Earth Summit of world political leaders held in Rio de Janeiro in June 1992, a conference was held in Vienna in November 1991 to set a scientific agenda for environment and development into the next century (Dooge et al. 1992:244). The authors concluded that natural scientists are not going to find "incontestable fact(s) about global environmental process" that would lead to "the emergence of universally shared perspectives on the structure of the problems to be solved." They asserted that "the social sciences, principally such disciplines as law, economics, geography and sociology, have begun to be incorporated into international and national environmental research programs as subordinate to the natural sciences." They criticized this subordinate role, arguing that the "critical uncertainties . . . are turning out to be less uncertainties of a physical, technical kind, than social, cultural and institutional." They and we are not calling for less natural science, but for much more social science.

The sorry status of social science in risk analysis in the United States was elegantly summarized by Richard Andrews (1994:1670) in a letter to the editor of *Science* in response to a statement of EPA administrator Carol Browner about the EPA's need to base decisions of the best possible science: "Notwithstanding the many unanswered questions in the natural and engineering sciences . . . , many of the most important uncertainties for improving EPA's policies lie not in these fields, but in the socioeconomic disciplines. If EPA is truly to base its decisions on the best possible science, it will need not only to improve the quantity and quality of its research but also to correct the profound imbalance in what research it supports and to address equally important socioeconomic factors that determine the effectiveness of its policies. A likely result will be the discovery of many risk-reduction opportunities that are less costly and more effective than present policies."

Pressure to elevate the social sciences comes from the political failures of many environmental laws to produce cost-effective and equitable results. At the time this book was written, only two environmental laws, the Toxic Substances Control Act (TSCA) and the Federal Insecticide, Fungicide, and Rodenticide Act (FIFRA), required the EPA to balance the benefits and costs of regulations. But the large cost-to-benefit ratios discussed earlier in this chapter are driving other organizations to insist on economic analyses. For example, the DOE, having agreed to clean up waste sites at costs exceeding billions of dollars, is requesting economic analyses to help guide those cleanups. Community opposition to siting new facilities and redeveloping old ones has led to the call for two-way risk communication.

We recommend more social science with trepidation. First, as noted above, social science surveys should not determine policies any more than natural science research. Second, social scientists are as capable as their natural science counterparts of tunneling themselves into jargon and treating residents of environmentally devastated neighborhoods as subjects rather than real people. Frankly, we fear that perfunctory economic and social studies may be done in multihazard neighborhoods under the social science label. For example, one or two focus-group meetings with people can give the pretense of risk communication. But good risk communication should consist of focus groups to elicit key issues, community surveys such as those used in this book, follow-up work with a representative group to formulate a mutually satisfactory plan, and follow through on implementation as part of a subcommittee.

A cost-and-benefit analysis can be an inadequate rudimentary comparison of three engineering cost proposals against the overall benefits to the municipality. It should also address the specifics of health, environmental quality, and property damage benefits. It should address who benefits and for how long; what is the likelihood the benefits will really be realized; what factors could reduce these benefits; and whether there is a disproportional distribution of benefits and costs.

Turf Protection. Will bureaucratic turf protection block this policy? In December 1993, Henry Cisneros, secretary of Housing and Urban Development, in an interview with *Time,* spoke frankly about turf problems: "You can't move this massive machinery or relate it too massive machinery in other departments real easily. You move with concrete blocks tied to your arms and legs. I can't believe how gridlocked the system is, how it runs counter to common sense sometimes, how irrelevant it is to things that are happening out in the country."

With respect to neighborhood redevelopment, Logan and Molotch (1987) see state and federal regulators, entrepreneurs, and neighborhood residents as combatants in a struggle to achieve their opposing goals. Readers will not be surprised to learn that reviewers told us that in addition to cost, laws and resistance by federal and state bureaucrats are the biggest obstacles to our poor quality, multiple-hazard neighborhood policy. American environmental laws developed as a series of narrowly focused responses to specific problems. Agency administrators/directors have little, if any, flexibility to respond to broader environmental problems. Simply put, the EPA administrator cannot take money from the Superfund program and give it to the local housing authority or police chief.

As part of a settlement of a law suit against a responsible party, the EPA administrator could permit some money to go to the housing authority. An anonymous reviewer suggested that industry lawyers would seize upon the idea as proof that expensive cleanups were not required. However, Sandman (1994) argued that companies might not object to a reallocation of funds into hazard and outrage components and might favor a reallocation, especially if their total costs were reduced. Another anonymous reviewer added that a private party might be willing to pay less to Superfund or another law and more into general revenues. This would allow the various levels of government to fight over the distribution.

Several reviewers suggested that environmental groups might object to placing the needs of people before the needs of fauna and flora. We do not agree. Based on their recent efforts, we think many will applaud the idea of trying to accomplish both. For example, the Natural Resources Defense Council (*Amicus Journal* 1994) recently joined in efforts to help redevelop poor quality areas such as the South Bronx.

Even if industry and environmental advocate groups did not object, it seems clear that the EPA and every other federal and state agency would have no reason to engage in projects that are not part of their environmental jurisdiction. Allowing agencies to search for reallocation within their existing mandates is a much more politically feasible option for agencies such as the EPA, Housing and Urban Development, and the Department of Transportation. For example, the EPA might be willing to reallocate money to lead and asbestos removal in a neighborhood where a hazardous-waste site is being remediated. At least the turf battle would take place within a single agency.

A special policy for multiple-hazard neighborhoods will be blocked by disinterested and/or turf protecting agencies and legislators unless important elected officials send unambiguous messages to federal and state agencies and legislators. Agencies and legislatures might be more inclined to cooperate and less defensive about their turf if Congress changed their mandate to allow for a broader definition of environment and charged them with looking for opportunities to work with other organizations around neighborhood environmental problems.

Opposition might turn to grudging cooperation if agencies that cooperated were given financial carrots, such as the availability of a special pot of money allocated only for addressing poor quality, multiple-hazard neighborhoods. The outsider method of initiating internal projects, described earlier in the chapter, proposes a special fund of money for this purpose.

Local governments have much to gain from our policy. They can demonstrate to local voters that they can obtain neighborhood improvement funds from outside sources. However, there is a potential trap for local officials. The proposed neighborhood development plan may be opposed by some local people who could use it to oppose local officials in elections. Given the slow pace of obtaining and spending federal and state funds, local officials are risking running in an election in which some people oppose their plans and others are distressed because the funds have not been secured or used.

The role of neighborhood residents and organizations must be central to the process of designing and implementing the insider project. Clay and Hollister (1983) argue that the neighborhood is uniquely able to represent people's needs to the larger society. Jane Jacobs (1961) sees the neighborhood district as the mediator between politically powerless street neighborhoods and powerful city governments. In 1978, Congress passed the Neighborhood Self-Help Development Act (NSHD), which provided funds directly to support local development projects. After spending less than $15 million, the program was cut during the Reagan administration. Despite a few highly publicized successes, such as the Dudley Street neighborhood in Boston (Medoff and Sklar 1994), Miller, Rein, and Levitt (1990) report that organizations in poor neighborhoods are relatively rare and operate on a shoestring. They assert that advocacy groups or regional agencies often assume the political role in these neighborhoods.

For example, the east Elizabeth planner indicated a need for stronger ties with the community to form a plan that can attract investments. Sometimes advocacy groups fill the void. The Regional Planning Association (RPA) of New Jersey (1994) identified more than one hundred abandoned or underused sites in Union County, New Jersey, that could be redeveloped. One of the sites is the northern boundary of the Elizabethport neighborhood described in chapter 5. Working with the City of Elizabeth and federal and state agencies, the RPA has developed a plan to build a major commercial center that would create one thousand jobs in one of the poorest quality neighborhoods in our study. While we applaud this multiple-agency effort, we point out that the EPA spent more than $40 million remediating the Chemical Control Waste site, the U.S. Department of Transportation has spent millions building a noise barrier and building a road to Newark Airport, and Exxon, Tosco, and other companies have spent millions on their production facilities in the area. Our policy would provide funds to allow the City of Elizabeth to move forward with more police and housing redevelopment and address other missing links in redevelopment. That is, our policy would foster comprehensive redevelopment of the area, rather than a fragmented one aimed at pollution control in some parts of the area, commercial and retail development in others, and transportation enhancement in others.

Summary

We argue that a policy should be developed to redevelop poor quality, multiple-hazard neighborhoods. This policy must be able to respond to behavioral, blight, and massive technology site hazards in neighborhoods with or without strong neighborhood organizations. Our fifteen hundred surveys suggest that a policy that responds to one problem in a piecemeal fashion will not substantially raise neighborhood quality. In this chapter, we have proposed a target-of-opportunity policy and implementation options that would take advantage of outsider plans to address one or more neighborhood problems. The policy would provide funds to insiders to address hazards not addressed by the outsider projects. In other words, it would tackle other critical problems and potentially improve neighborhood quality. With caveats noted about economic risk and neighborhood political realities, we conclude that health and safety should be improved and investment efficiency increased as a result of the policy. Distributional inequities are addressed by restricting funds to poor and perhaps fair quality neighborhoods with multiple hazards. Lastly, neighborhood consent for the outside project should be easier to obtain because the neighborhood plays a direct role in the complementary inside project.

Organizational acceptability is likely to be the biggest constraint. The inside initiative would probably face the least political opposition, but it would also limit the number of opportunities for neighborhood redevelopment. The outside initiative method would encounter strong opposition from fiscal conservatives and those who would perceive our program as wasting resources on unproductive segments of society.

No one has a monopoly on wisdom about what a proper environmental protection program should be. Nor does anyone really know what constitutes a just solution for those living in the worst neighborhoods. Because a true scientific understanding and political consensus are lacking, neighborhood residents, if they can form a consensus, should be given the opportunity to express their opinion in the form of innovative inside projects. Surely, this is a healthy approach in a democracy.

Appendix 1:
Closed and Fully Labeled
Survey Instrument

All neighborhoods have characteristics and conditions, some of which concern people. Please help us understand how you feel about your *present* neighborhood by answering the following set of questions.

A. Please circle Yes or No.	Does your neighborhood have the following?		If yes, does the condition bother you?		Is it so disturbing that you would like to move?	
1. Abandoned houses?	Yes	No	Yes	No	Yes	No
2. Abandoned factories and businesses?	Yes	No	Yes	No	Yes	No
3. Occupied buildings in poor or dangerous condition?	Yes	No	Yes	No	Yes	No
4. Inadequate street lighting?	Yes	No	Yes	No	Yes	No
5. Streets, roads, and sidewalks in disrepair or open ditches?	Yes	No	Yes	No	Yes	No
6. Motor vehicle noise and heavy traffic?	Yes	No	Yes	No	Yes	No
7. Noise from airplanes?	Yes	No	Yes	No	Yes	No
8. Noise from trains?	Yes	No	Yes	No	Yes	No
9. Litter or trash in streets, empty lots, or properties?	Yes	No	Yes	No	Yes	No
10. Odors or smoke?	Yes	No	Yes	No	Yes	No
11. Petroleum refinery or tank farm?	Yes	No	Yes	No	Yes	No
12. Incinerator?	Yes	No	Yes	No	Yes	No
13. Chemical plant?	Yes	No	Yes	No	Yes	No
14. Metal for furniture plant?	Yes	No	Yes	No	Yes	No
15. Junkyard, gasoline station, and other nonresidential activities?	Yes	No	Yes	No	Yes	No
16. Sites with hazardous wastes?	Yes	No	Yes	No	Yes	No
17. Recreational facilities that attract noisy/rowdy people?	Yes	No	Yes	No	Yes	No

A. Continued Please circle Yes or No.	Does your neighborhood have the following?		If yes, does the condition bother you?		Is it so disturbing that you would like to move?	
18. Right-of-way for a utility?	Yes	No	Yes	No	Yes	No
19. Unfriendly neighbors?	Yes	No	Yes	No	Yes	No
20. High crime rate?	Yes	No	Yes	No	Yes	No
21. Dogs, cats, or other uncontrolled animals?	Yes	No	Yes	No	Yes	No

B. Are these reasons you to live in this neighborhood? (Please circle Yes or No.)

1. Convenient to job	Yes	No
2. Convenient to friends/relatives	Yes	No
3. Convenient to leisure activities	Yes	No
4. Convenient to public transportation	Yes	No
5. Convenient to hospital	Yes	No
6. Convenient to shopping	Yes	No
7. Good schools	Yes	No
8. Other public services	Yes	No
9. Housing is inexpensive	Yes	No
10. House was inherited	Yes	No
11. Other (please describe below)	Yes	No

C. How would you rate your *present* neighborhood as a place to live?
   1. Excellent   2. Good   3. Fair   4. Poor

D. How would you rate your *present* neighborhood compared to your *previous* (old) neighborhood?
   1. Better   2. Same   3. Worse   4. Not Applicable

E. Please tell us about yourself so that we can understand who is disturbed by certain neighborhood conditions. Circle the answer that describes yourself.

1. What is your age?
   a. 18–30 years   b. 31–50 years   c. 51–70 years   d. 70+ years

2. What is your sex?
   a. Male   b. Female

3. Do you own or rent your residence?
   a. Own   b. Rent   c. Other

4. How long have you lived in your *present* neighborhood?
    a. 0–6 months   b. 6 months–2 years
    c. 2–5 years   d. 5–10 years
    e. 10 years or more

5. What is the last grade you completed in school?
    a. 1–8   b. 9–11
    c. Graduated High School   d. Technical School
    e. Some College   f. Graduated College

Is there anything else you would like to tell us about your neighborhood that we did not ask?

_____

_____

Thank you for helping us understand your neighborhood concerns.

Appendix 2:
Open-ended Survey
Instrument

Surveyor Question Sheet

[Read this statement to all potential respondents.]

Hello my name is ———. I am a graduate student in the Department of Urban Planning and Policy Development at Rutgers University. I would like to ask you a few questions about neighborhoods. Professors Michael Greenberg and Dona Schneider have been surveying people in New Jersey and Pennsylvania in order to try to better understand how Americans think about neighborhoods. This interview is completely voluntary. If I come to a question which you do not want to answer, just let me know and I will go to the next question. This interview should take about 10–15 minutes. We will not use your name or any other identifier. The survey is completely confidential.

A. *Feelings about neighborhoods:* Please choose two neighborhoods. The first should be one that is great—you enjoy being in it, you would go out of your way to spend time in it. The second should be one that you think is terrible—that is, you hate being in it, and you would avoid it.

> A1. *Great neighborhood.* Imagine that you are walking, biking, or riding through the neighborhood you think is great. Consider why you *feel* as you do about this neighborhood. List your feelings about the neighborhood you like. Make sure that these are your *feelings,* not a list of physical characteristics of the neighborhood. [If they don't know what we mean by feelings, pick love. Responses should be anger, fear, ugly, revulsion, happiness, jubilation, sense of openness, friendliness, newness, light, warm, dark, love, hate, beauty.] [Write down the list of feelings about the great neighborhood on the accompanying sheet.]

> A2. *Terrible neighborhood.* Imagine that you are walking, biking, or riding through the neighborhood you dislike. Consider why you *feel* as you do about this neighborhood. List your feelings about the neighborhood you dislike. Make sure that these are your *feelings,*

not a list of physical characteristics of the neighborhood. [Write down the list of feelings about the terrible neighborhood on the accompanying sheet.]

B. *Terrible neighborhood characteristics:* I am particularly interested in your feelings about the terrible neighborhood. Consider why you feel as you do about the terrible neighborhood. Which *characteristics* are most related to your feelings of distress about this neighborhood? Close your eyes and tell me what you see that distresses you [characteristics should be: abandoned housing, abandoned factories and businesses, airplanes overhead, automobile traffic, bars that attract rowdy people, broken sidewalks and streets, chemical plants, crime, dilapidated housing, drugs, inadequate street lighting, public transportation, shopping, medical facilities, police protection, sanitation services, recreation facilities, fire protection, gas tanks, petrochemical facilities, landfills and hazardous-waste sites, noise, not enough trees, shrubs, and grass, not enough parking, recreational facilities that attract rowdy people, odors, power lines for utility, rats, raccoons, isolation from other people, sewage treatment plant, smoke, stray dogs and cats, trains, unfriendly neighbors.] [List characteristics which most distress respondent on the accompanying sheet.]

C. *Interaction of distressing characteristics:* How do these distressing characteristics interact in your thinking? That is, do they reinforce one another, act independently? [Try to get examples from people. This is the sort of response to expect: A house down the street has been abandoned and I'm afraid to let my children go near it because drug addicts hang out there. Tractor noise from the waste site wakes me up night and neighbors argue all the time which keeps me up. I see a raccoon and worry about my children getting bitten because the town won't send someone to get rid of the raccoon.] [Write the elicited answers on the accompanying sheet.]

D. *Improving the terrible neighborhood:* Imagine that you had the money and power to improve the neighborhood you dislike. What would you choose to do? [Prompts: more police, repair abandoned housing, fix playground, clean up hazardous-waste site.] [Write the responses on the accompanying sheet.]

E. *The fixed problem:* If the respondent did not mention the hazardous-waste site, or whatever we identified as the massive technology site problem, ask why. [Write the answer on the accompanying sheet.]

ANSWER PAGE

A1. Feelings about the great neighborhood

A2. Feelings about the terrible neighborhood

B. Characteristics of terrible neighborhood

C. Interaction of distressing characteristics

D. Improving the terrible neighborhood

E. Fixed problem comments

F. Please tell us about yourself so that we can understand who is disturbed by certain neighborhood conditions.

    1. What is your age?
    a. 18–30 years   b. 31–50 years   c. 51–70 years   d. 70+ years

    2. What is your sex?
    a. Male   b. Female

    3. Do you own or rent your residence?
    a. Own   b. Rent   c. Other

    4. How long have you lived in your *present* neighborhood?
    a. 0–6 months   b. 6 mo–2 years c. 2–5 years
    d. 5–10 years   e. 10+ years

    5. What is the last grade you completed in school?
    a. 1–8   b. 9–11   c. Graduated high school

d. Some college   f. Technical or trade school
g. Armed services training   h. Graduated college

6. Which of the following have you done during the past two years?
(Circle all that apply.)
a. Attended a public meeting
b. Voted in a local election
c. Contacted an elected official about a problem
d. Called the police
e. Had your blood pressure checked
f. Had your cholesterol checked
g. Visited a doctor for a checkup
h. Visited a dentist for a checkup
i. Volunteered for a civic or church function
j. Had an eye examination

7. How would you rate your health?
a. Excellent   b. Very good   c. Good
d. Fair   e. Poor

Is there anything else you would like to tell us about *your* neighborhood?

[Please thank them for answering our questions.]

References

Adams, P. 1992. "Television as Gathering Place." *Annals of the Association of American Geographers* 82:117–35.

Agency for Toxic Substances and Disease Registry. 1992. "Hazardous Waste Sites: Priority Health Conditions and Research Strategies—United States." *MMWR* 41:72–74.

Aitken, S. 1990. "Local Evaluations of Neighborhood Change." *Annals of the Association of American Geographers* 80:247–67.

Amicus Journal. 1994. "A Pioneering Partnership: Recycling and Jobs in the South Bronx." 16:4.

Andrews, P. 1994. Letter to the editor. *Science* 263:1670.

Appleyard, D., and M. Lintell. 1972. "Environmental Quality of City Streets: The Residents' Viewpoint." *Journal of the American Institute of Planners* 38:84–101.

Baldassare, M., and C. Katz. 1992. "The Personal Threat of Environmental Problems as Predictor of Environmental Practices." *Environment and Behavior* 24:602–16.

Baxter, R. 1990. "Some Public Attitudes About Health and the Environment." *Environmental Health Perspectives* 86:261–69.

Beatley, T. 1994. *Ethical Land Use.* Baltimore: Johns Hopkins University Press.

Behrman, R., and V. Vaughan. 1987. *Nelson Textbook of Pediatrics.* 13th ed. Philadelphia: W. B. Saunders.

Blocker, T., and E. Eckberg. 1989. "Environmental Issues as Women's Issues: General Concerns and Local Hazards." *Social Science Quarterly* 70:586–93.

Bowermaster, J. 1993. "A Town Called Morrisonville." *Audubon* (July–August): 42–51.

Brown, M. 1981. *Laying Waste: The Poisoning of America by Toxic Chemicals.* New York: Washington Square Press.

Brown, P., and E. Mikkelsen. 1990. *No Safe Place: Toxic Waste, Leukemia, and Community Action.* Berkeley and Los Angeles: University of California Press.

Buckley, W. 1993. "Poverty, Racism Don't Explain Black Crime." *Newark Star-Ledger,* 5 January, p. 14.

Bullard, R. 1990. *Dumping on Dixie: Race, Class, and Environmental Quality.* Boulder, Colo.: Westview Press.

Burgess, J. 1974. "Stereotypes and Urban Images." *Area* 6:167–91.

Burton, I., R. Kates, and G. White. 1978. *The Environment as Hazard.* New York: Oxford University Press.

Buttel, F. 1987. "New Directions in Environmental Sociology." *Annual Review of Sociology* 13:465–88.

Calabresi, G., and P. Bobbit. 1978. *Tragic Choices.* New York: Norton.

Callow, A. 1965. *The Tweed Ring.* New York: Oxford University Press.

Campbell, A., P. Converse, and W. Rodgers. 1976. *The Quality of American Life: Perceptions, Evaluations, and Satisfactions.* New York: Russell Sage Foundation.

Carlin, A. 1990. *Environmental Investments: The Cost of Clean Environment: A Summary.* Washington, D.C.: Environmental Protection Agency.

Carnay, J. 1986. "Youth Gangs Plague South." *Time,* 18 August, 17.

Carnegie Commission. 1993. *Risk and the Environment: Improving Regulatory Decision Making.* New York: Carnegie Commission.

Carter, K., J. Jaffe, and K. Dilworth. 1995. "Carteret, Union City, Mt. Holly, Pleasantville, Named Enterprise Zones." *Newark Star-Ledger,* 12 January, p. 13.

Chemical Manufacturers Association. 1991. *Summary Report: Baseline for Improvement, Public Perceptions of the Chemical Industry, 1989–1990.* Toledo, Ohio: National Family Opinion.

Cisneros, H. 1993. Interview. *Time,* 6 December, 31.

Citizen Fund of New Jersey. 1993. *Poisons in Our Neighborhoods: Toxic Pollution in New Jersey.* Washington, D.C.: Citizen Fund of New Jersey.

Clay, G. 1976. *Right Before Your Eyes: Penetrating the Urban Environment.* Washington, D.C.: American Planning Association Press.

Clay, P., and R. Hollister, eds. 1983. *Neighborhood Policy and Planning.* Lexington, Mass.: Lexington Books, D.C. Heath.

Collin, R. 1992. "Environmental Racism: A Law and Planning Approach to Environmental Racism." *Virginia Environmental Law Journal* 11:495–546.

Commission for Racial Justice, United Church of Christ. 1987. *Toxic Wastes and Race in the United States.* New York: United Church of Christ.

Committee on Remedial Action Priorities for Hazardous Waste Sites, National Research Council. 1994. *Ranking Hazardous-Waste Sites for Remedial Action.* Washington, D.C.: National Academy Press.

Commoner, B. 1971. *The Closing Circle: Nature, Man, and Technology.* New York: Bantam Books.

Cutter, S. 1985. *Rating Places.* Washington, D.C.: Association of American Geographers.

———. 1993. *Living with Risk: The Geography of Technological Hazards.* Boston: Edward Arnold.

Dahmann, D. 1983. "Subjective Assessments of Neighborhood Quality by Size of Place." *Urban Studies* 20:31–45.

Davis, J. 1993. Analyst, Port Authority of New York and New Jersey. Personal communication, 19 October.

Detwyler, T., and M. Marcus. 1972. *Urbanization and Environment*. Belmont, Calif.: Duxbury Press.

Dickens, C. 1960. *Hard Times*. New York: Harper and Row.

Diefenbach, M., N. Weinstein, and J. O'Reilly. 1993. "Scales for Assessing Perceptions of Health Hazard Susceptibility." *Health Education Research: Theory and Practice* 8:181–92.

Dienemann, E., R. Ahlert, and M. Greenberg. 1991. "Remediation of the Lipari Landfill, America's #1 Ranked Superfund Site." *Impact Assessment Bulletin* 9:13–30.

Dixon, P., M. Bobo, and R. Stevick. 1984. "Response Differences and Preferences for All-Category-Defined and End-Defined Likert Formats." *Educational and Psychological Measurement* 44:61–66.

Dodge K., J. Bates, and G. Petit. 1990. "Mechanisms in the Cycle of Violence." *Science* 250:1678–83.

Dooge, J., G. Goodman, J. La Riviere, J. Marton-Lefevre, T. O'Riordan, and F. Praderie, eds. 1992. *An Agenda of Science for Environment and Development in the 21st Century*. Cambridge: Cambridge University Press.

Douglas, M. 1985. *Risk Acceptability According to the Social Sciences*. New York: Russell Sage Foundation.

Drane, J. 1991. "Imputing Nonresponses to Mail-Back Questionnaires." *American Journal of Epidemiology* 134:908–12.

Dunne, M., P. Burnett, J. Lawton, and B. Raphael. 1990. "The Health Effects of Chemical Waste in an Urban Community." *Medical Journal of Australia* 152:592–97.

Edelstein, M. 1988. *Contaminated Communities: The Social and Psychological Impacts of Residential Toxic Exposure*. Boulder, Colo.: Westview Press.

Elton, B. 1989. *Stark*. London: Sphere Books.

Environmental Enterprise Center. 1994. *Evergreen Community Environmental Success Stories*. Victoria, B.C.: Environmental Enterprise Center.

Epstein, S., L. Brown, and C. Pope. 1982. *Hazardous Waste in America*. San Francisco: Sierra Club Books.

Fallows, J. 1971. *The Water Lords*. New York: Bantam Books.

Fedarko, K. 1992. "The Other America: Who Could Live Here? 'Only People with No Other Choice.'" *Time,* 20 January, 20–23.

Findley, S., and J. Ford. 1993. "Reversals in the Epidemiological Transition in Harlem." Paper presented at the Population Association of America Conference, 1–3 April, Cincinnati, Ohio.

Finkel, A., and D. Golding, eds. 1994. *Worst Things First? The Debate Over Risk-Based National Environmental Priorities*. Washington, D.C.: Resources for the Future.

Fischer, G., M. Morgan, B. Fischhoff, I. Nair, and L. Lave. 1991. "What Risks Are People Concerned About?" *Risk Analysis* 11:303–14.

Fitchen, J. 1989. "When Toxic Chemicals Pollute Residential Environments:

The Cultural Meanings of Home and Homeownership." *Human Organization* 48:313–24.

Flynn, J., P. Slovic, and C. Mertz. 1993. "The Nevada Initiative: A Risk Communication." *Risk Analysis* 13:497–502.

Folkman, S., and R. Lazarus. 1988. "The Relationship Between Coping and Emotion: Implications for Theory and Research." *Social Science and Medicine* 26:309–17.

Foster, K., D. Bernstein, and P. Huber, eds. 1993. *Phantom Risks: Scientific Inference and the Law.* Cambridge, Mass.: MIT Press.

Freeman, H. 1988. "Psychiatric Aspects of Environmental Stress." *Journal of Mental Health* 17:13–23.

Freud. 1952. Chicago: Great Books.

Gallagher, W. 1993. *The Power of Place: How Our Surroundings Shape Our Thoughts, Emotions and Actions.* New York: Poseidon Press.

Gallup Organization for Charles F. Kettering Foundation and Charles Stewart Mott Foundation. 1977. *State of the Cities Survey.* Princeton, N.J.: Gallup.

Galton, F. 1880. "Psychometric Experiments." *Brain* 2:149–62.

Gannon, B. 1993. "3 Firms Agree to Pay $52 Million to Cover Cleanup of Lipari Landfill." *Newark Star-Ledger,* 20 January, p. B1.

Gans, H. 1962. *The Urban Villagers: Group and Class in the Life of Italian-Americans.* New York: Free Press.

Gelles R. 1973. "Child Abuse as Psychopathology: A Sociological Critique and Reformulation." *American Journal of Orthopsychiatry* 43:611–21.

Ginzberg, E., H. Berliner, and M. Ostow. 1993. "Changing U.S. Health Care: A Study of Four Metropolitan Areas." Boulder, Colo.: Westview Press.

Glass, D., and J. Singer. 1978. "Some Effects of Uncontrollable Noise." In *Humanscape: Environments for People,* edited by S. Kaplan and R. Kaplan, 259–2620. Belmont, Calif.: Wadsworth.

Goetze, R. 1976. *Building Neighborhood Confidence.* Cambridge, Mass.: Ballinger Press.

Goin, P. 1991. *Nuclear Landscapes.* Baltimore: Johns Hopkins University Press.

Gold, J. 1980. *An Introduction to Behavioural Geography.* New York: Oxford University Press.

Goldman, B. 1991. *The Truth About Where You Live: An Atlas for Action on Toxins and Mortality.* New York: Times Books, Random House.

Gould, J. 1986. *Quality of Life in American Neighborhoods: Levels of Affluence, Toxic Waste, and Cancer Mortality in Residential Zip Code Areas.* Boulder, Colo.: Westview Press.

Gray, J. 1992. "Peace Corps' Training Using Camden Schools." *New York Times,* 9 November, p. B5.

Grayson, M., and T. Shepard. 1972. *The Disaster Lobby: Prophets of Ecological Doom and Other Absurdities.* Chicago: Follett.

Greenberg, M. 1979. *A Primer on Industrial Environmental Impact.* New

Brunswick, N.J.: Center for Urban Policy Research, Rutgers University.

Greenberg, M., and S. Amer. 1989. "Self-Interest and Direct Legislation: Public Support of a Hazardous Waste Bond Issue." *Political Geography Quarterly* 8:67–78.

Greenberg, M., and R. Anderson. 1984. *Hazardous Waste Sites: The Credibility Gap.* New Brunswick, N.J.: Center for Urban Policy Research, Rutgers University.

Greenberg, M., and J. Hughes. 1992. "The Impact of Hazardous Waste Superfund Sites On the Value of Houses Sold in New Jersey." *Annals of Regional Science* 26:147–53.

———. 1993. "Impact of Hazardous Waste Sites on Property Values and Land Use: Tax Assessors' Appraisal." *Appraisal Journal* 61:42–51.

Greenberg, M., D. Krueckeberg, M. Kaltman, W. Metz, and C. Wilhelm. 1986. "Local Planning V. National Policy." *Town Planning Review* 57:225–37.

Greenberg, M., F. Popper, and B. West. 1990. "The TOADS: A New American Epidemic." *Urban Affairs Quarterly* 25:435–54.

———. 1991. "The Fiscal Pit and the Federalist Pendulum: Explaining Differences Between U.S. States in Protecting Health and the Environment." *Environmentalist* 11:95–104.

Greenberg, M., F. Popper, B. West, and D. Schneider. 1992. "TOADS Go to New Jersey: Implications for Land Use and Public Health in Mid-Sized and Large U.S. Cities." *Urban Studies* 29:117–25.

Greenberg, M., D. Sachsman, P. Sandman, and K. Salomone. 1989. "Risk, Drama, and Geography in the Coverage of Environmental Risk by Network TV." *Journalism Quarterly* (Summer): 267–76.

Greenberg, M., and D. Schneider. 1994. "Violence in American Cities: Young Black Males is the Answer, but What Was the Question?" *Social Science and Medicine* 39:179–87.

Greenberg, M., D. Schneider, and J. Martell. 1994. "Health Promotion Priorities of Economically Stressed Cities." *Journal of Health Care for the Poor and Underserved* 6:10–22.

Greenberg, M., and D. Wartenberg. 1990. "How Epidemiologists Can Improve Television Network News Coverage of Disease Clusters Reports." *Epidemiology* 1:168–70.

Hall, A. 1994. "EPA Names Firm to Clean Worst Landfill." *Courier Post,* 7 January, p. 1.

Hall, B., and M. Kerr. 1991. *1991–1992 Green Index.* Washington, D.C.: Island Press.

Hamilton, L. 1985. "Who Cares About Water Pollution? Opinions in a Small-Town Crisis." *Sociological Inquiry* 55:170–81.

Hapgood, F. 1979. "Risk-Benefit Analysis." *Atlantic* 243:1, 35–37.

Hardy, D. 1993. "State Fines Chester Trash Plant $112,000 for Emissions of Gases." *Inquirer,* 18 March, p. B4.

Hare, T. 1991. *Toxic Waste.* New York: Aladdin Books, Gloucester Press.

Harries, K. 1992. *Serious Violence: Patterns of Homicide and Assault in America.* Springfield, Ill.: Charles C. Thomas.

Harris, R., and D. Burmaster. 1992. "Restoring Science to Superfund Risk Assessment." *Environ Report* 6:6–11.

Hart, J. 1994. "Sigh of Relief." *Delaware County Daily Times,* 23 March, p. 5.

Hawkes, N. 1991. *Toxic Waste and Recycling.* New York: Aladdin Books, Franklin Watts Pubs.

Heimstra, N., and L. McFarling. 1978. *Environmental Psychology.* 2d ed. Monterey, Calif.: Wadsworth.

Himmelberger, J., S. Ratick, and A. White. 1991. "Compensation for Risks: Host Community Benefits in Siting Locally Unwanted Facilities. *Environmental Management* 15:647–58.

Hinkle, L., and W. Loring. 1977. *The Effect of the Man-Made Environment on Health and Behavior.* DHEW Pub. No. CDC 77-8318. Washington, D.C.: Centers for Disease Control.

Hinshaw, M., and K. Allott. 1972. "Environmental Preferences of Future Housing Consumers." *Journal of the American Institute of Planners* 38:102–7.

Hoehn, J., M. Berger, and G. Blomquist. 1987. "A Hedonic Model of Interregional Wages, Rents, and Amenity Values." *Journal of Regional Science* 27:605–20.

Hohenemser, C., R. Kates, and P. Slovic. 1983. "The Nature of Technological Hazards." *Science* 220:378–84.

Home News. 1990. "Wave of Murders Sweeps U.S. Cities." 7 December, p. A11.

———. 1992. "Landfill Cleanup Proceeds." 28 June, p. 3.

Hoyle, T. 1990. *The Last Gasp.* London: Grafton.

Ittelson, W., H. Proshansky, L. Rivlin, and G. Winkel. 1974. *An Introduction to Environmental Psychology.* New York: Holt, Rinehart, and Winston.

Jacobs, J. 1961. *The Death and Life of Great American Cities.* New York: Vintage Books.

Jakle, J., and D. Wilson. 1992. *Derelict Landscapes: The Wasting Away of America's Built Environment.* Savage, Md.: Rowman and Littlefield Books.

Judd, D. 1988. *The Politics of American Cities.* 3d ed. Glenview, Ill.: Scott, Foresman.

Kachigan, S. 1991. *Multivariate Statistical Analysis.* 2d ed. New York: Radius Press.

Kaplan, S., and R. Kaplan. 1978. *Humanscape: Environments for People.* Belmont, Calif.: Wadsworth.

Kasper, R. 1980. "Perceptions of Risk and Their Effects in Decision Making." In *Societal Risk Assessment, How Safe Is Safe Enough?,* edited by R. Schwing and W. Albers Jr., 71–84. New York: Plenum Press.

Kasperson, R., O. Renn, P. Slovic, H. Brown, J. Emel, R. Goble, J. Kasperson, and S. Ratick. 1988. "The Social Amplification of Risk: A Conceptual Framework." *Risk Analysis* 8:177–87.

Kates, R., and J. Kasperson. 1983. "Comparative Risk Analysis of Technological Hazards." *Proceedings of the National Academy of Sciences* 80:7027–38.

Kent, B. 1986. "Real Estate: 12 Great Towns That You Can Still Afford." *New Jersey Monthly* 11 (5 March): 77–98.

Kerner Commission. 1968. *Report of the National Advisory Commission on Civil Disorders.* New York: Bantam Books.

Kotlowitz, A. 1991. *There Are No Children Here.* New York: Anchor Books, Doubleday Books.

Krauss, C. 1995. "New York City Crime Falls, but Just Why is a Mystery." *New York Times,* 1 January, p. 1.

Krimsky, S., and A. Plough. 1988. *Environmental Hazards: Community Risks as a Social Process.* Dover, Mass.: Auburn House.

Kryter, K. 1970. *The Effects of Noise on Man.* New York: Academic Press.

Kunreuther, H., D. Easterling, W. Desvousges, and P. Slovic. 1990. "Public Attitudes Toward Siting a High-Level Nuclear Waste Repository in Nevada." *Risk Analysis* 10:469–84.

Kunreuther, H., L. Susskind, and T. Aarts. 1991. *The Facility Siting Credo: Guidelines for an Effective Facility Siting Process.* Philadelphia: University of Pennsylvania Publication Services.

Kuntsler, J. 1993. *The Geography of Nowhere.* New York: Simon and Schuster.

Lake, L. 1983. "The Environmental Mandate: Activists and the Electorate." *Political Science Quarterly* 98:215–33.

Landy, M. 1986. "Cleaning Up Superfund." *Public Interest* 85:58.

Landy, M., M. Roberts, and S. Thomas. 1990. *The Environmental Protection Agency: Asking the Wrong Questions.* New York: Oxford University Press.

Lee, R. 1993. *Doing Research on Sensitive Topics.* Newbury Park, Calif.: Sage.

Lee, T. 1968. "Urban Neighborhood as a Socio-Spatial Schema." *Human Relations* 21:241–68.

———. 1976. *Psychology and the Environment.* London: Methuen.

Leighton A. 1959. *My Name Is Legion: Foundations for a Theory of Man in Relation to Culture.* New York: Basic Books.

Lewis, P., D. Lowenthal, and Y. F. Tuan. 1973. *Visual Blight in America.* Washington, D.C.: Association of American Geographers.

Lindell, M., and T. Earle. 1983. "How Close is Close Enough: Public Perceptions of the Risks of Industrial Facilities." *Risk Analysis* 3:245–53.

Logan J., and H. Molotch. 1987. *Urban Fortunes: The Political Economy of Place.* Berkeley and Los Angeles: University of California Press.

Lowrance, W. 1976. *Of Acceptable Risk.* Los Altos, Calif.: W. Kaufmann.

McClelland, G., W. Schulze, and B. Hurd. 1990. "The Effect of Risk Beliefs on Property Values: A Case Study of a Hazardous Waste Site." *Risk Analysis* 10:485–97.

McCord, C., and H. Freeman. 1990. "Excess Mortality in Harlem." *New England Journal of Medicine* 322:173–77.

McKelvie, S. 1978. "Graphic Rating Scales—How Many Categories?" *British Journal of Psychology* 69:185–202.

Maize, K. 1976. "Can EPA Clean Up U.S. Steel?" *Environmental Action* 8:4–8.

Marks, P. 1994. "Electric Fields Create Nebulous Peril but Real Fear on L.I." *New York Times,* 6 January, pp. B1, B7.

Mason, J. 1992. *A Public Health Service Progress Report on Healthy People 2000: Violent and Abusive Behavior.* Washington, D.C.: U.S. Department of Health and Human Services.

Mathews, J. 1991. "Superfund Boondoggle." *Washington Post,* 6 September, p. A21.

Medoff, P., and H. Sklar. 1994. *Streets of Hope: the Fall and Rise of an Urban Neighborhood.* Boston: South End Press.

Meek, R., and J. Straayer. 1971. *The Politics of Neglect: The Environmental Crisis.* New York: Houghton Mifflin.

Meining, D., ed. 1979. *The Interpretation of Ordinary Landscapes.* New York: Oxford University Press.

Meislin, R. 1984. "In a Devastated Mexican Area—the Anger Persists." *New York Times,* 6 December, p. A12.

Michalos, A., ed. 1974. *Philosophical Problems of Science.* Boston: Allyn and Bacon.

Michelson, W. 1970. *Man and His Urban Environment: A Sociological Approach.* Reading, Mass.: Addison-Wesley.

Miller, S., M. Rein, and P. Levitt. 1990. "Community Action in the United States." *Community Development Journal* 25:356–68.

Milton, J. [1667] 1952. *Paradise Lost* (1667). In *Milton: Great Books of the Western World,* edited by R. Hutchins. Chicago: Encyclopedia Britannica.

Minard, R. 1991. *Hard Choices: States Use Risk to Refine Environmental Priorities.* South Royalton, Vt.: Northeast Center for Comparative Risk, Vermont Law School.

Moore, G., and R. Golledge, eds. 1976. *Environmental Knowing.* Stroudsburg, Pa.: Dowden, Hutchinson, and Ross.

Murdie, R. 1969. *Factorial Ecology of Metropolitan Toronto, 1951–1961.* Department of Geography Research Paper no. 116. Chicago: University of Chicago.

National Research Council. 1991. *Environmental Epidemiology: Public Health and Hazardous Waste.* Washington, D.C.: National Academy Press.

———. 1994. *Building Consensus Through Risk Assessment and Management of the Department of Energy's Environmental Remediation Program.* Washington, D.C.: National Academy Press.

Nelkin, D. 1981. "Wisdom, Expertise, and the Application of Ethics." *Science, Technology, and Human Values* 6 (34): 16–17.

New Jersey Department of Environmental Protection. 1989. *Hazardous Waste Site Program: Site Status Report.* Trenton: N.J. Department of Environmental Protection.

New Jersey Department of Health. 1989. A Report on the Health of Residents Living Near the Lipari Landfill. Trenton: New Jersey Department of Health.

New York Times. 1989. "Landfill Linked to Causes of Leukemia and Low Birthweight." 5 February, p. 33.

————. 1992. "Gunshot Wounds Labeled Epidemic." 11 June, p. B10.

Orme, T. 1992. "Superfund: Is it Bulldozing Our Public Health Dollars?" *Priorities* (Summer): 1–4.

Ostman, R., and J. Parker. 1987. "Impact of Education, Age, Newspapers, and Television on Environmental Knowledge, Concerns, and Behaviors." *Journal of Environmental Education* 19:3–9.

Palen, J. 1987. *The Urban World.* New York: McGraw-Hill.

Passell, P. 1991. "Experts Question Staggering Costs of Toxic Cleanups." *New York Times,* 1 September, p. 1.

Peck, D., ed. 1989. *Psychological Effects of Hazardous Toxic Waste Disposal on Communities.* Springfield, Ill.: Charles C. Thomas.

Peet, J. 1993. "Cleanup Completed at Chemical Control." *Newark Star-Ledger,* 15 December, pp. 1, 18.

Piller, C. 1991. *The Fail-Safe Society, Community Defiance and the End of American Technological Optimism.* Berkeley and Los Angeles: University of California Press.

Pocock, D., and R. Hudson. 1978. *Images of the Urban Environment.* New York: Columbia University Press.

Pomper, G., ed. 1984. *The Election of 1984: Reports and Interpretations.* Chatham, N.J.: Chatham House.

Porteous, J. 1977. *Environment and Behavior.* Reading, Mass.: Addison-Wesley.

Prato, L. 1991. *Covering the Environmental Beat.* Washington, D.C.: Environmental Reporting Forum, the Media Institute.

Randall, A., J. Hoehn, and D. Brookshire. 1983. "Contingent Valuation Survey for Evaluating Environmental Assets." *National Resource Journal* 23:635–48.

Rapoport, A. 1977. *Human Aspects of Urban Form.* New York: Basic Books.

Rawls, J. 1971. *A Theory of Justice.* Cambridge: Harvard University Press.

Regional Plan Association of New Jersey. 1994. *Union County Model Site Redevelopment Project: Final Report.* Newark: Regional Plan Association of New Jersey.

Robertson, K. 1994. "Realistic Estimates of Risk. America at a Critical Juncture." *AIHC Journal* (Spring): 3–15.

Robinson, J. 1987. Letter to editor. *Science* 237:19.

Rodriguez-Trias, H. 1993. "Violence: Our Greatest Public Health Threat." *Nation's Health* 23:2.

Rogerson, R., A. Findlay, A. Morris, and M. Coombes. 1989. "Indicators of Quality of Life: Some Methodological Issues." *Environment and Planning A* 21:1655–66.

Rohrman, B. 1985. "Categorical Scaling Versus Magnitude Scaling—A Practicability-Oriented Comparison." In *Measurement and Personality Assessment,* edited by E. Roskam, 155–63. North Holland, N.Y.: Elsevier Science.

Roper Organization. 1990. *The Environment: Public Attitudes and Individual Behavior.* Racine, Wisc.: S. C. Johnson and Sons.

Rose, H., and P. McClain. 1990. *Race, Place, and Risk: Black Homicide in Urban America.* Albany: SUNY Press.

Rosenberg, M., and M. Fenley, eds. 1991. *Violence in America: A Public Health Approach.* New York: Oxford University Press.

Russell, M. 1987. "Risk Communication: Informing Public Opinion." *EPA Journal* 134:20–21.

Russell, M., E. Colglazier, and M. English. 1991. *Hazardous Waste Remediation: The Task Ahead.* Knoxville, Tenn.: Waste Management Research and Education Institute.

Rutala, W., and D. Weber. 1991. "Infectious Waste: Mismatch Between Science and Policy." *New England Journal of Medicine* 325 (8): 578–82.

Saarinen, T. 1976. *Environmental Planning: Perception and Behavior.* Boston: Houghton Mifflin.

Salvesen, D. 1994. "EPA Offers Brownfield Development Incentives." *Planning* (October): 27.

Sandman, P. 1994. Risk communication consultant. Personal communication, 17 May.

Sandman, P., P. Miller, B. Johnson, and N. Weinstein. 1993. "Agency Communication, Community Outrage, and Perception of Risk: Three Simulation Experiments." *Risk Analysis* 13:585–98.

Sandman, P., D. Sachsman, M. Greenberg, and M. Gochfeld. 1987. *Environmental Risk and the Press.* New Brunswick, N.J.: Transaction Press.

Sanoff, H. 1975. *Seeing the Environment: An Advocacy Approach.* Raleigh, N.C.: Learning Environments.

Schneider, D., and M. Greenberg. 1994. "Homicide and Suicide in New Jersey: Trends, Patterns, and Social Context." *New Jersey Medicine* 91:843–45.

Schneider, K. 1993. "Rules Easing for Urban Toxic Cleanups." *New York Times,* 20 September, p. A12.

Schuman, H., and J. Scott. 1987. "Problems in the Use of Survey Questions to Measure Public Opinion." *Science* 236:957–59.

Schwab, D. 1993. "Jerseyans Lash Out at Jet Noise Hearing." *Newark Star-Ledger,* 6 January, pp. 1, 8.

Schwaneberg, R. 1991. "Violent Crime Jumps to Record High in State." *Newark Star-Ledger,* 22 June, p. 1.

Science Advisory Board, U.S. Environmental Protection Agency. 1990. *Reducing Risk: Setting Priorities and Strategies for Environmental Protection.* Washington, D.C.: U.S. Environmental Protection Agency.

Sheehan, H., and R. Wedeen, eds. 1993. *Toxic Circles: Environmental Hazards from the Workplace into the Community.* New Brunswick, N.J.: Rutgers University Press.

Shevky, E., and W. Bell. 1972. *Social Area Analysis: Theory, Illustrative Application, and Computational Procedures.* Westport, Conn.: Greenwood Press.

Shrader-Frechette, K. 1985. *Risk Analysis and Scientific Method: Methodological and Ethical Problems with Evaluating Societal Hazards.* Boston: D. Reidel.

———. 1991a. "Reductionist Approaches to Risk." In *Acceptable Evidence: Science and Values in Risk Management,* edited by D. Mayo and R. Hollander, 218–44. New York: Oxford University Press.

———. 1991b. *Risk and Rationality: Philosophical Foundations for Populist Reforms.* Berkeley and Los Angeles: University of California Press.

Silbergeld, E. 1993a. *Investing in Prevention: Opportunities to Reduce Disease and Health Care Costs Through Identifying and Reducing Environmental Contributions to Preventable Disease.* Washington, D.C.: Environmental Defense Fund.

———. 1993b. "Risk Assessment: The Perspective and Experience of U.S. Environmentalists." *Environmental Health Perspectives* 101:100–104.

Singer, E., and P. Endreny. 1993. *Reporting on Risk.* New York: Russell Sage Foundation.

Singer, G. 1993. Chief, Bureau of Community Relations, N.J. Department of Environmental Protection. Personal communication, 11 January.

Skaburskis, A. 1989. "Impact Attenuation in Conflict Situations: The Price Effects of a Nuisance Land Use." *Environment and Planning A* 21:375–83.

Slovic, P. 1993. "Perceived Risk, Trust, and Democracy." *Risk Analysis* 13:675–82.

Slovic, P., B. Fischhoff, and S. Lichtenstein. 1979. "Rating the Risks." *Environment* 21:14–20,36–39.

———. 1980. "Facts and Fears: Understanding Perceived Risk." In *Societal Risk Assessment: How Safe is Safe Enough,* edited by R. Schwing and W. Albers Jr. 181–216. New York: Plenum Press.

Slovic, P., M. Layman, N. Kraus, J. Flynn, J. Chalmers, and G. Gesell. 1991. "Perceived Risk, Stigma, and Potential Economic Impacts of a High-Level Nuclear Waste Repository in Nevada." *Risk Analysis* 11:683–702.

Smith, V., and W. Desvousges. 1987. "An Empirical Analysis of the Economic Value of Risk Changes." *Journal of Political Economy* 95:89–113.

Smith, W., and A. Smith. 1975. *Minamata.* New York: Holt, Rinehart, and Winston.

Society for Risk Analysis. 1994. "Risk Analysis High Priority in White House." *Risk Newsletter* 14 (2): 1–2.

Stafford, R. 1981. "Why Superfund was Needed." *EPA Journal* 7 (June): 8–10.

Newark Star-Ledger. 1993. "Superfund Cleans Ill-Famed Dump." 7 January, p. 21.

Starr, C. 1969. "Social Benefit VS. Technological Risk." *Science* 165:1232–38.

Stengel, R. 1985. "When Brother Kills Brother." *Time,* 16 September, 32–36.

Sternlieb, G. 1966. *The Tenement Landlord.* New Brunswick, N.J.: Rutgers University Press.

Sternlieb, G., and J. Hughes. 1990. *New Jersey Home Prices.* Rutgers Regional Report, Vol. 2. New Brunswick, N.J.: Center for Urban Policy Research, Rutgers University.

Stillman, C. 1975. "The Fair Land." In *Landscape Assessment,* edited by E. Zube, R. Brush, and J. Fabos, 18–30. New York: Halsted Press.

Stoffle, R., M. Traugott, J. Stone, P. McIntyre, F. Jensen, and C. Davidson. 1991. "Risk Perception Mapping: Using Ethnography to Define the Locally Affected Population for a Low-Level Radioactive Waste Storage Facility in Michigan." *American Anthropologist* 93:611–35.

Stranahan, S. 1993. "State Approves Infectious-Waste Treatment Plant for Chester." *Inquirer,* 14 July, p. 7.

Sutherland, H., G. Lockwood, D. Tritchler, F. Sem, L. Brooks, and J. Till. 1991. "Communicating Probabilistic Information to Cancer Patients: Is There 'Noise' on the Line?" *Social Science and Medicine* 32:725–27.

Talcott, F. 1992. "How Certain is that Environmental Risk Estimate?" *Resources* 107:10–15.

Taylor, A., and J. Hart. 1994. "Blast Levels Tank; 19 Injured." *Delaware County Daily Times,* 22 March, pp. 2–3.

Taylor, D. 1989. "Blacks and the Environment. Toward an Explanation of the Concern and Action Gap Between Blacks and Whites." *Environment and Behavior* 21:175–205.

Teal, J., and M. Teal. 1969. *Life and Death of the Salt Marsh.* New York: Ballantine Books.

Thompson, D. 1992. "Living Happily Near a Nuclear Trash Heap." *Time,* 11 May, 53–54.

Thrill, J-C., and D. Sui. 1993. "Mental Maps and Fuzziness in Space Preferences." *Professional Geographer* 45:264–76.

Time. 1980. "The Poisoning of America." 22 September, front cover.

———. 1992a. "Camden, N.J. Child Welfare and the Poor: Who Could Live Here?" 20 January, 20–23.

———. 1992b. "Children in the Danger Zone: For Black Youngsters, it Is Often a Short Trip from Cradle to Grave." 15 June, 24.

Tod, I., and M. Wheeler. 1978. *Utopia.* New York: Harmony Books.

Torres, J. 1989. *Fire and Fear.* New York: Warner Books.

Traver, N. 1992. "Children without Pity." *Time,* 26 October, 46–51.

U.S.A. Today. 1991. "19 Cities Set Records for Murder." 2 January, p. 1.

U.S. Bureau of the Census. 1983. *Geographic Identification Code Scheme.* Washington, D.C.: U.S. Government Printing Office.

———. 1994. *County and City Data Book: 1994.* Washington, D.C.: U.S. Government Printing Office.

U.S. Council on Environmental Quality. 1980. *Public Opinion on Environmental Issues: Results of a National Public Opinion Survey.* Washington, D.C.: U.S. Government Printing Office.

U.S. Department of Commerce. 1983–1991. *American Housing Survey for the United States.* Volumes for 1981, 1983, 1985, 1987, and 1989. Washington, D.C.: U.S. Government Printing Office.

———. 1992. *1990 Census of Population and Housing STF3A.* CD-ROM. Washington, D.C.: U.S. Government Printing Office.

U.S. Department of Health and Human Services. 1985. *Report of the Secretary's Task Force on Black and Minority Health.* Vol. 5, *Homicide, Suicide, and Unintentional Injuries.* Washington, D.C.: U.S. Department of Health and Human Services.

———. 1990. "Homicide Among Young Black Males: United States, 1978–1987." *Morbidity and Mortality Weekly Report* 39:869–73.

———. 1991. *Healthy People 2000.* Washington, D.C.: U.S. Department of Health and Human Services.

———. 1992. "Unintentional Firearm-Related Fatalities Among Children and Teenagers—United States, 1982–1988." *Morbidity and Mortality Weekly Report* 41:442–51.

U.S. Environmental Protection Agency. 1973. *Fish Kills Caused by Pollution in 1973.* Washington, D.C.: Superintendent of Documents.

———. 1974. *Information on Levels of Environmental Noise Requisite to Protect Public Health and Welfare with an Adequate Margin of Safety.* Washington, D.C.: U.S. Environmental Protection Agency.

———. 1980. "Chemical Waste Exploding!" *EPA Journal* 6, front cover.

———. 1987. *Unfinished Business: A Comparative Assessment of Environmental Problems.* Washington, D.C.: U.S. Environmental Protection Agency.

———. 1992. *Environmental Equity: Reducing Risk for All Communities.* Washington, D.C.: U.S. Environmental Protection Agency.

Van Houtven, G., and M. Cropper. 1994. "When Is a Life Too Costly to Save? The Evidence of Environmental Regulations?" *Resources* 114 (Winter): 6–10.

Van Liere, K., and R. Dunlap. 1980. "The Social Basis of Environmental Concern: A Review of Hypotheses, Explanations, and Empirical Evidence." *Public Opinion Quarterly* 44:181–97.

Veronis, N. 1993. "Site Panel Sets Dates for Meetings, Final Vote on GAF Incinerator Plan." *Newark Star-Ledger,* 10 December, p. 89.

Versluis, A. 1987. *Telos.* New York: Arkana.

Von Allem, S., M. Greenwell, H. Hansen, S. Perdue, P. Price, and C. Schmidt. 1992. *Quality of Life and ATSDR's Mission.* Atlanta: Agency for Toxic Substances Disease Registry.

Wallace, McCarg, Roberts, and Todd Planners. 1977. *City of Camden Comprehensive Plan, 1977–1992.* Philadelphia: Wallace, McCarg, Rogerts, and Todd Planners.

Wallace, R. 1981. "Fire Service Productivity and the New York City Fire Crisis." *Human Ecology* 9:433–64.

——. 1988. "A Synergism of Plagues: Planned Shrinkage, Contagious Housing Destruction and AIDS in the Bronx." *Environmental Research* 47:1–33.

——. 1989. "Homelessness, Contagious Destruction of Housing and Municipal Service Cuts in New York City: 1. Demographics of a Housing Deficit." *Environment and Planning A* 21:1585–1603.

Wallsten, T., D. Budescu, A. Rapoport, R. Zwick, and B. Forsyth. 1986. "Measuring the Vague Meanings of Probability Terms." *Journal of Experimental Psychology: General* 115:348–65.

Ward, C. 1989. *Welcome, Thinner City: Urban Survival in the 1990s.* London: Bedford Square Press.

Ward, D. 1989. *Poverty, Ethnicity, and the American City, 1840–1925, Changing Conceptions of the Slums and the Ghetto.* New York: Cambridge University Press.

Warner, S. 1978. *Streetcar Suburbs: The Process of Growth in Boston, 1870–1900.* Boston: Harvard University Press.

Webber, M. 1963. "Order in Diversity: Community Without Propinquity." In *Cities and Space,* edited by L. Wingo, 23–54. Baltimore: Johns Hopkins University Press.

Weinberg, D. 1980. "We Almost Lost Elizabeth." *New Jersey Monthly* 41 (August): 35–39, 97–113.

Weinstein, N. 1988. *Attitudes of the Public and the Department of Environmental Protection Toward Environmental Hazards.* Trenton: New Jersey Department of Environmental Protection.

Weir, D. 1987. *The Bhopal Syndrome.* London: Earthscan.

Whelan, E. 1993. *Toxic Terror: The Truth Behind the Cancer Scares.* Buffalo: Prometheus Books.

Whyte, A., and I. Burton. 1980. *Environmental Risk Assessment—SCOPE 15.* New York: John Wiley and Sons.

Will, G. 1992. "The Toughest Epidemic of All: Violence." *New York Times,* 30 November, p. A8.

Winograd, E., and U. Neisser, eds. 1992. *Affect and Accuracy in Recall.* New York: Cambridge University Press.

Wyckoff, P. 1994. " 'Mist' Fells Toll Takers, Shuts Pike Interchange." *Newark Star-Ledger,* 1 January, pp. 1, 4.

Yankelovich, Skelly, and White Organization. 1979. *The General Mill's American Family Report, 1978–1979.* Minneapolis: General Mills.

Zabrin L., J. Hardy, E. Smith, and M. Hirsch. 1986. "Substance Use and Its Relation to Sexual Activity Among Inner-City Adolescents." *Journal of Adolescent Health Care* 7:320–31.

Zehner, R. 1972. "Neighborhood and Community Satisfaction: A Report on New Towns and Less-Planned Suburbs." In *Environment and the Social Sciences,* edited by J. Wohlwill and D. Carson, 169–83. Washington, D.C.: American Psychological Association.

Zeigler, D., J. Johnson, and S. Brunn. 1983. *Technological Hazards.* Washington, D.C.: Association of American Geographers.

Zeiss, C. 1989. "Property-Value Guarantees for Waste Facilities." *Journal of Urban Planning and Development* 115:123–35.

Zeiss, C., and J. Atwater. 1987. "Waste Facilities in Residential Communities: Impacts and Acceptance." *Journal of Urban Planning and Development* 113:19–34.

Zielhuis, R., and A. Wibowo. 1989. "Standard Setting in Occupational Health: 'Philosophical Issues.'" *American Journal of Industrial Medicine* 16:569–98.

Zwick, D. 1971. *Water Waste-Land.* New York: Bantam.

Index

accidents, environmental, 15, 81, 110–112, 131

age: and perceptions, 32; as ratings factor, 87, 99 table, 123 table, 145, 151 table, 174

agencies: competition between, xiv; private, xiv; public, xiv; reallocation of funds from, 207–208; for redevelopment, 38–39, 82; for subsidized housing, 34

Agency for Toxic Substances and Disease Registry, 203

AIDS, 24, 26, 212, 213

airports, 1, 16, 41, 50 table, 55 table, 109–110, 112, 141

Air Products and Chemicals, 81

amenities, 3, 6 table, 28–30, 51 table, 93, 95 table, 147 table, 176 table, 194–195; access to work, 3, 51 table, 68, 71, 90 table, 117 table; defining, 3; friends and family, 3, 51 table, 93, 108, 117 table; inexpensive housing, 3, 32, 51 table, 72, 90 table, 93, 119, 153–154, 177, 178, 194; public transportation, 3, 51 table, 68, 72, 90 table, 93, 117 table, 172, 177, 194; as ratings factor, 40; religious services, 3, 5; schools, 3, 51 table, 90 table, 97, 117 table, 122

American Cyanamid, 139–140, 141, 144, 146 table, 151 table, 156, 156 table, 157

American Housing Survey, 37, 47–51, 50–51 table, 51 table, 66, 130, 187, 196, 198

American Public Health Association, 26

Andrews, Richard, 226

animals: aesthetic problems with, 25; bites from, 25; rodents, 23, 24, 25; and spread of disease, 25; uncontrolled, 1, 24, 25, 49, 50 table, 90 table, 91 table, 101 table, 120 table, 121, 124, 125 table, 147 table, 155, 170–171, 175, 178, 216

arson, 1

asbestos, 24

bars, 22

Bayonne, N.J., 134, 138, 144, 146 table, 151 table, 200, 212, 213

Bayway refinery, 110, 111

behaviors, 6, 77; abusive, 26; criminal, 24–27; as ratings factor, 76, 130; sexual, 24

Bhopal (India), 20

Bhopal Syndrome (Weir), 17

Biomedical Waste Systems Inc., 82

blight, xiii, 22–24, 23, 50 table, 108, 142, 191, 206, 213, 216; Camden, 171, 174, 178; Chester, 85; Elizabeth, 216; and loss of control, 22–23; Marcus Hook, 96; physical, 23; as ratings factor, 130; and violence, 23

Boston (Massachusetts), 29

About the Authors

Michael Greenberg and Dona Schneider are professors in the Department of Urban Studies and Community Health at Rutgers University.

Dr. Greenberg is Codirector of the New Jersey Graduate Program in Public Health, Director of the Policy Division of the Environmental and Occupational Health Sciences Institute, and Director of the Policy Division of the Hazardous Substances Management Research Center. He has served on a National Academy of Sciences Committee on Remedial Action Priorities for Hazardous Waste Sites, and is the author of numerous articles and books on environmental health policy. Dr. Greenberg's list of publications include: *Urbanization and Cancer Mortality* (1983), *Hazardous Waste Sites: the Credibility Gap* (1984), *Public Health and the Environment* (1987), *Environmental Risk and the Press* (1987), and *Reporter's Environmental Handbook* (1995).

Dona Schneider is Chair of the Medical Geography Specialty Group of the Association of American Geographers and serves as Cochair of the Advisory Group on Cancer Prevention and Control for the New Jersey Commission on Cancer Research. Elected to the American College of Epidemiology in 1992, Dr. Schneider has written numerous articles on childhood cancer, child and minority health, and risk behaviors, including violence. Her publications include *Public Health and Public Health Services: The Connecticut–New Jersey– New York Tri-State Region* (1992) and *American Childhood: Risks and Realities* (1995).

Together, Professors Greenberg and Schneider have published more than a dozen articles on health and the environment in such journals as *American Journal of Epidemiology, Environmentalist, Environmental Health Perspectives, International Journal of Epidemiology, Journal of Environment and Health, Milbank Quarterly, Policy Studies Journal, Risk Analysis, Social Science and Medicine,* and *Urban Studies.* Their next book is in the planning stage.